## NRA Hunter Skills Series

# HOW TO TALK ABOUT HUNTING

*Research-Based Communications Strategies*

NRA Hunters' Leadership Forum

© 2020 by National Rifle Association

All rights reserved. Printed in the United States of America. No part of this book may be reproduced in whole or part without written permission.

Produced by the NRA Hunters' Leadership Forum. For information on the Hunter Skills series or NRA Hunters' Leadership Forum, contact the National Rifle Association, 11250 Waples Mill Road, Fairfax, Virginia 22030 or online at nrahlf.org.

Main entry under title:
*How to Talk About Hunting – NRA Hunter Skills Series*

ISBN 978-0-935998-49-8

# Acknowledgments

### AUTHOR
Mark Damian Duda,
*Executive Director, Responsive Management*

### PROJECT MANAGER
Peter Churchbourne,
*Director, NRA Hunters' Leadership Forum*

### CO-AUTHOR
Martin Jones,
*Senior Research Associate, Responsive Management*

### CONSULTANTS
Samuel Nelson, A-Game Speech and Debate Consulting
John Stowell, A-Game Speech and Debate Consulting
Armands Revelins, A-Game Speech and Debate Consulting
Karen Mehall Phillips, Director of Communications,
NRA Hunters' Leadership Forum

### ILLUSTRATOR
Todd Telander, Telander Galleries and Todd Telander Fine Art

Don't raise your voice;
improve your argument.[1]

# Contents

Introduction .................................................. ix

Chapter 1: Why Public Opinion on Hunting Matters ............ 1

Chapter 2: Why Words Matter ................................ 23

Chapter 3: Participation in Hunting ........................ 29

Chapter 4: Attitudes Toward Hunting ........................ 53

Chapter 5: Attitudes Toward Animal Rights, Animal Welfare,
    and Dominionism ........................................ 75

Chapter 6: Arguing for Hunting: What Works and What Doesn't .. 89

Chapter 7: Participation in Sport Shooting ................. 113

Chapter 8: Attitudes Toward Sport Shooting ................. 129

Chapter 9: Debating About Hunting .......................... 137

Chapter 10: Developing Formal Communications Programs
    in Support of Hunting .................................. 151

Chapter 11: Talking About Hunting: Don'ts and Dos .......... 187

Endnotes ................................................... 201

About the Authors & Consultants ............................ 227

# Introduction

**EACH YEAR, MORE THAN ELEVEN** million Americans go hunting. Most hunt with firearms or archery equipment, typically pursuing deer, turkey, waterfowl, or small game species. The meat of animals harvested by hunters is rarely wasted, being either consumed by hunters and their families or donated.[2] Hunters also contribute significantly to the U.S. economy: in a recent year, their expenditures on equipment, lodging, and other items totaled more than $26 billion.[3]

Hunting is consistent with the values and beliefs of most Americans. For decades, surveys have found that a large majority of Americans approve of legal hunting. Surveys also show that most Americans identify with an animal welfare philosophy allowing for the humane use of animals by humans—in other words, Americans largely do *not* support the animal rights position of banning the use of animals entirely. In line with these beliefs, most Americans consume meat and use products derived from animals.

Just as millions of Americans hunt, millions more know a friend or family member who hunts. Even if one does not hunt, there are compelling reasons to support hunting, including the desire to maintain America's wildlife populations. Each year, hunters, through their purchases of licenses and conservation taxes levied on their equipment, contribute hundreds of millions of dollars in funding for species recovery efforts, habitat improvement projects, and other conservation work carried out by the nation's fish and wildlife agencies. On the non-government side, hunters account for hundreds of millions of dollars in donations to nonprofit conservation organizations and on purchases of private recreational lands that provide habitat and rest areas for wildlife. A decline in hunting means diminished revenue for conservation—this means less material support for fish and wildlife management activities that benefit *all* Americans, not just hunters.

Despite all of this, the facts cannot speak for themselves—even though hunting is ingrained in America's conservation success story, it remains vulnerable to opposition. The evidence alone is not enough to effectively build public support for hunting.

---

> "Hunting is one of the oldest of human practices. Indeed, according to some it has been the primary basis for our species' social, intellectual, and evolutionary development. Perhaps 99 percent of human tenure on earth has been as a hunter-gatherer."[4]
>
> —Dr. Stephen R. Kellert

---

Not only can opposition to hunting interfere with the right of Americans to legally hunt, it can prevent wildlife managers from carrying out the work entrusted to them. For example, recent legislative challenges organized by anti-hunters in Maine and Florida have sought to limit the use of hunting as a scientific tool for managing black bear populations in these two states.[5] This management through public opinion often has adverse effects, such as when unchecked bear populations begin to exceed biological and cultural carrying capacity.

Formal debates about hunting can also sway public opinion. In attempting to build a case for hunting using facts alone, proponents of hunting are often overwhelmed by the skillful rhetoric, misdirection, and persuasion of their well-trained anti-hunting opponents. In a recent debate, anti-hunters successfully convinced the audience that hunters do not conserve wildlife, despite all evidence put forth to the contrary.[6] Such setbacks reflect the vulnerable reputation of hunting in the eyes of the public.

To protect hunting from the consequences of unwarranted controversy and damaging misperceptions, hunters and their advocates must learn how to communicate deliberately and thoughtfully about hunting. This means making use of the key principles of persuasion advocated by the ancient philosopher Aristotle: *ethos*, *pathos*, and *logos*.

Ethos refers to credibility, especially the trustworthiness of knowledgeable professionals like agency biologists and game wardens; pathos refers to emotion, such as the fact that hunter conservationists care deeply about wildlife and other universal values that resonate even with non-hunters; and logos refers to logic, or the factual reasons why hunting matters. *Building support for hunting depends on all three elements.*

This book provides the tools necessary to effectively talk about and debate on behalf of hunting. The communications strategies presented here are research-based; they draw on more than 30 years of survey research, focus groups, and other data sources that reflect Americans' attitudes toward hunting, the use of animals, and related topics (endnotes are used throughout the book to cite sources referenced in the text).

Because most hunting is done with firearms, it is not unusual for discussions about hunting to lead to discussions about firearms. Firearms, too, are prominent in American society: just under half of all Americans live in a household with a firearm, and roughly fifty-two million went target or sport shooting in 2018.[7] Additionally, sport shooting is often a gateway to hunting. For this reason, the book addresses sport shooting and how it relates to communications about hunting.

*In 1900, there were around 40,000 Rocky Mountain elk; today there are 1 million. This recovery was possible largely because of the conservation funding provided by hunters.*

Each chapter begins with a summary of main points and ends with a list of key takeaways from the material. The final chapter of the book discusses the definitive "don'ts" and "dos" of talking about hunting.

The future of hunting in America depends on social acceptance. To gain this support, proponents of hunting must use language that resonates with non-hunters and those unfamiliar with hunting. To this end, this book focuses on the research-based communications that will build the most support for hunting.

By following the guidelines and strategies described in this book, hunters and their advocates will learn how to communicate about hunting in the most persuasive and compelling ways possible.

# CHAPTER 1

# Why Public Opinion on Hunting Matters

**MAINTAINING PUBLIC SUPPORT FOR HUNTING** *is essential. Despite its importance as a food source, a wildlife management tool, and a crucial source of funding for conservation in the United States, hunting remains vulnerable to misinformation, a lack of information, and general negative attention. This can encourage support for restrictive legislation and other measures. Facts alone will not be enough to move public opinion about hunting—the hunting community must appeal to non-hunters through common goals, motivations, and values.*

## HUNTING IN A HISTORICAL AND CONTEMPORARY CONTEXT

Hunting has been around almost as long as people have, in many ways being embedded in the evolutionary path of human beings. Before the innovations of farming and agriculture, most people depended on hunting and gathering to eat.[8]

Hunting remains an important source of food today. Across all categories of game species, hunting in the United States produces roughly a billion pounds of meat each year, enough for close to four billion individual meals with a four-ounce serving of protein.[9] One survey found that about four in ten Americans had eaten wild-caught game meat of some kind (e.g., venison, turkey, boar, duck) in the past year.[10]

Just as the earliest hunters passed down their knowledge and skills to others to ensure the survival of the group, the average hunter today was initiated into hunting by another hunter, often a father or father figure.[11] The social component of hunting remains important, with many hunters still participating for reasons of tradition or family bonding.[12]

> Today, every state fish and wildlife agency across the country is legislatively mandated to manage and provide opportunities for hunting.
>
>

Legal hunting is grounded in science: it is managed by trained biologists to ensure the health of wildlife populations. Wildlife cannot thrive without properly managed habitat, and the lands and natural areas maintained for game benefit a myriad of other species as well. Moreover, the selective culling of herds based on biological data means that hunting is good for biodiversity. Hunters are subject to numerous laws regulating when, where, and how they may hunt certain species—in this way, hunting is managed to ensure the sustainability of wildlife populations.

Today, every state fish and wildlife agency across the country is legislatively mandated to manage and provide opportunities for hunting, meaning every American has the right to hunt in accordance with all laws and regulations. A recent survey of fish and wildlife agency employees found 95 percent of employees in support of legal hunting, with similar overwhelming majorities supportive of hunting for meat and hunting for wildlife management.[13]

Hunting is both a traditional pastime and a right: almost half of the country's states have passed bills or amended their constitutions to include language explicitly protecting the right of citizens to hunt.[14]

The idea of hunting as a legal right subject to management and regulation is based on a set of principles known as the North American Model of Wildlife Conservation.[15] The North American Model evolved in part to address the wanton abuse, market hunting, and resulting decimation of certain species that had occurred in America by the early part of the twentieth century. The Model rests on a series of guiding components, including the concept that wildlife resources are a public trust belonging to everyone. The Model calls for allocation of wildlife by law and permits the killing of wildlife only for a legitimate purpose; it eliminates wildlife markets and identifies science as the proper tool for wildlife policy. It also calls for democracy of hunting, which is why hunting today is managed primarily on the state level by the nation's individual fish and wildlife agencies.

> "Wildlife does not exist by accident. It thrives today in North America because of a wondrous network of policies, laws and financial support structures largely put in place and maintained by the small percentage of us who hunt and fish. Perhaps in some distant future society at large will pay for what we have carried for a century or more; but even if this were true would not the history of our achievement be worth telling? The reality is that no feasible alternative model for wildlife conservation is yet within our reach, and may never be."[16]
> 
> —*Shane Mahoney*

## How Hunters Help Fund Wildlife Conservation

Hunting is important not just for historical and practical reasons—it is also an essential funding mechanism for wildlife conservation in America. In this sense, even those who do not hunt and feel no particular way about hunting stand to benefit from the contributions of hunters. Through their purchases of taxable equipment, licenses, stamps, and other items, hunters represent one of the most important constituencies for conservation funding in the United States. (This is to say nothing of the national economic impact of hunters' expenditures—this benefit of hunting is discussed in detail in Chapter 3.)

### FEDERAL AID IN WILDLIFE RESTORATION ACT

With the passage of the Federal Aid in Wildlife Restoration Act[17] in 1937, Congress (supported by fish and wildlife agencies, equipment manufacturers, conservation groups, garden clubs, and hunters themselves) established a dedicated funding mechanism for wildlife management and conservation through an excise tax on sporting arms and ammunition—at the time, items purchased mostly by hunters. A key reason for the legislation was the decline in game and other wildlife populations at the time due to habitat loss, wanton waste of the wildlife resources, and inadequate management. Commonly known as the Pittman-Robertson Act for its sponsoring legislators, Nevada Senator Key Pittman and Virginia Congressman A. Willis Robertson, the Act initially created an 11-percent excise tax on firearms and ammunition; amendments in later years added a 10-percent tax on pistols, revolvers, and handguns, and an 11-percent tax on bows, arrows, and other archery equipment.

---

"I believe we have a commitment to sportsmen and women who pay the excise taxes that for 46 years have supported wildlife conservation through the Pittman-Robertson program. They and the manufacturers whose products are taxed are strong backers of the program. Years ago in fact, when it was decided that a number of excise taxes should be eliminated, hunters and the manufacturers urged Congress to retain the taxes on sporting arms and ammunition to continue the wildlife restoration efforts which they support. How often have you encountered that situation?"[18]

—*Senator Malcolm Wallop
in 1983*

---

Excise tax revenues are transferred to a dedicated Wildlife Restoration Trust Fund and then apportioned to fish and wildlife agencies in all 50 states and the 5 major territories based on a formula accounting for population, land area, and hunting license sales. The Trust Fund supports a number of individual conservation efforts through the Wildlife Restoration Program, including species recovery, habitat improvements, and other conservation work. States are required to pay for a quarter of the total cost of these projects, with Federal Aid Wildlife Restoration funds making up the other 75 percent.[19] Crucially, original language included in the Federal Aid in Wildlife Restoration legislation by Congressman Robertson specified that states, in order to be eligible to receive the federal aid, would not be allowed to divert the revenues from license fees paid by hunters for any purpose other than the work of the state fish and wildlife agency—thus guaranteeing a revenue stream committed to conservation. This is a key reason why the Pittman-Robertson Act is often thought of as being more important for wildlife than any other legislative effort.[20]

> Since its passage in 1937, the Wildlife Restoration Act has generated almost $19 billion for conservation work. Between 2015 and 2019 alone, an average total of $606 million was apportioned to states through the Wildlife Restoration Program.

In addition to major conservation projects, the Wildlife Restoration Trust Fund allocates funding for hunter safety programs, other wildlife- and nature-related educational programs (enjoyed by hunters and non-hunters alike), the construction of new shooting ranges, and Multistate Conservation Grant projects that address the regional and national priorities of state fish and wildlife agencies. In 2019, the Wildlife Restoration Act was amended to allocate additional money toward a new Modern Multistate Conservation Grant program for projects to recruit, retain, and reactivate hunters.[21] Finally, interest earned through the Trust Fund goes to the North American Wetlands Conservation Fund, which in turns supports a landmark wetlands habitat program managed by the U.S. Fish and Wildlife Service.

Since the passage of the Wildlife Restoration Act, purchases of firearms, ammunition, and other taxable equipment have generated almost $19 billion for conservation work. Between 2015 and 2019 alone, an average total of $606 million was apportioned to states through the Wildlife Restoration Program.[22] In essence, as long as sales of firearms, ammunition, and archery equipment continue, Pittman-Robertson excise tax revenues will remain a reliable source of funding for U.S. conservation efforts year in and year out—this means that programs can be implemented consistently over time instead of proceeding in fits and starts.

The diagram on the next page provides a breakdown of the excise tax funding sources created through the Wildlife Restoration Act, the efforts they support, and the amounts deducted from the Trust Fund for each program.

**How to Talk About Hunting** ⊕ *Research-Based Communications Strategies*

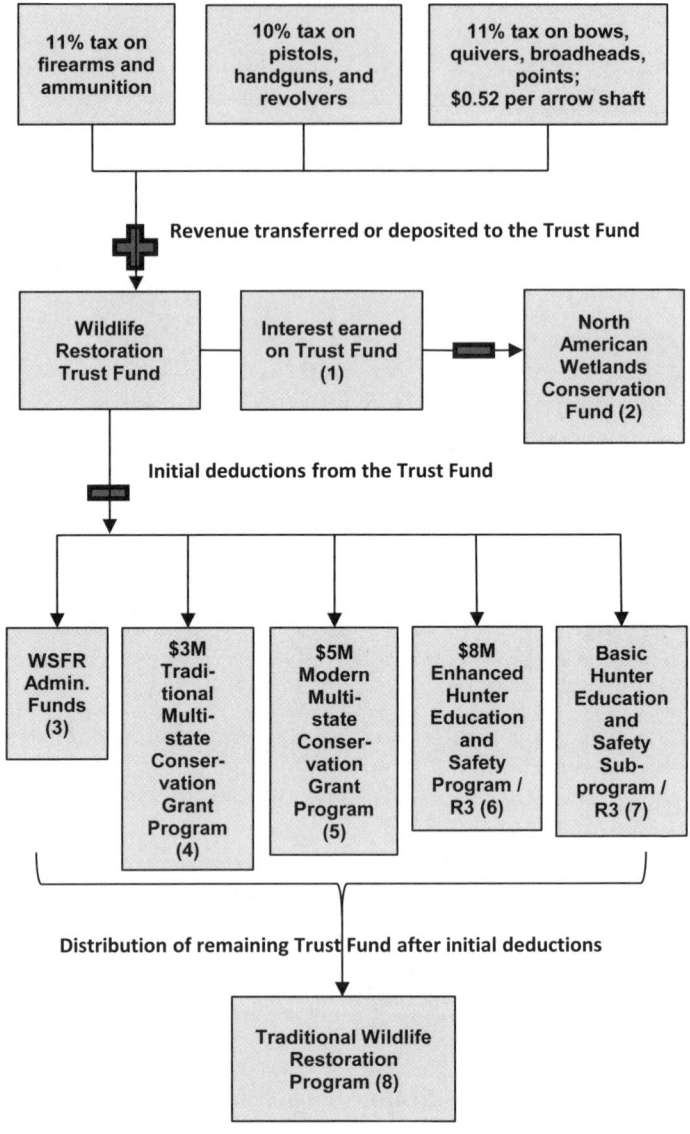

Source: U.S. Fish and Wildlife Service.

1. 16 U.S.C. 669b(b)
2. The North American Wetlands Conservation Fund was created by the North American Wetlands Conservation Act (NAWCA). The Act created a wetlands habitat program administered by the U.S. Fish and Wildlife Service. It is a non-regulatory, incentive-based, voluntary wildlife conservation program that provides matching grants to protect and manage wetland habitats for migratory birds and other wetlands wildlife in the U.S., Mexico, and Canada.

   It supports the North American Waterfowl Management Plan, an international agreement that provides a strategy for the long-term protection of wetlands and associated uplands habitats needed by waterfowl and other migratory birds in all of North America.

   NAWCA stimulates public-private partnerships to protect, restore, and manage wetland habitats. Such efforts include restoring wetlands that have been altered, enhancing water availability, and reducing soil erosion and the likelihood of floods. Many of the projects provide opportunities for wildlife watching, fishing, and hunting. NAWCA is widely recognized as helping once-decimated populations of waterfowl rebound to healthy levels.
3. Taken from total taxes; $ based on prior year amount, adjusted to CPI [16 U.S.C. 669c(a)]
4. Taken from total taxes [16 U.S.C. 669h-2(a)(1)(A)]
5. Taken from taxes on bows, quivers, broadheads, arrows, and points [16 U.S.C. 669h-2(a)(1)(B)]
6. Taken from total taxes [16 U.S.C. 669h-1(a)]
7. 1/2 of taxes collected on pistols, revolvers, handguns, bows, quivers, broadheads, arrows, and points [16 U.S.C. 669c(c)]
8. Remaining funds from taxes on firearms, ammunition, pistols, revolvers, handguns, bows, quivers, broadheads, arrows, and points [16 U.S.C. 669c(b)]

*Source: U.S. Fish and Wildlife Service.*

## CONSERVATION WORK FUNDED THROUGH THE WILDLIFE RESTORATION PROGRAM

To fully appreciate the scale of hunters' contributions to conservation, it is worth taking a closer look at the individual efforts funded with Pittman-Robertson excise tax revenues.

Almost two thirds of Pittman-Robertson funds are used by states to purchase, develop, and maintain wildlife management areas (or WMAs, as they are commonly known). WMAs are set aside specifically for wildlife and wildlife-related recreation, meaning they are used by both hunters and non-hunters. In total, states have purchased approximately 5 million acres for WMA use; another 40 million acres are managed for wildlife via agreements with private landowners. For comparison, this total acreage for wildlife management purposes exceeds the size of more than half of the states in the United States, including Missouri (44.0 million acres), Oklahoma (43.9 million acres), and Washington (42.5 million acres).[23]

There are numerous individual land management and habitat enhancement efforts made possible through Wildlife Restoration Program funding. Just a few examples include the planting of tree and shrub cover for wildlife, controlled burns of brush and grass to improve habitat, and various water management projects.

Species recovery makes up another critical area of the Wildlife Restoration Program. As a result of the ongoing management work done in this area over the years, the populations of numerous wildlife species that were once threatened or endangered have returned to healthy levels (note that one of the original goals of the Pittman-Robertson Act was to reverse the decline in the populations of various wildlife species). Prominent examples of species brought back thanks to funding through the Wildlife Restoration Program include game animals like the white-tailed deer, wild turkey, wood duck, Rocky Mountain elk, and tundra swan, as well as nongame animals like the bald eagle, trumpeter swan, and brown pelican (see the summary on the next page for examples of recovered species and their current population estimates).

## Hunters' Contributions to Wildlife: Endangered and Threatened Species Brought Back

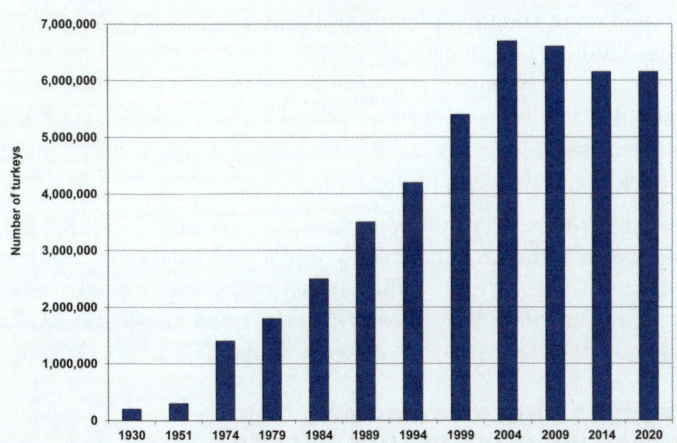

Source: *National Wild Turkey Federation.*

Thanks to the dedicated management and ongoing conservation work made possible through hunter dollars, the populations of numerous wildlife species have rebounded over the past century:[24]

|  | Population in 1900 | Population Today |
| --- | --- | --- |
| Wild turkey | 100,000 | 6-7 million |
| White-tailed deer | < 500,000 | 32 million |
| Wood duck | extremely rare | 6 million |
| Rocky Mountain elk | 40,000 | 1 million |
| Pronghorn antelope | 13,000 | 1 million |
| Bighorn sheep | < 20,000 | > 85,000 |

Additionally, by 1963, there were just 412 breeding pairs of bald eagles left in the contiguous U.S. Today, there are an estimated 15,000 breeding pairs in the contiguous U.S. and another 30,000 individual eagles in Alaska.

The resurgence of these once-endangered populations is due to the scientific management of the fish and wildlife community, guided by the principles of the North American Model of Wildlife Conservation and supported by the financial contributions of hunters.

## STATE-LEVEL HUNTING LICENSES, TAGS, AND PERMITS

Some of the most important wildlife conservation work in the United States is implemented at the state level by the individual fish and wildlife agencies, and many of these agencies are funded through sales of hunting and fishing licenses (a recent estimate indicates that about a third of all state fish and wildlife agency funding comes from these license sales).[25]

At last count, roughly 15 million licensed hunters generated more than $900 million in a single year through their purchases of state-level licenses, tags, and permits.[26] This funding is used to administer agency programs not only for species recovery and habitat maintenance but also enforcement and education (again, efforts that benefit not only hunters but the wider non-hunting public as well).

The collective reach of the state agencies in terms of their impact on wildlife is vast: each year, the agencies contribute a total of $5.6 billion to conservation. State fish and wildlife agency conservation work is carried out by more than 50,000 employees managing 464 million acres of land and 167 million acres of lakes, reservoirs, wetlands, and riparian areas.[27]

## THE FEDERAL DUCK STAMP AND THE NATIONAL WILDLIFE REFUGE SYSTEM

Since 1934, all U.S. waterfowl hunters have been required to purchase a Federal Migratory Bird Hunting and Conservation Stamp (commonly known as a Duck Stamp), with the proceeds used to preserve wetlands and other habitat through the National Wildlife Refuge System (the Duck Stamp is also purchased by collectors and non-hunters who wish to contribute). Since the program's inception, Federal Duck Stamp sales have produced more than $800 million, directly funding the purchase of more than 6 million acres of wetlands habitat.[28]

The 568 National Wildlife Refuges in the United States encompassing approximately 850 million acres provide habitat for a diverse range of fish and wildlife, including threatened and endangered species. For example, Florida's Hobe Sound National Wildlife Refuge (encompassing 980 acres) is home to loggerhead and green sea turtles; Mississippi's Sandhill Crane National Wildlife Refuge provides more than 19,000 acres for its namesake species; and Wildlife Refuges throughout California offer habitat for the California condor, the long-toed salamander, the least tern, and Lange's metalmark butterfly, among other species. These essential areas would not be possible without funding from the Federal Duck Stamp.

The Refuge System is economically important in its own right. In a recent year, more than 50 million people visited the National Wildlife Refuges, contributing $3.2 billion for local economies and helping to generate nearly 41,000 American jobs.[29] Hunting is allowed on more than half of the Refuges, which helps to ensure that game populations do not expand beyond biological carrying capacity—such scenarios can result in habitat degradation, leading to starvation or disease.

**NONPROFIT CONSERVATION ORGANIZATIONS**

Hunters also help to fund U.S. conservation efforts by joining and supporting nonprofit organizations dedicated to species recovery and habitat preservation. Major conservation organizations like the Rocky Mountain Elk Foundation, Ducks Unlimited, the National Wild Turkey Federation, and Pheasants Forever all have membership numbers in the hundreds of thousands, and most members are hunters. These organizations typically fund significant habitat restoration work on both public and private lands.

Another example of wildlife conservation work by a nonprofit organization that is mostly funded by hunters is the Rocky Mountain Elk Foundation's protected elk range. Using a combination of acquisitions, match dollars from partners, and access agreements and easements, the Foundation has secured protection for elk winter and summer ranges, migration corridors, and calving grounds. Overall, the Foundation and its partners have implemented almost 12,000 conservation projects benefiting more than 7.4 million acres of wildlife habitat. The cumulative value of these projects exceeds $1.1 billion.[30]

## The Vulnerability of Hunting to Public Opinion

Surveys consistently find that a sizable majority of Americans approve of legal hunting (see Chapter 4 for a closer look at attitudes toward hunting). Yet despite this tacit support, hunting remains vulnerable to the volatile nature of public opinion. Even though millions of Americans take to the fields and forests each year without incident to connect with nature and harvest game meat, viral photos on social media and high-profile news stories about the killings of celebrity animals can fuel anti-hunting sentiment and have practical consequences.

At times, vociferous public opposition to hunting has compelled private companies to make concessions to the outcry. For example, in the wake of the highly publicized killing of an African lion by an American dentist, several major airlines announced a ban on the import of hunting trophies from other countries.[31] Around the same time, Google refused to run an ad from the Rocky Mountain Elk Foundation depicting a legal elk hunt in New Mexico (after appeals from legislators, Google reversed its decision and allowed the ad).[32]

Organized opposition to legal hunting can also manifest at the ballot box. Over the years, various state-level ballot initiatives and referenda have been used to attempt to restrict or eliminate certain legal hunting activities, even when the state fish and wildlife agency is on record as opposing the measure in the interests of proper scientific wildlife management.[33] It is also the case that some citizen-sponsored initiatives and referenda benefit from lobbying and funding from out-of-state interests, including prominent national animal rights organizations.[34]

While acknowledging the need to listen to the public, biologists and other wildlife professionals have noted that such "management through referendum" can undercut a central tenet of the North American Model of Wildlife Conservation—that science, not public sentiment, be the principal tool used to manage wildlife.[35] Anti-hunting legislative measures also reinforce the need for agencies to communicate with the public about how and why wildlife management decisions are made.

The reputation of hunting is also susceptible to the rhetorical skills of its defenders and attackers. Formal debates about hunting can be particularly risky propositions when the pro-hunting side fails to make a persuasive case. A prominent example occurred in May 2016, when Intelligence Squared U.S., a nonprofit, nonpartisan organization committed to public discourse, hosted a live debate over the claim that hunters conserve wildlife.[36] Two speakers on each side argued for and against the claim. One of the pro-hunting debaters was the editor of *Field and Stream* magazine; the anti-hunting side included the president of the Humane Society of the United States.

The pro-hunting side diligently provided information explaining how hunters fund conservation efforts and how hunting is managed according to science. Yet, in relying primarily on factual information about hunting and its benefits, the pro-hunting side failed to anticipate the emotionally charged cherry-picked exaggerations and outright inaccuracies offered by the opposition—an approach that proved much more compelling to the debate audience. For example, at one point, an anti-hunting debater compared wildlife agency biologists supporting hunting to tobacco company scientists ignoring the health hazards of smoking—an abhorrent insult to the thousands of professionals who staff the nation's fish and wildlife agencies. The anti-hunters also spent several minutes attacking whale hunting—a topic completely unrelated to the concept of legal, regulated hunting in the United States. Nevertheless, the association was enough to muddy the waters and cast doubt on the pro-hunting arguments. Biological data, the principles of the North American Model of Wildlife Conservation, and all the successes of the modern conservation movement were all largely ignored in favor of sensationalism. According to an audience poll, a third of viewers before the debate said they were against the assertion that hunters conserve wildlife; afterward, based on the arguments offered by the two sides, two thirds were against the idea that hunters conserve wildlife.[37]

## Shaping Public Opinions and Attitudes

According to Dr. Thomas Heberlein of the University of Wisconsin, people's attitudes may tend toward consistency but are not bound by consistency.[38] This helps to explain how a solid majority of Americans can approve of hunting in surveys while, at the same time, a notable segment of the public can be persuaded to vote for ballot initiatives and support causes that limit or restrict hunting. Along the same lines, 13 percent of Americans identify as animal rights proponents (believing that animals have rights like humans and should not be used in any way), yet consume meat and wear leather.[39]

Hunters cannot make assumptions about which arguments for hunting will resonate with non-hunters. For example, defending hunting on the basis of tradition alone may invite opponents to counter that hunting today is done out of choice, not necessity. Hunters also should not assume that the lawful right of people to hunt is, by itself, a reason to support hunting: history is filled with examples of things that were once legal which are now understood to be immoral.

The outcome of the Intelligence Squared debate demonstrates that logic and facts alone will not be enough to move public opinion on hunting. It is not enough to recite basic information about how hunting benefits conservation, even though ample such evidence exists: as detailed earlier, hunting is critical as both a funding mechanism for conservation work and as a practical wildlife management tool.

> Research on persuasive communications highlights
> the importance of motivation, rather than
> information, in changing attitudes and behaviors.
>
>

The philosopher Aristotle observed that effective arguments consist not just of logic (logos) but of credibility (ethos) and emotion (pathos) as well. Thus, merely pointing out logical inconsistencies (like the hypocrisy of eating meat but opposing hunting), while important for winning a formal debate, will not necessarily win over the hearts and minds of those who are neutral or negative about hunting.

A few observations drawn from research on Americans' values and the types of communications most likely to change attitudes can inform the right approach forward. First, hunters must understand that Americans' attitudes toward wildlife have shifted in recent years. According to Dr. Michael Manfredo and Dr. Tara Teel of Colorado State University and their colleagues at the Ohio State University, modernization in the United States (encompassing urbanization and increasing levels of income and education) has changed how Americans view wildlife: as people move farther away from wildlife and into urban areas, they increasingly view wildlife in protective terms, becoming less approving of the consumptive use of animals.[40] (Chapter 5 provides more detail on Americans' attitudes toward wildlife, animal rights, and animal welfare issues.)

Research on persuasive communications highlights the importance of motivation, rather than information, in changing attitudes and behaviors.[41] On this, hunters should feel encouraged, as they likely share with most non-hunters common motivations like self-interest, social responsibility, and self-transcendence.[42] These motivations are readily applied to attitudes toward hunting and the use of animals. For example, the motivations of self-interest and social responsibility lie at the heart of hunting to obtain food in a safe and environmentally responsible way. Focusing on shared motivations, such as concern for the health of wildlife populations or the desire to consume healthy, organic protein, may help to reframe hunting by encouraging people to think about its purpose and benefits.

Today, the fish and wildlife community devotes significant time and resources to the recruitment, retention, and reactivation of hunters (collectively referred to as "R3"). Notably, a recent amendment to the Federal Aid in Wildlife Restoration Act allocated a portion of the excise tax revenues from archery equipment specifically for this purpose. Beyond the efforts of the state fish and wildlife agencies and their associations, industry groups and national nonprofits are committed to increasing participation in hunting as well. For example, the Council to Advance Hunting and the Shooting Sports, a national nongovernmental organization, currently develops tools and other resources to assist states with R3 planning and program implementation. However, without favorable public opinion on hunting, efforts to bring new hunters into the fold will be fruitless, just as future Federal Aid funding for conservation will be threatened. Public support for legal, regulated hunting is essential.

## Hunters Protect Habitat

Chincoteague National Wildlife Refuge is often referred to as "an ecological treasure."[43] The refuge protects critical coastline, coastal marsh and maritime forest habitats along an ever-urbanizing East Coast. At various times of the year, it is home to more than 320 species of birds, including bald eagles, peregrine falcons, songbirds, waterfowl, and shorebirds such as the endangered piping plover.

Chincoteague provides important habitat for 30 species of mammals including red fox, river otters, white-tailed deer, and the endangered Delmarva fox squirrel. Active wildlife management programs are working toward restoring the endangered piping plover and Delmarva fox squirrel from the brink of extinction. Chincoteague also provides important habitat for people—it is the sixth-most visited National Wildlife Refuge in the nation with almost 1.5 million visitors a year.

Over the years this refuge has provided habitat protection, wildlife restoration, and recreation for millions of Americans. Hunters were the primary drivers of the purchase of the Chincoteague National Wildlife Refuge in 1943 through their purchases of Migratory Bird Hunting and Conservation Stamps (known as Federal Duck Stamps). Refuges set aside using these funds include those shown in the accompanying list.

## Refuges of more than 1,000 acres with 95 percent or more of acreage secured with the Migratory Bird Conservation Fund, with acreage and percentage secured using the Fund[44]

Overflow (AK), 13,426 acres, 100%
Wapanocca (AK), 5,629 acres, 100%
Butte Sink (CA), 11,044 acres, 98%
Delevan (CA), 5,797 acres, 100%
Merced (CA), 3,806 acres, 100%
Sacramento (CA), 10,819 acres, 99%
Sutter (CA), 2,590 acres, 100%
Tulare Basin (CA), 4,279 acres, 96%
Willow Creek-Lurline (CA), 5,978 acres, 99%
Bombay Hook (DE), 16,331 acres, 95%
St. Vincent (FL), 12,494 acres, 99%
Camas (ID), 10,657 acres, 98%
Kootenai (ID), 2,774 acres, 100%
Muscatatuck (IN), 7,802 acres, 99%
Desoto (IA), 3,503 acres, 98%
Union Slough (IA), 2,916 acres, 100%
Quivira (KS), 22,019 acres, 99%
Reelfoot (KY), 2,040 acres, 100%
Upper Quachita (LA), 54,198 acres, 96%
Eastern Neck (MD), 2,286 acres, 100%
Monomoy (MA), 7,914 acres, 99%
Parker River (MA), 4,757 acres, 98%
Hamden Slough (MN), 3,223 acres, 99%
Sherburne (MN), 29,678 acres, 99%
Tamarac (MN), 35,198 acres, 99%
Coldwater River (MS), 2,482 acres, 96%
Mathews Brake (MS), 2,415 acres, 99%
Morgan Brake (MS), 7,464 acres, 97%
St. Catherine Creek (MS), 25,091 acres, 99%
Yazoo (MS), 12,943 acres, 100%
Clarence Cannon (MO), 3,750 acres, 99%
Mingo (MO), 21,661 acres, 99%
Lee Metcalf (MT), 2,800 acres, 96%
Swan River (MT), 1,569 acres, 100%
Bosque Del Apache (NM), 57,331 acres, 99%
Las Vegas (NM), 8,672 acres, 100%
Iroquois (NY), 10,828 acres, 99%
Pea Island (NC), 5,834 acres, 99%
Pee Dee (NC), 8,467 acres, 99%
Chase Lake (ND), 4,449 acres, 100%
White Lake (ND), 1,040 acres, 100%
Ankeny (OR), 2,796 acres, 100%
Baskett Slough (OR), 2,492 acres, 100%
William L. Finley (OR), 5,706 acres, 100%
Dakota Grassland (SD), 2,794 acres, 100%
Hatchie (TN), 11,556 acres, 97%
Big Boggy (TX), 4,526 acres, 97%
Brazoria (TX), 45,764 acres, 96%
Little Sandy (TX), 3,802 acres, 100%
McFaddin (TX), 58,861 acres, 100%
Moody (TX), 3,517 acres, 100%
Texas Point (TX), 8,952 acres, 100%
Horicon (WI), 21,414 acres, 99%

## Species Restored: A Tale of Two Birds

Hunters are collectively one of the most important sources of funding for wildlife conservation in the United States. Through licenses, fees, excise taxes (see the Federal Aid in Wildlife Restoration Act, or Pittman-Robertson Act, of 1937[45]), and private donations, hunters contribute an estimated $1.6 billion annually for conservation programs and efforts.[46] This funding is responsible for saving many wildlife species, including the gray wolf, peregrine falcon, California condor, and Canada goose. Many people are also aware of the recovery of the bald eagle, a much-celebrated success. Perhaps less well-known but no less important, however, is the recovery of wild turkey in the U.S. And hunters played a large role in making these recoveries possible.

Both the bald eagle and the wild turkey are quintessentially American symbols. The bald eagle is a striking bird of prey commonly associated with the values of freedom and liberty. The wild turkey is a standard centerpiece of America's colonial history and Thanksgiving tradition, which celebrates our abundance of food from the harvest but has also become a symbolic representation of appreciation of more than just food.

Both the eagle and the turkey are prominent figures in the American psyche as emblems of the strength and abundance inherent to our country.

In the first half of the 20th century, the bald eagle population declined and was facing extinction. While bald eagles were once very common in the U.S., an estimated 412 nesting pairs were left in the contiguous U.S. by the 1960s.[47] The primary contributing factors to the population decline were habitat destruction and degradation, use of pesticides (particularly DDT, which made female eagles sterile or caused thinning of the egg shells, preventing hatching), and illegal shooting. Federal efforts to protect and restore bald eagles included the Bald and Golden Eagle Protection Act (1940), the banning of DDT (1972), and the Endangered Species Act (1973).[48] In June 2007, the bald eagle was removed from the list of threatened and endangered species, and there are now an estimated 15,000 breeding pairs in the contiguous U.S. (and another 30,000 individual eagles in Alaska).[49] During recovery, state fish and wildlife agencies were intricately involved in the conservation efforts, such as habitat restoration and protection, as well as relocating and breeding eagles.[50] Funds for those efforts came from hunters, largely through hunting license fees and the Federal Aid in Wildlife Restoration program.[51]

Much like the bald eagle, wild turkey populations were abundant early in the history of our nation, providing an important food source for Native Americans and early settlers. Hunting pressure and habitat loss, as well as too much market hunting, negatively impacted wild turkey populations, and by the 1920s the wild turkey had disappeared from 18 of the 39 states in which it was originally found.[52] The wild turkey population in the U.S. eventually declined to only 30,000 birds nationwide.[53] Restoration efforts began in the 1930s, with state fish and wildlife commissions and agencies dedicating resources to research and efforts in the field. Although initial efforts at releasing pen-raised birds did not prove successful, eventually relocation of wild turkeys into suitable habitat led the way. Today, thriving wild turkey populations can be found in 49 U.S. states (as well as in Canada and Mexico), with an estimated population of 6 to 7 million turkeys.[54] Conservation efforts again were largely funded by hunters' and sportsmen's dollars through license fees and the Federal Aid in Wildlife Restoration program.

## Be Patient: Americans Care About Wildlife but Don't Know Much About It

### Overall Public Knowledge Grades

Public knowledge of fish and wildlife management was graded based on responses to 18 questions.

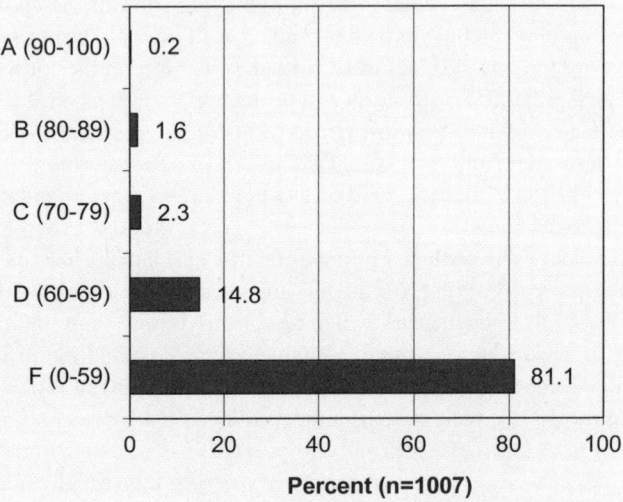

Source: *Responsive Management.*[55]

Hunters and non-hunters share a lot of common ground, especially a love of wildlife. But research shows that most Americans have fairly low knowledge about wildlife management issues. In one state survey, most general population residents "failed" a series of knowledge questions about wildlife, habitat, and fish and wildlife agency responsibilities, typically answering less than half of the questions correctly.

It's useful to remember that concepts widely understood by hunters—such as basic wildlife management and the role of hunting in conservation—may not be as obvious to the average non-hunting member of the public.

This means that hunters must craft their messages and arguments carefully, using the right words, concepts, and phrases. Perhaps above all else, hunters must be patient.

## Key Takeaways

- Hunting has functioned as a food source for more than a million years; more recently, it has become important as a tool for wildlife management.

- Through their purchases of firearms, ammunition, and archery equipment taxed through the Federal Aid in Wildlife Restoration Act (also known as the Pittman-Robertson Act), hunters are one of the most important sources of funding for conservation in the United States.

- Negative public opinion on hunting can result in practical consequences such as restrictions on legal hunting activities.

- Anti-hunting sentiment can also encourage support for ballot initiatives and referenda that attempt to limit or prohibit hunting activities.

- Information alone will not be enough to change public opinion on hunting.

- The hunting community must focus on persuasive messages based on motivations and values that resonate with the public.

- Remember that increasing cultural acceptance of hunting is different than increasing participation in hunting. But the former must precede the latter—hunting can only take place in a society that accepts it.

- The hunting community should work to bridge the gap between hunters and non-hunting recreationists. While a relatively small percentage of Americans hunt, tens of millions of Americans enjoy hiking, camping, and viewing wildlife. These activities benefit from the healthy habitat and wild, undeveloped areas made possible through funding provided by hunters.

## CHAPTER 2

# Why Words Matter

**WORDS MATTER WHEN IT COMES** *to talking about hunting. Certain words resonate while others have the opposite effect, eliciting disapproval or misunderstanding. Those who advocate for hunting must think about the impact of the words they use. Most importantly, they should follow communications and messaging recommendations based on research over their own assumptions about the language that will reach non-hunters.*

Explaining a bedrock principle of communication, pollster Frank Luntz notes that it's not what you say—it's what they hear.[56] In other words, hunters cannot assume that the terms and phrases that are meaningful to them are the same ones that will resonate with non-hunters. Individual words have specific connotations—they imply, evoke, or suggest certain things based on cultural or historical associations, whether accurately or not. Using the right words and phrases to talk about hunting can mean the difference between building new support or hardening existing opposition.

Understanding the importance of words is not a theoretical or abstract notion—as this and later chapters will show, there are quantifiable differences in the way certain words resonate better than others. These differences matter when constructing the most effective formal messages and communications campaigns in support of hunting, but also when having productive conversations about hunting in more casual settings.

## How Phrasing Impacts Perception

The extent to which wording can affect perceptions of the intended or implied meaning is evident in the following examples. Note that the selection of these examples and the brief commentary that accompanies them are not meant to imply any political or social positions; rather, the examples have been chosen because of their usefulness in illustrating the impact of phrasing. Consider the differences in the following:

- *"Illegal alien"* versus *"undocumented worker."* These examples show how carefully chosen adjectives can be used to emphasize certain traits or details.
- *"Death tax"* versus *"estate tax."* In these examples, the concept in question is alternately framed as something that would apply to everyone or to only a subset of people.
- *"Assault rifle"* versus *"modern sporting rifle."* The first of the two terms shown here represents a more incendiary approach by including a word evocative of violent conflict ("assault").
- *"Trophy hunting"* versus *"hunting for meat."* This last example is important, as research has shown that Americans are far more likely to approve of hunting for meat than hunting for a trophy.[57] Accordingly, opponents of hunting will often seek to define *all* hunting as trophy hunting specifically, precisely because of the polarizing connotations of the word "trophy." According to one focus group participant, "I think there are two classes of hunters: subsistence [or] as a way of life, and pure sport and trophy hunting."[58]

(See Chapter 4 for more detailed discussion on how approval of hunting varies depending on the explicit reason given.)

## Measuring Approval of Hunting Using Specific Terms

On a basic level, wording affects how people perceive hunting. In the early 1990s, focus group discussions conducted by Responsive Management with members of the general public revealed the tendency for some people to interpret the term "hunting" by itself as being synonymous with "poaching." Further discussion (and subsequent survey research) suggested that some people view recreational hunting (that is, hunting managed and regulated by state fish and wildlife agencies) as being a threat to certain wildlife populations.[59] For these reasons, public opinion studies on hunting often now ask about "legal" or "regulated" hunting as opposed to simply "hunting."

Incorporating the word "regulated" alone, however, can also lead to potential misperceptions, as when people mishear or misinterpret the phrase "regulated hunting" (as in hunting that is subject to rules and regulations) as *"regulating* hunting" (as in applying additional rules or regulations to hunting that did not exist before).

A comparison of surveys[60] measuring approval of hunting may illustrate the potential effect of this minor but crucial difference in wording. The first survey asked about approval of "regulated hunting," while the second survey asked about approval of "legal hunting." In these studies, 61 percent of respondents expressed approval of "regulated hunting," compared to 79 percent who expressed approval of "legal hunting." Of course, while it is impossible to verify that some of the respondents in the first survey misinterpreted the phrase "regulated" as referring to additional rules or regulations on hunting, the potential implications of the wording difference are nonetheless useful to keep in mind.

Hunting that is described as both legal *and* regulated may be met with the most approval. For example, one survey that used this wording had 88 percent of respondents expressing approval, with more than half expressing *strong* approval.[61] It may be that the added specificity helps to communicate hunting in a positive way as a carefully managed and controlled activity.

## Employing Words Known to Resonate

Chapter 6 of this book is devoted to the most effective individual arguments and messages in support of hunting; this chapter shows how the inclusion of specific words can result in measurable differences in the impact of messages. First, though, it is worth making some general observations about some specific terms and phrases of interest.

In his book, *Words That Work*, Frank Luntz draws on the findings of extensive opinion research to offer observations about the relative impact of certain words.[62] Some of these words have been tested in research specifically about hunting, with the results generally confirming their effectiveness. Several key words are presented below as examples that may be particularly relevant to conversations about hunting. Consider the following:

- "*Lifestyle.*" Luntz describes this term as "self-defined and aspirational," and hunting is clearly an example of a lifestyle choice with social, biological, nutritional, and economic benefits.
- "*Efficient.*" Luntz notes the tendency for people to associate the term "efficient" with the idea of getting more for less, or the wise use of resources. Hunting, being an expression of self-sufficiency, is also certainly an efficient use of resources in terms of the consumption of meat. For instance, in some cases, the venison from a single deer yields enough meat to last an entire season; in other cases, it is gifted

to the friends and family of the hunter or is donated to charitable programs like Hunters for the Hungry.
- *"Investment."* Another term described by Luntz as evoking the responsible use of resources, the purchase of a hunting license can be seen as an investment in the future of America's natural resources thanks to the funding it provides for essential conservation and wildlife management work. Additionally, the very act of learning to hunt marks an important personal and social investment.
- *"Independent."* Luntz's research emphasizes "independent" as an effective way to communicate the state of having no constrictions. Again, the concept of an "independent consumer" ties in effectively with the appeal of hunting as an activity of self-sufficiency and self-reliance.

Other research[63] suggests the particular appeal of the term *"healthy,"* as might be applied in conversations about healthy habitat, healthy wildlife, healthy people, and healthy food (note that all of these concepts have some overlap with hunting). Separate research[64] has shown that terms relating to *"children"* and *"family"* can be effective at encouraging people to support and take part in nature-based outdoor activities.

## Effective Ways to Describe Hunting as a Food Source

Hunting is unique from other recreational activities in that it offers a number of benefits as a food source. Terms like "organic," "all-natural," and "free-range" have become increasingly popular as descriptors suggestive of healthy, chemical-free choices in food products, including meat (sales of products labeled "organic" have grown in recent years, attributed in part to consumer interest in the healthiest options available).[65]

The adjective "humane" has also gained traction among consumers who have ethical concerns about the origins of the meat they consume. Comments in focus groups suggest that some Americans are uneasy with the factory farming practices of the industrial meat industry, desiring a more humane alternative to meat production.

Hunting for food is consistent with all of these things: the meat from hunting is organic, all-natural, and sourced in a humane way from a free-ranging animal. In this way, the right words can be used to communicate hunting as an environmentally friendly method of sourcing meat that reduces animal suffering while connecting people with their food.

## *Not Just Theoretical: Words Affect Attitudes*

A practical example of the impact phrasing can have on public opinion comes from a Responsive Management survey of Pennsylvania residents, in which different phrases measured support for essentially the same thing. One version of the survey question asked respondents if they supported using "lethal methods" to manage the deer population, while the other version asked about support for "legal, regulated hunting" to manage deer. Even though both phrases implied that deer would be killed, support for the latter wording was more than 20 percent higher among the same respondents.

**In general, do you support or oppose lethal methods to manage deer populations in Pennsylvania?**

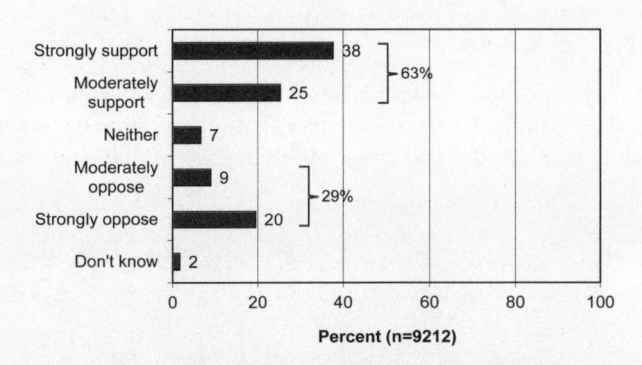

| Response | Percent |
|---|---|
| Strongly support | 38 |
| Moderately support | 25 |
| Neither | 7 |
| Moderately oppose | 9 |
| Strongly oppose | 20 |
| Don't know | 2 |

Support: 63%; Oppose: 29%
Percent (n=9212)

**How about legal, regulated hunting? (Do you support or oppose this method of controlling deer populations in Pennsylvania?)**

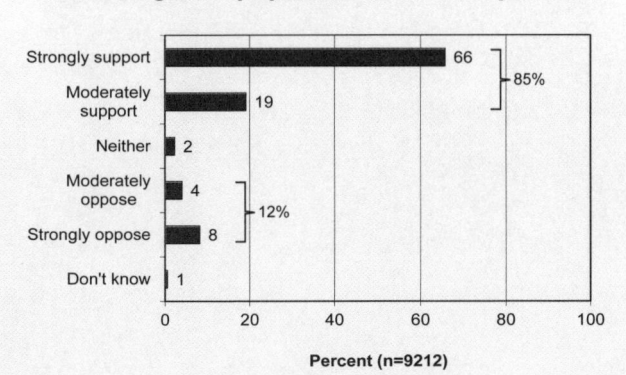

| Response | Percent |
|---|---|
| Strongly support | 66 |
| Moderately support | 19 |
| Neither | 2 |
| Moderately oppose | 4 |
| Strongly oppose | 8 |
| Don't know | 1 |

Support: 85%; Oppose: 12%
Percent (n=9212)

Source: *Responsive Management.*[66]

## Key Takeaways

- Words matter when talking about hunting.

- Hunters should not talk about hunting based on what they assume will resonate with non-hunters. Instead, they should listen to what the research says about effective messaging and communications on hunting.

- The phrase "trophy hunting" provokes a strong negative reaction among many non-hunters. Strictly in terms of the language surrounding hunting, advocates should attempt to separate the concept of hunting in general from trophy hunting specifically.

- Terms like "healthy," "organic," "all-natural," and "free-range" can be particularly effective when communicating the food-related benefits of hunting.

- Employ words and phrases known to resonate—for example, say "legal, regulated hunting" to let non-hunters know that hunting is controlled and regulated and that it helps lead to healthy wildlife populations.

## CHAPTER 3

# Participation in Hunting

**THIS CHAPTER DETAILS VARIOUS ASPECTS** *of Americans' participation in hunting, including the characteristics of hunters and their contributions to the U.S. economy. The chapter also examines hunting participation trends and the most important threats that legal hunting in America faces today.*

## Hunting Participation Numbers and Trends

To communicate about hunting effectively, it is necessary to first understand the entire picture of hunting participation in the United States, including recent trends and the characteristics and preferences of American hunters. This information provides useful context for discussions about hunting, especially by illustrating the degree to which hunting is ingrained in American society.

### NUMBER OF HUNTERS

There are more than 11 million active hunters in the United States today. According to the most recent *National Survey of Fishing, Hunting, and Wildlife Associated Recreation*, 11.5 million people age 16 and older participated in hunting in 2016.[67] This is approximately 4.4 percent of the U.S. population age 16 and older in 2016.[68]

The *National Survey*, conducted every 5 years since 1955 by the U.S. Fish and Wildlife Service and the U.S. Bureau of the Census, however, is only one of several major sources of data on participation in hunting. Other major data sources measuring hunting participation result in varying estimated numbers of hunters in the U.S. that are based on different ways of both defining and measuring participation. See the table below for the total number of U.S. hunters from several major data sources.

### Number of Hunters in the United States

| Source of Data | Number of Hunters | Year | Comments |
|---|---|---|---|
| 2016 National Survey | 11.5 million | 2016 | 1-year timeframe; any participation at all (number shown for age 16 and older who participated in 2016) |
| | 1.8 million | 2016 | 1-year timeframe; any participation at all (number shown for ages 6 to 15 who participated in 2015) |
| Federal Aid License Data | 15.6 million | 2016 | 1-year timeframe; paid license holders |
| NSGA | 18.1 million | 2019 | 1-year timeframe; firearm hunters; participated more than once in previous year; age 7 and older |
| Cornell University | 41.2 million | 2013 | Consider themselves an active hunter; age 18 and older (number calculated from survey results and U.S. Census Bureau population estimate for age 18 and older in 2013) |

Sources: *U.S. Fish and Wildlife Service/U.S. Census; U.S. Fish and Wildlife Service (license holders data); National Sporting Goods Association; Cornell University.*[69]

For reference, the *National Survey* determines the number of participants based on participation rates in a large random sample of U.S. households. Data for the *National Survey* are collected and reported separately for two age groups (those who are ages 6 to 15 and those age 16 and older). (Note that the 2016 survey measured hunting participation in 2016 among those age 16 and older; however, for those ages 6 to 15, participation was not measured for 2016 but for 2015, as well as for 2014 and 2013.) For those age 16 and older, participation is measured only for a single year, which can lead to the exclusion of some who do not hunt every year.

Hunting license sales provide another source of data on hunting participation. License sales data are collected by each state and submitted to the U.S. Fish and Wildlife Service to be compiled as part of the Federal

Aid in Wildlife Restoration Act (also known as the Pittman-Robertson Act; see Chapter 1 for an extensive discussion of this legislation). The data are "de-duplicated" within each state to account for individuals who purchased more than one license or permit, thereby determining the actual number of hunters in the state. The timeframe for the data is again a single year. The data include youth but do not include anyone exempt from having to purchase a license to hunt, such as private landowners hunting on their own land.

The National Sporting Goods Association (NSGA) measures hunting participation in a single year for individuals ages 7 and older.

Additional sources of periodic hunting participation data include the Sports & Fitness Industry Association (SFIA), which publishes participation data through the Outdoor Foundation, and the *National Survey on Recreation and the Environment* (NSRE). While each of these sources measures participation, the timeframe, age range and definitions of participation vary.

> Research suggests that at least a third of hunters do not hunt every year—in any given year, there are more people who self-identify as hunters than actually hunt.

A notable disadvantage to measuring participation for only one year is that churn is a well-documented aspect of hunting. Churn refers to the proportion of hunters who do not hunt each year. In addition to extremely avid hunters who hunt each year, there is a group of hunters who skip occasional years or do not find an opportunity to go every year due to work, health, or other factors.

Research suggests that at least a third of hunters do not hunt every year—in any given year, there are more people who self-identify as hunters than actually hunt. Among active hunters (those who had hunted in the past 2 years), only 63 percent had hunted all 5 of the previous 5 years (37 percent had not hunted all 5 of the previous 5 years).[70]

Some researchers choose to measure hunting participation by determining the proportion of the population that has hunted within the past 3 years or even 5 years to account for churn. Other researchers have used self-identification rather than participation to determine the proportion of the population that is encompassed by the term, *hunters*.

The 2013 Cornell *National Social Survey* found that about 17 percent of Americans considered themselves active hunters.[71] Using U.S. Census population estimates for 2013,[72] 17 percent of the population means approximately 41.2 million adults age 18 and older in the U.S. considered themselves hunters at the time. Although Cornell surveyed those age 18 or older and the *National Survey* measured participation among those age 16 or older, Cornell still estimates three to four times as many hunters as the 2011 and 2016 *National Survey* estimates.

## HUNTING PARTICIPATION TRENDS

The *National Survey* indicates that participation in hunting has declined since the 1980s. Note, however, that the *National Survey* methodology indicates that the most recent survey is best compared to past surveys beginning with 1991. When looking at absolute numbers (top graph) or at the rate in the population (bottom graph), there has been a decline in participation, going from 14.1 million hunters (a rate of 7.4 percent of the U.S. population 16 years old and older) in 1991 to 11.5 million (4.5 percent) in 2016. The values are included for hunting overall in each of these two figures.[73]

**Number of hunters (in millions).**

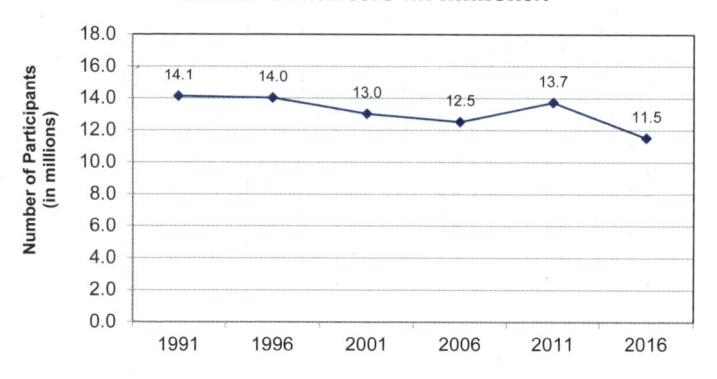

| Year | Number (millions) |
|---|---|
| 1991 | 14.1 |
| 1996 | 14.0 |
| 2001 | 13.0 |
| 2006 | 12.5 |
| 2011 | 13.7 |
| 2016 | 11.5 |

**National hunting participation rate.**

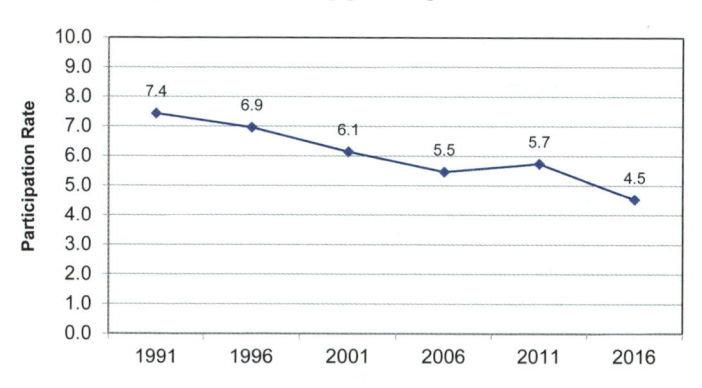

| Year | Participation Rate |
|---|---|
| 1991 | 7.4 |
| 1996 | 6.9 |
| 2001 | 6.1 |
| 2006 | 5.5 |
| 2011 | 5.7 |
| 2016 | 4.5 |

Source: U.S. Fish and Wildlife Service/U.S. Census Bureau (ages 16 years old and older).[74]

Looking at Federal Aid license data from 1980 to 2018, the number of hunting license holders in the United States has hovered around 15 million.[75] Also shown are the *National Survey* numbers for comparison starting in 1991.

**Hunting License Holders (Federal Aid Data) and Number of Hunters (National Survey Data)**

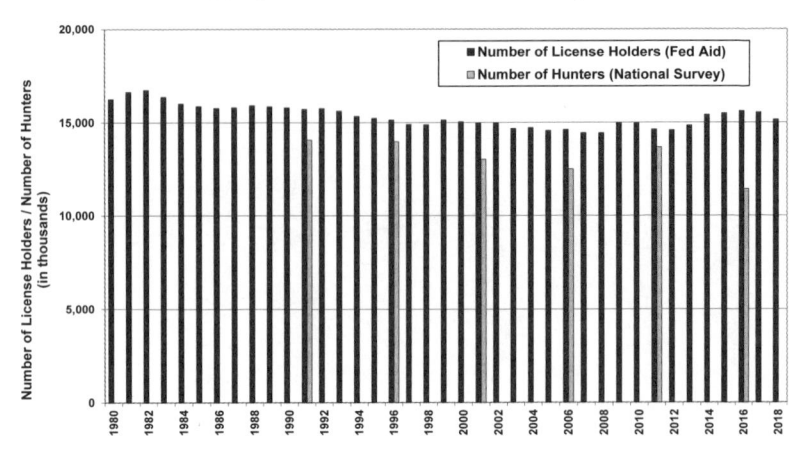

*Source: U.S. Fish and Wildlife Service (for license holder data); U.S. Fish and Wildlife Service/U.S. Census Bureau (ages 16 years old and older) (for Survey data).*

## HUNTING INITIATION

Understanding how hunters become hunters helps us understand participation trends. Perhaps most importantly, research indicates that it takes a hunter to make a hunter. Hunters come from hunting families, and hunting families produce hunters. Therefore, it is logical to expect that hunting participation may continue to decline if there are fewer hunting families to initiate new hunters.

Almost all hunters are initiated when they are young by family members. Hunters initiated this way hunt more frequently and are more likely to be avid hunters throughout their life when compared to hunters initiated in some other way. The presence of other family members who hunt, the exposure to hunting, and the presence of the hunting culture are of utmost importance in hunting initiation (as well as continuation).[76]

Initiation into hunting is also most commonly through male family members, particularly the father or stepfather, but also through uncles, brothers, and grandfathers. The majority of active hunters were first taken hunting by their father (68 percent), followed by friends (8 percent), grandfather (7 percent), spouse (6 percent), and uncle (6 percent).[77]

PARTICIPATION IN HUNTING

*Female participation in hunting has increased over the past two decades. Additionally, archery continues to play an important role in hunting, with a third of all U.S. hunters using some type of archery equipment to hunt.*[78]

In contrast, those who are introduced to hunting by friends instead of family typically start hunting as young adults and are more likely to quit hunting within a few years because they lack the family support. And very few individuals start and continue hunting without any mentor at all to introduce them to the sport.[79] However, this axiom may be changing a little, with more "adult onset" hunters taking up the sport outside of family—an encouraging sign but still an exception to the rule. Some of these encouraging signs include indications that the number of female hunters is rising through the targeted recruitment of new female hunters.

## General Characteristics of U.S. Hunters

This section looks at the general characteristics of hunters in the United States, including the species that they hunt, the equipment that they use, and their motivations for hunting. Characteristics relating to hunter education are examined as well.

### HUNTING PARTICIPATION BY SPECIES

Hunters most commonly hunt big game like deer and elk, small game such as rabbit and squirrel, and migratory birds including waterfowl. According to the 2016 *National Survey*, 9.2 million hunters (of 11.5 million hunters age 16 and older total) hunted big game in 2016, followed by 3.5 million small game hunters and 2.4 million migratory bird hunters.[80] Note that the sum of hunters by species type is more than the total of 11.5 million because hunters may have hunted multiple species. Deer is, by far, the most hunted species in the United States with 8.1 million hunters hunting deer in 2016, followed by wild turkey as the next most hunted species with 2.0 million hunters.

### HUNTING PARTICIPATION BY EQUIPMENT USED

Hunters most often hunt with firearms such as rifles and shotguns, although many hunt with bows and other archery equipment. A study in 2008 found that rifles (typically used by 69 percent of hunters) and shotguns (55 percent) were the most used hunting equipment, while 23 percent of hunters typically used archery equipment and 13 percent used muzzleloader rifles.[81] Research in 2018 showed that among hunters who hunted with firearms, 68 percent used a shotgun and 63 percent used a rifle to hunt, followed by 44 percent who used archery equipment.[82]

**Hunting participation by species type.**

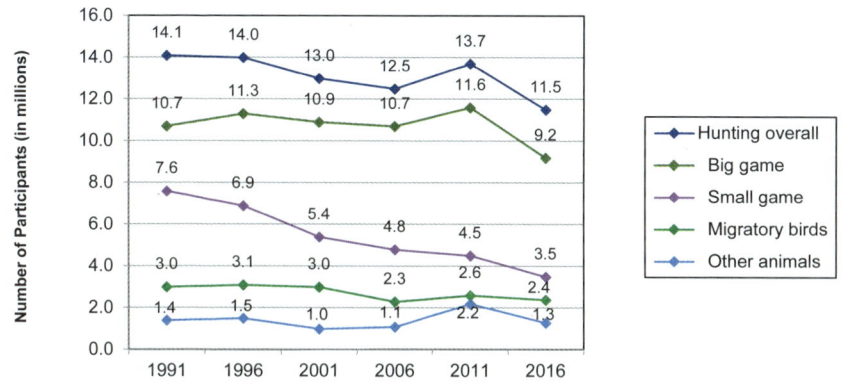

*Source: U.S. Fish and Wildlife Service/U.S. Census Bureau (ages 16 years old and older).*

The data from the 2008 and 2018 studies suggest hunting with archery equipment, or bowhunting, may be increasing. Other sources of participation data also suggest bowhunting is either increasing or has stayed relatively stable just as hunting overall has declined. For example, NSGA data show that the number of bowhunters has increased by 28 percent from 4.72 million in 2001 to 6.04 million in 2019 while the same source shows hunting participation overall increased by only 2 percent over that same time period.[83] Moreover, about a third of bowhunters say that their participation in the activity has increased over the past 5 years. Millennials (18 to 34 years old in 2017), who are the newest generation of adult hunters, have the highest percentage in the "increased participation" group in contrast to older age groups.[84]

## HUNTER MOTIVATIONS

Studies show that the top motivations for hunting are largely recreational, social, or naturalistic. However, hunting for the meat is also increasing as interest in natural and organic food sources continues to grow (the locavore movement that sprang out of this interest is discussed later in this chapter). Hunting for a trophy remains extremely low in importance.

In 2011, hunters were asked to name their most important reasons for hunting. The top two responses were enjoyment (37 percent) and aesthetic reasons (28 percent). The utilitarian reason of hunting for the meat was named by 24 percent. Hunting for a trophy was low in the ranking at less than 0.5 percent.[85]

More recently, research shows that American hunters most often name the meat as their most important reason for hunting, and that the percentage of hunters who hunt mainly for the meat continues to grow. Responsive Management, which has tracked hunting participation for almost three decades, periodically asks hunters to choose their single, most important reason for hunting from a list that includes for a trophy, to be close to nature, to be with family and friends, for the sport or recreation, or for the meat. In 2017, about two in five hunters nationwide selected for the meat—by far the most popular answer. (While research shows that hunters hunt for numerous reasons, this question was designed to identify their *top* reason for hunting.)[86]

Rather than a new development, this finding is instead the latest data point in a continuing trend. Hunting for the meat was once the most important reason for hunting (in 1980) but fell for a while (1995 through 2006), and then rose again in importance in 2013 and 2017. Although hunting for the meat is increasing in importance, hunting for the sport or recreation has always been one of the most important reasons why hunters participate, and it remains an important reason today. By contrast, hunting for a trophy is *not* an important reason for the vast majority of hunters.

**Motivations for hunting.**

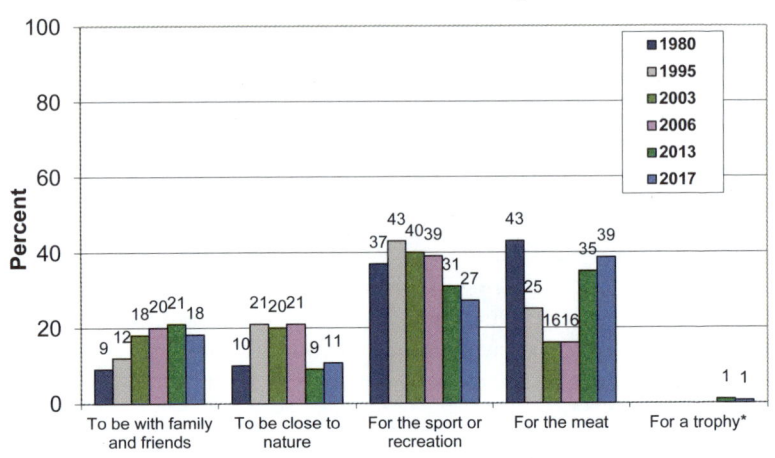

*Included in answer set only in 2013 and 2017

Sources: S. Kellert, Responsive Management, National Shooting Sports Foundation.[86]

The reasons for the growing emphasis on game meat as a primary motivator for hunting range from the economic to the sociocultural—the shift cannot be attributed to a single reason alone. An important benefit of hunting is its potential as a source of food that hunters can acquire themselves in a cost-effective manner, especially during times of economic downturn or other turmoil, such as the 2020 Coronavirus pandemic.

Another reason for the uptick in hunters who went out mostly for the meat is the locavore movement, a growing national trend reflecting interest in eating locally and taking a more active role in the acquisition of food, especially organic, free-range, chemical- and hormone-free meat. Through the locavore movement, individuals from nontraditional hunting backgrounds have sought lessons and seminars offering instruction on how to hunt and process game meat. Locavore hunters are often educated millennials who hail from urban and suburban areas; lacking traditional hunting mentors, they nonetheless have been moved to take up hunting as adults for reasons of self-sufficiency, health, sustainability, or a desire to reconnect with nature.

## HUNTER EDUCATION REQUIREMENTS

New hunters are required to complete a state-certified hunter education program. Hunter education began in the 1940s in an effort to reduce hunting-related accidents and fatalities and to promote responsible hunter behavior. Hunter education is now required and programs are offered in all 50 states. Hunter education has helped to make hunting safer by reducing the number of hunting-related incidents in the field.

Today, the International Hunter Education Association reports that hunting-related incidents are at their lowest in the history of documenting such injuries and fatalities.[87] For example, in 1968, Texas recorded 105 hunting-related incidents, with 37 fatalities; approximately 855,000 hunting licenses were sold that year. Although the Texas Parks and Wildlife Department had only started tracking such incidents two years prior in 1966, the incidence figures remain the historical high since tracking began in the state. Nearly 30 years after hunter education became state law in Texas, the Department recorded only 21 firearm-related accidents, with 2 fatalities, in 2017, when nearly 1.25 million hunting licenses were sold.[88]

## Not Just Rural, White Males: Nontraditional Locavore Hunters Seek Healthy Organic Meat

While motivations for hunting vary, more Americans today are heading afield specifically to obtain local, healthy meat. Driven by an interest in organic food, sustainability, and self-sufficiency, the growing cohort of "locavore" hunters is notable because they are somewhat demographically distinct from the typical rural, white male hunter: locavore hunters often include urban and suburban residents of both genders who were not initiated into hunting as children, instead developing an interest as adults.

A number of state fish and wildlife agencies now offer "learn to hunt" programs that provide instruction on hunting as a way to source local proteins. Such programs are often advertised at farmers markets and other areas popular with "foodies." In his book, *The Mindful Carnivore*, author Tovar Cerulli writes about the phenomenon of "adult-onset hunting" via his own experiences taking up the activity for food- and health-related reasons. The locavore hunter movement has also inspired community programs and cookbooks devoted to locally sourced foods, including meat obtained through hunting.

The motivation to hunt specifically for the meat is an important one, as Americans overwhelmingly approve of hunting for this reason.

Today, hunting-related incidents are at their lowest in the history of documenting such injuries and fatalities.

⊕

Texas serves as an example of a state (just one of many) with effective hunter education laws. The NRA designed the first hunter education program in 1949 and continues to provide this important service today through a free online course designed to help new hunters of all ages learn how to hunt safely and responsibly. As the accident statistics bear out, hunter education works.

## The Economic Contribution of U.S. Hunters

Hunters contribute a significant amount of money to the U.S. economy, both through direct spending and through multiplier effects impacting tax revenues and jobs.

In 2016, expenditures from hunters totaled more than $26 billion in the United States. In addition to licenses and equipment, hunters spend money on food and lodging, transportation, membership dues, land leases, magazines and books, and more. This spending benefits not only wildlife and natural resource management and conservation but also supports businesses, jobs, and the economy overall.

The contribution hunters make to the U.S. economy is substantial. When a hunter spends money on a hunting trip, the value of that money is not limited to that immediate transaction—calculating the overall economic impact using the multiplier effect, the value of hunting has been estimated at approximately $36 billion, supporting as many as 525,000 jobs nationwide. Additionally, through license and permit fees, excise taxes, and donations, hunters contribute approximately $1.6 billion a year for conservation programs and wildlife management efforts.

⊕

According to the 2016 *National Survey*, hunters spent an estimated $800 million on licenses and permits, $7.4 billion on hunting equipment, $3.2 billion on transportation, and $3.1 billion on food and lodging for their hunting trips.[89] The *National Survey* calculations include additional spending categories for auxiliary and special equipment, land leasing, and more, ultimately totaling $26.2 billion. Southwick Associates used the *National Survey* data to further calculate hunter expenses and estimates that the average cost of each hunting trip taken in 2016 is $184.[90]

The contribution hunters make to the U.S. economy through hunting is substantial. When a hunter spends money on a hunting trip, the value of that money does not stop with that transaction; the expense supports the store, helps pay the wages of store employees, helps pay the supplier and manufacturer of the product, and more. The progression of the money through several levels and industries within our economy is called the multiplier effect. The multiplier effect spreads and continues to impact the U.S. economy beyond the initial transaction. Using the multiplier effect to calculate impact, the value of hunter spending in 2016 has been estimated at approximately $36 billion for the economy, supporting as many as 525,000 jobs in many different sectors, not just the outdoor industry.

Hunter spending contributes directly to wildlife and natural resources management and conservation as well through state-level hunting licenses, tags, and permits; Pittman-Robertson excise taxes on hunting and shooting equipment and ammunition; the Federal Duck Stamp; and membership in and donations to non-profit conservation organizations (see Chapter 1 for more detailed information on hunters' financial contributions to conservation). Through licenses, fees, excise taxes, and donations, hunters contribute approximately $1.6 billion a year for conservation programs and wildlife management efforts.[91] Southwick Associates estimates the total contribution to conservation to be even higher at $1.8 billion.[92]

## Threats to Hunting in the United States

While it is clear that hunting is both ecologically and financially important to wildlife management and conservation, hunting participation has been mostly declining since the 1980s. Important issues negatively affecting hunting participation in the United States today include the following:

- The changing demographic makeup of the United States.
- Lack of access.

- Lack of opportunity.
- Poor hunter behavior.
- Low public knowledge about wildlife and conservation.
- Anti-hunting sentiment.

## CHANGING DEMOGRAPHICS IN THE UNITED STATES

Changing demographic factors in the United States are driving the trend of decreasing hunting participation. Five key demographic trends run counter to what is optimal for hunting: an increase in the total U.S. population and increases in urban residents, minority and immigrant residents, and older residents.

Each year the U.S. population increases, but the total number of hunters has experienced an overall decline according to most sources, including the *National Survey,* since the 1980s and 1990s. This decline is especially important to note as the U.S. population growth rate averaged 11 percent to 13 percent from the 1980s to the 2000s.[93] With a declining number of participants, the rate of national hunting participation also decreased, but that decrease was made even more substantial by the growing population.

The increase in the total U.S. population is accompanied by urbanization, which often leads to increased housing, decreased habitat, and encroachment into rural areas, all conditions that decrease places to hunt and access to hunting areas. Fewer hunting opportunities means less hunting participation.

Further compounding the decline is that much of the population growth has been among groups not strongly associated with hunting: urban residents, minority groups, and immigrants. Data shows that rural residents hunt at a higher rate than do urban residents. Increases in the minority and immigrant proportions of the population, including the increase in those of Hispanic origin, mean an increase in two other population groups with lower rates of hunting.

Another important demographic trend that influences hunting participation is an aging society. The increasing age of the U.S. population is especially detrimental to hunting participation because young and middle-aged adults are more likely to hunt than older adults due to attrition naturally associated with aging.[94]

As a result of the growing population overall, as well as among groups less likely to hunt, a smaller proportion of the U.S. population participates in hunting each year.[95] In short, the proportion of the U.S. population that is most likely to hunt is getting smaller.

## LACK OF ACCESS

Access is an increasing problem, in part, because of one of the previously discussed demographic trends: the increase in the total U.S. population and the resulting urban sprawl. Urbanization causes the loss of huntable areas and the fragmentation of habitat. However, evidence suggests access is also becoming more difficult because landowners who are not affected by urbanization are increasingly disallowing hunting.

Access issues comprise two components: physical access and social/psychological aspects of access. Physical access refers to the actual land available for hunting. Social/psychological aspects involve the perceptions and assumptions of those physical aspects but also include things unrelated to the physical access, such as simple knowledge of land available for hunting.

The first two aspects of physical access are the actual land and the ability to get to and from that land. As an example of the latter, public land can become surrounded by private lands on every side. If access is not provided by design, the land can truly become "acreage open for hunting" that is actually not available for hunting. (This phenomenon is a common problem among anglers who fish in lakes and ponds, where all the shorefront property is bought up and then posted.) In a Responsive Management study on access, private land blocking access to public land was described as a major problem by 9 percent of hunters and as a moderate or a minor problem by another 20 percent.[96]

The social/psychological aspects of access include the perception of access. For the hunter looking to go hunting, perception of access is more important than the actual access. For instance, if a hunter has problems finding a place to park his car at a certain location, he may never return, even if the place nearly always has room but simply did not on that day. In this case, perception (that there is never available parking there) does not match reality (usually there is available parking), but the perception wins out and the hunter never returns.

Another important aspect of social/psychological access is awareness of access, a factor that fish and wildlife agencies *can* influence through dissemination of information. A hunter without any nearby hunting lands is the same as a hunter who does have hunting lands nearby if the latter does not know about those lands.

Access programs should consider both physical and social/psychological access. The aforementioned research on access and the effectiveness of access programs overall reviewed more than 60 access programs. Some programs found to be quite effective included walk-in access programs and mapping/atlas programs. Not surprisingly, the first of these combines both physical access (providing a place to hunt) and social/psychological access (in that it alleviates hunters' worries about whether they will find a place to hunt). The second—atlas and mapping programs (and now smartphone apps)—is completely in the realm of social/psychological aspects, as it lets hunters know where the land for hunting can be found.

## LACK OF OPPORTUNITY

Lack of opportunity must be considered as separate from access because it refers to wildlife populations themselves. In areas where there is no game to hunt, all other issues, including access to hunting lands, are a moot point.

As mentioned previously, loss and fragmentation of habitat can harm the viability of species, with the urban sprawl associated with the growing U.S. population destroying available habitat.

Invasive species are another potential problem that could affect wildlife. While they do not yet appear to have notably affected huntable species, invasive species already have drastically changed some fisheries, to the detriment of some anglers' fishing experiences. This threat may start to negatively affect hunting by impacting huntable species directly or by affecting habitat.

While threats like urbanization and lack of access overlap with an increasing lack of opportunity, another important element is the potential effect of climate change on wildlife. A study conducted for the National Wildlife Federation found that 70 percent of hunters and anglers nationwide strongly or moderately agreed that global warming is a serious threat to wildlife. Many respondents indicated they had already observed phenomena that they believed to be a result of climate change, which 73 percent believed was or would soon impact hunting and fishing conditions.[97]

How to Talk About Hunting ⊕ Research-Based Communications Strategies

## POOR HUNTER BEHAVIOR

Paired with some non-hunters' uneasiness over certain methods of hunting is their uneasiness about the behaviors of some hunters. Some non-hunters even say they approve of hunting in general but have a problem with hunters themselves. This perception is not wholly without reason—as with any group, there are a few bad apples who tarnish the reputation of the entire sport. For instance, many non-hunters believe that hunters who commit hunting violations are aware of the violations but intentionally commit them anyway.[98]

Public perceptions of poor hunter behavior can be more damaging than the reality. An example from 2015 involved an American hunter who paid a guide for the opportunity to hunt a lion in what he thought was a legal hunt. When the legality of the hunt was later questioned, the reaction in the United States was severe (note that the American hunter was not charged with any crimes; charges against the guide were later dropped). Following the incident, the man temporarily went into hiding as protesters decried his actions.

The incident amounted to a notable black eye for recreational hunting, with consequences that included new rules issued by the U.S. Fish and Wildlife Service on the importation of trophies from other countries and a ban by some airlines on carrying certain trophies as cargo.[99]

Hunters must be aware of how their actions are perceived—actions that are seen as harmful or unethical can damage support for hunting overall. The aforementioned incident with the African lion was mentioned prominently by the anti-hunting side in a live debate[100] about hunting held soon after the story came to light, allowing the anti-hunting side to steer the debate discussion toward the types of animals that most Americans do not want to see hunted and toward the motivations for hunting that are not widely supported. (See Chapter 4 for a more thorough discussion of trophy hunting.)

## LOW PUBLIC KNOWLEDGE ABOUT WILDLIFE AND CONSERVATION

According to the Wildlife Management Institute, in the 2012 elections, 46 of 57 statewide, municipal, and county ballot initiatives across the country concerning funding and support for conservation-related causes passed—an 81 percent passage rate.[101] Additionally, based on data from the Trust for Public Land and the National Conference of State Legislatures, in the 2014 elections, 41 of 57 statewide, municipal, and county ballot initiatives, referenda, and bond measures concerning wildlife, land preservation, sportsmen's rights, and other conservation-related issues passed—a 72-percent passage rate.[102] The results demonstrate that people care about wildlife and natural resource conservation issues.

However, despite the care and concern, there is a pronounced lack of awareness and knowledge about wildlife in general, how wildlife is managed, the role of hunting in that management, how wildlife management is funded, and who manages wildlife.

For instance, in a survey conducted by Responsive Management in the 16 member states of the Southeastern Association of Fish and Wildlife Agencies, less than half of state residents (only 38 percent) could name their state agency or a close derivative of the agency name. Additionally, when asked how their state fish and wildlife agency is funded, most residents do not really know. Common answers are "taxes" or "state taxes," but the reality in many states is that little, if any, general state taxes go to these agencies. Furthermore, knowledge of the excise taxes on hunting and fishing equipment (including firearms and ammunition) is very low. Amazingly, this is true even of those who consider themselves to be hunters or anglers.[103]

The danger of this relatively low level of knowledge is that the public does not generally understand the biological principles upon which wildlife management is based. They also may not support or understand the methods—including hunting—that are used to manage wildlife.

## ANTI-HUNTING SENTIMENT

The anti-hunting movement is, fortunately, a fringe movement. The large majority of Americans approve of hunting, even if they do not personally hunt. Roughly three quarters of U.S. residents approve of legal hunting.[104] The increase in anti-hunting rhetoric and activism beginning in the 1980s and 1990s might lead one to believe that public approval of hunting has decreased, but the research does not support that with studies showing public attitudes have remained relatively stable since Stephen Kellert's landmark study on attitudes toward hunting in 1978.[105]

An important nuance of this general approval of hunting is that it is not constant for all species, for all reasons to hunt, or across all hunting methods. This is evident in the results of a Responsive Management survey that found while a large majority of Americans approve of hunting deer, wild turkey, small game and waterfowl, only 60 percent approve of hunting elk, and less than a majority approve of hunting black bear, mountain lion, or mourning dove.[106]

---

> A large majority of Americans approve of hunting for the meat, to protect humans from harm, for animal population control, and for wildlife management.

---

Likewise, a large majority of Americans approve of hunting for the meat, to protect humans from harm, for animal population control, and for wildlife management. Each reason has more than 80 percent of Americans expressing approval. But only 71 percent of Americans approve of hunting to protect property, just more than half approve of hunting for the sport, and less than a majority approve of hunting to supplement income, hunting for the challenge, or hunting for a trophy.[107]

In looking at various hunting methods and equipment, a Responsive Management survey found that more than half of Americans are opposed to hunting using high-tech gear such as remote trail-cameras and hearing devices. Also, just more than half oppose hunting in a high-fenced preserve. Hunting over bait and hunting using scents that attract game also have relatively high levels of opposition, some of which comes from hunters themselves over concern about fair chase principles.[108]

The danger to hunting is that robust opposition to some types of hunting can be exploited to reduce support for hunting overall. For instance, the Humane Society of the United States supported a ballot referendum in Maine that sought to ban three methods of bear hunting that do not have high public approval: baiting, hunting with dogs, and trapping.[109] While the referendum did not pass, certainly some of those who supported it were doing so to chip away at the right of Maine residents to go hunting at all.

## Hunter Profiles: Composition of Hunters

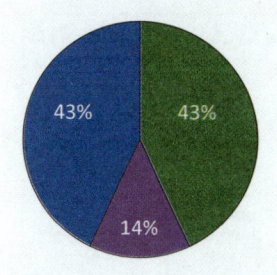

- Active hunter (has hunted in the past 2 years): 43%
- Recently lapsed hunter (has hunted in the past 5 years, but not in the past 2 years): 14%
- Long-ago lapsed (has hunted, but not in the past 5 years): 43%

Research (*The Future of Hunting and the Shooting Sports: Research-Based Recruitment and Retention Strategies,* produced in 2008 by Responsive Management) shows that ACTIVE hunters are more likely than are inactive hunters to have the following characteristics:

- Is very interested in going hunting in the next year.
- Has taken somebody new to the sport of hunting.
- Currently has family members who hunt. ← Social support
- Has fished in the past 5 years.
- Has camped in the past 5 years.
- Has friends who hunt.
- Is very interested in going target or sport shooting in the next year.
- Is between 18 and 34 years old. ← Younger
- Has gone boating in the past 5 years.
- Has been invited to go hunting with a friend.
- Has had a child ask to be taken hunting.
- Has gone hiking in the past 5 years.
- Rates access for hunting in state of residence as excellent or good.
- Has viewed wildlife in the past 5 years.
- Is male.
- Was first taken hunting by his or her father. ← Initiated by father
- Rates access to private lands for hunting as excellent or good.
- Has gone water-skiing in the past 5 years.
- Lives in a small city or town or a rural area.
- Has been a member or donated to a conservation or sportsman's organization in the past 2 years.
- Rates access to public lands for hunting as excellent or good.
- Goes sport shooting in addition to hunting.
- Grew up in a household with firearms.
- Has visited a state or national park in the past 5 years.
- Thinks few or no hunters drink alcohol while hunting.
- Was younger than the median age when first went hunting. ← Initiated at young age
- Had a group or person who taught him or her to hunt.
- Has a household income of less than $80,000.

*Source: Responsive Management.*

## Hunter Profiles: Composition of Hunters

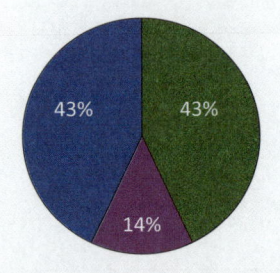

- Active hunter (has hunted in the past 2 years): 43%
- Recently lapsed hunter (has hunted in the past 5 years, but not in the past 2 years): 14%
- Long-ago lapsed (has hunted, but not in the past 5 years): 43%

Research (*The Future of Hunting and the Shooting Sports: Research-Based Recruitment and Retention Strategies,* produced in 2008 by Responsive Management) shows that INACTIVE hunters are more likely than are active hunters to have the following characteristics:

- Is very interested in going hunting in the next year.
- Did not indicate interest in going hunting in the next year.
- Has not taken somebody hunting who is new to the sport of hunting.
- Did not indicate interest in going target or sport shooting in the next year.
- Does not currently have family members who hunt. ← **No social support**
- Does not have friends who hunt.
- Has not been invited to go hunting with a friend.
- Has not had a child ask to be taken hunting.
- Is 65 years old or older. ← **Older**
- Is female.
- Was not first taken hunting by his or her father. ← **Not initiated by father**
- Lives in a large city/urban area or a suburban area. ← **Urban**
- Has not been a member of nor donated to a conservation or sportsman's organization in the past 2 years.
- Did not grow up in a household with firearms.
- Rates access for hunting in state of residence as fair or poor.
- Thinks most or some hunters drink alcohol while hunting.
- Is between 35 and 64 years old.
- Did not have a group or person who taught him or her to hunt.
- Started hunting when older than the median initiation age of hunters. ← **Initiated at an older age**

*Source: Responsive Management.*

## Key Takeaways

- According to the *National Survey*, there are an estimated 11.5 million U.S. hunters. (Other sources offer estimates as high as 41 million.) However, at least a third of hunters do not hunt every year. This means that, in any given year, there are more people who self-identify as hunters than actually hunt.

- According to the *National Survey*, hunting participation overall has been declining since the 1980s.

- It takes a hunter to make a hunter. Most hunters are initiated into hunting as a child by a male family member. While more hunters today are entering the sport as adults (i.e., without familial support), they are a minority compared to those who are initiated via the traditional pathway.

- Hunters most commonly hunt big game like deer, followed by small game and migratory birds.

- Hunters most often hunt with firearms such as rifles and shotguns, but bowhunting is growing.

- The top motivations for hunting are largely recreational and social, but hunting for the meat has re-emerged as an important reason for hunting. Hunting for a trophy remains extremely low in importance.

- New hunters are required to complete a state-certified hunter education program.

- According to the *National Survey*, expenditures from hunters totaled $26.2 billion in the United States.

- Hunter spending contributes directly to wildlife and natural resources management and conservation. Through licenses, fees, excise taxes, and donations, hunters contribute approximately $1.6 billion a year for conservation programs and efforts.

**How to Talk About Hunting** ⊕ *Research-Based Communications Strategies*

## *Key Takeaways (continued)*

- Hunting is clearly important, both ecologically and financially, to wildlife management and conservation. Important issues negatively affecting hunting participation in the United States today include the following:
    - The changing demographic makeup of the United States.
    - Lack of access.
    - Lack of opportunity.
    - Poor hunter behavior.
    - Low public knowledge about wildlife and conservation.
    - Anti-hunting sentiment.
- Research shows that the most important variable related to support for hunting is knowing a hunter. The more hunters there are, the more likely it will be for members of the non-hunting public to support hunting.

# CHAPTER 4
# *Attitudes Toward Hunting*

**THIS CHAPTER COVERS AMERICANS' ATTITUDES** *toward hunting and related topics. The vast majority of Americans (including youth) approve of legal hunting, although approval varies based on the species being hunted, the method of hunting, and the motivation for hunting. For example, there is strong support for hunting for the meat and hunting for wildlife management purposes, but relatively little support for trophy hunting. While Americans are largely positive about hunters themselves, some damaging stereotypes and inaccurate assumptions persist, such as the belief that hunters practice unsafe behavior while hunting and that hunting as practiced in the United States endangers some wildlife populations.*

## Overall Approval of Hunting

Research shows that 8 out of 10 American adults approve of legal hunting in the general sense, without any conditions or qualifiers such as the reason for hunting.[110] The share of Americans saying that, regardless of their own personal opinion, others should have the right to hunt is even higher (9 out of 10 believe this).[111] In essence, Americans are overwhelmingly more positive than negative when it comes to the basic concept of hunting.

Approval of hunting in the United States has held steady for decades. In 1995, approval was at 73 percent, compared to 80 percent today.[112] (Neutral and "don't know" responses make up the remaining 7 percent.)

**Percent of American adults who...**

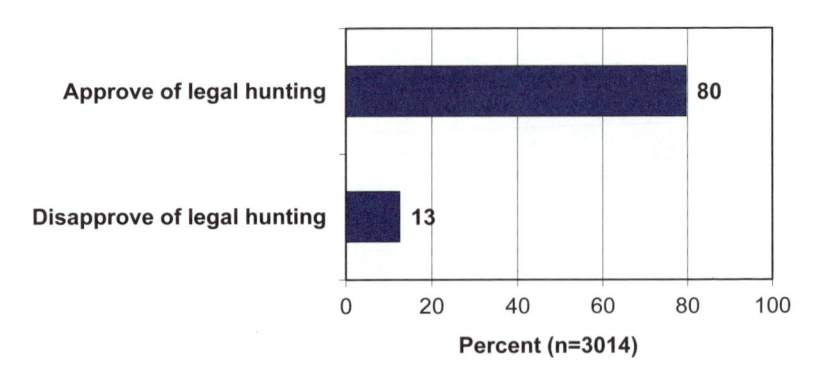

- Approve of legal hunting: 80
- Disapprove of legal hunting: 13

Percent (n=3014)

*Source: Responsive Management.*[113]

**Percent of American adults who...**

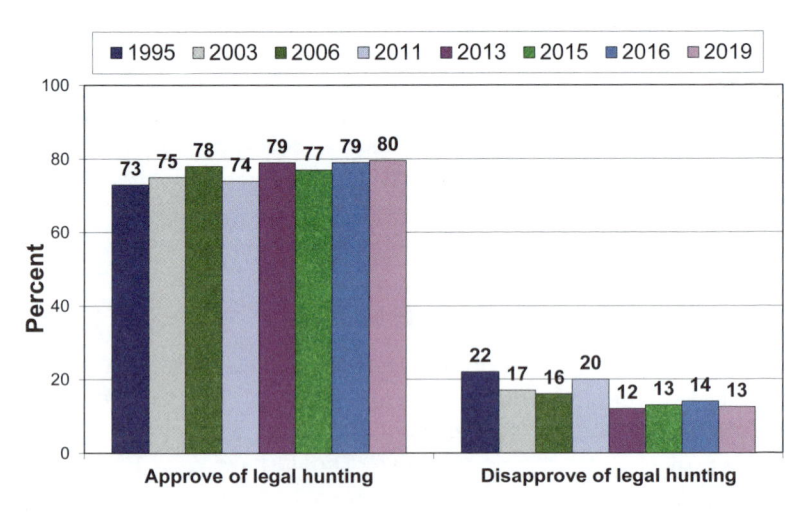

Legend: ■1995 ■2003 ■2006 ■2011 ■2013 ■2015 ■2016 ■2019

Approve of legal hunting: 73, 75, 78, 74, 79, 77, 79, 80

Disapprove of legal hunting: 22, 17, 16, 20, 12, 13, 14, 13

*Source: Responsive Management.*[114]

Approval of hunting is highest in the Midwest and lowest in the Northeast, with substantial differences in approval by demographic group. For example, some of the highest rates of approval are among

ATTITUDES TOWARD HUNTING

rural residents, white people, and males, while some of the lowest rates are among Hispanic people, black people, and females.

There are also dramatic differences in approval based on whether one grew up in a household with firearms (as shown in the graph below) as well as whether one knows a hunter (not included in the study below, but included in another study that entailed a similar analysis), which underscores the importance of social influence in helping to shape attitudes toward hunting.[115]

**Percent of each of the following groups approving of legal hunting:**

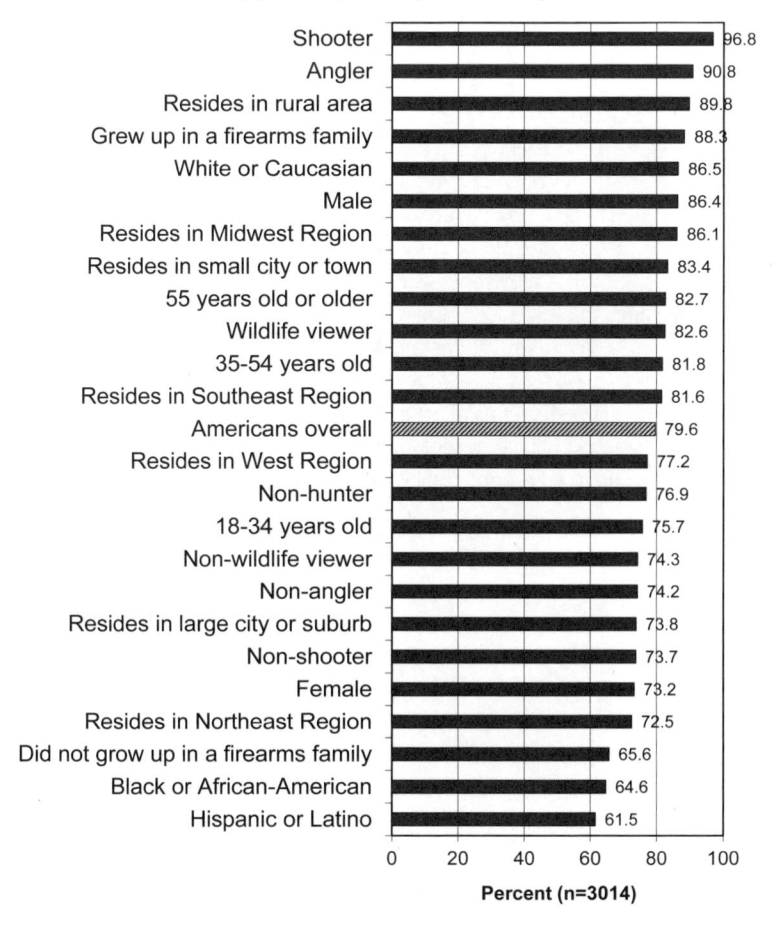

| Group | Percent |
|---|---|
| Shooter | 96.8 |
| Angler | 90.8 |
| Resides in rural area | 89.8 |
| Grew up in a firearms family | 88.3 |
| White or Caucasian | 86.5 |
| Male | 86.4 |
| Resides in Midwest Region | 86.1 |
| Resides in small city or town | 83.4 |
| 55 years old or older | 82.7 |
| Wildlife viewer | 82.6 |
| 35-54 years old | 81.8 |
| Resides in Southeast Region | 81.6 |
| Americans overall | 79.6 |
| Resides in West Region | 77.2 |
| Non-hunter | 76.9 |
| 18-34 years old | 75.7 |
| Non-wildlife viewer | 74.3 |
| Non-angler | 74.2 |
| Resides in large city or suburb | 73.8 |
| Non-shooter | 73.7 |
| Female | 73.2 |
| Resides in Northeast Region | 72.5 |
| Did not grow up in a firearms family | 65.6 |
| Black or African-American | 64.6 |
| Hispanic or Latino | 61.5 |

Percent (n=3014)

*Source: Responsive Management.*[116]

## Percent of each of the following groups disapproving of legal hunting:

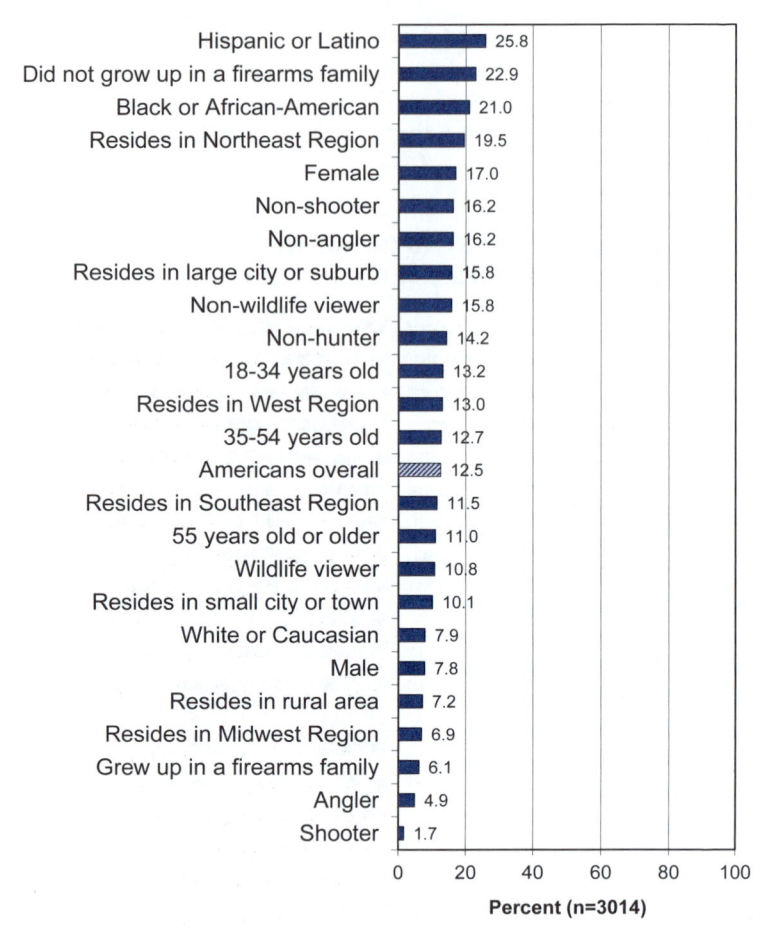

| Group | Percent |
|---|---|
| Hispanic or Latino | 25.8 |
| Did not grow up in a firearms family | 22.9 |
| Black or African-American | 21.0 |
| Resides in Northeast Region | 19.5 |
| Female | 17.0 |
| Non-shooter | 16.2 |
| Non-angler | 16.2 |
| Resides in large city or suburb | 15.8 |
| Non-wildlife viewer | 15.8 |
| Non-hunter | 14.2 |
| 18-34 years old | 13.2 |
| Resides in West Region | 13.0 |
| 35-54 years old | 12.7 |
| Americans overall | 12.5 |
| Resides in Southeast Region | 11.5 |
| 55 years old or older | 11.0 |
| Wildlife viewer | 10.8 |
| Resides in small city or town | 10.1 |
| White or Caucasian | 7.9 |
| Male | 7.8 |
| Resides in rural area | 7.2 |
| Resides in Midwest Region | 6.9 |
| Grew up in a firearms family | 6.1 |
| Angler | 4.9 |
| Shooter | 1.7 |

Percent (n=3014)

*Source: Responsive Management.*[117]

While an overwhelming majority of Americans approve of legal hunting *in general*, this approval tends to be conditional rather than absolute. In fact, approval of hunting varies rather significantly based on the species being hunted, the method of hunting, and the motivation for hunting.

## More Americans Support the Right of Others to Hunt Than Approve of Hunting Themselves

Attitudes toward hunting can be assessed both in terms of a person's *personal opinion* of hunting as well as their opinion regarding the *right of others* to hunt, as demonstrated in the following Responsive Management survey questions:

- Do you approve or disapprove of legal hunting?
- No matter your opinion on hunting, do you agree or disagree that it is okay for other people to hunt if they do so legally and in accordance with hunting laws and regulations?

As noted earlier in this chapter, the share of Americans saying that, regardless of their own opinion, others should have the right to hunt is even higher than the share who say that they themselves approve of hunting. Disapproving of something, however, is not necessarily the same as wanting to ban it outright. This means that there is likely a segment of people who personally disapprove of hunting but still do not want it banned.

The other question allows for this potential disapproval ("no matter your opinion on hunting") but focuses on the right of others to hunt. Other research (related to both hunting and sport shooting) demonstrates the extent to which "the right" to do something resonates with Americans. While the second question does not use the term "right" specifically, it gets at a similar concept through the wording "it is okay for other people to hunt."

The second question also includes qualifying language specifying that the hunting will be done responsibly ("…if they do so legally and in accordance with hunting laws and regulations")—this would likely soften some potential opposition. The qualifying language might also encourage people to think of hunting hypothetically in terms of a motivation that they find acceptable, like hunting for food or hunting for wildlife management (as opposed to hunting for a trophy).

## Approval of Hunting by Species

Surveys have found that Americans are far more likely to approve of hunting for ungulates, waterfowl, and small game than hunting for predators like mountain lion, wolf, or bear.[118] The differences in how the public views the hunting of various species may stem in part from a tendency for people to prioritize certain categories of animals over others: the most concern is for pets, followed by species perceived as being rare or endangered; game species thought of as common or plentiful garner the least amount of concern.[119] The concept of "charismatic megafauna" has also been used to refer to the favorable or even protective manner in which the public regards species that loom large in the popular consciousness.[120] (These concepts are discussed more in Chapter 5.)

**Percent of Americans who approve of hunting...**

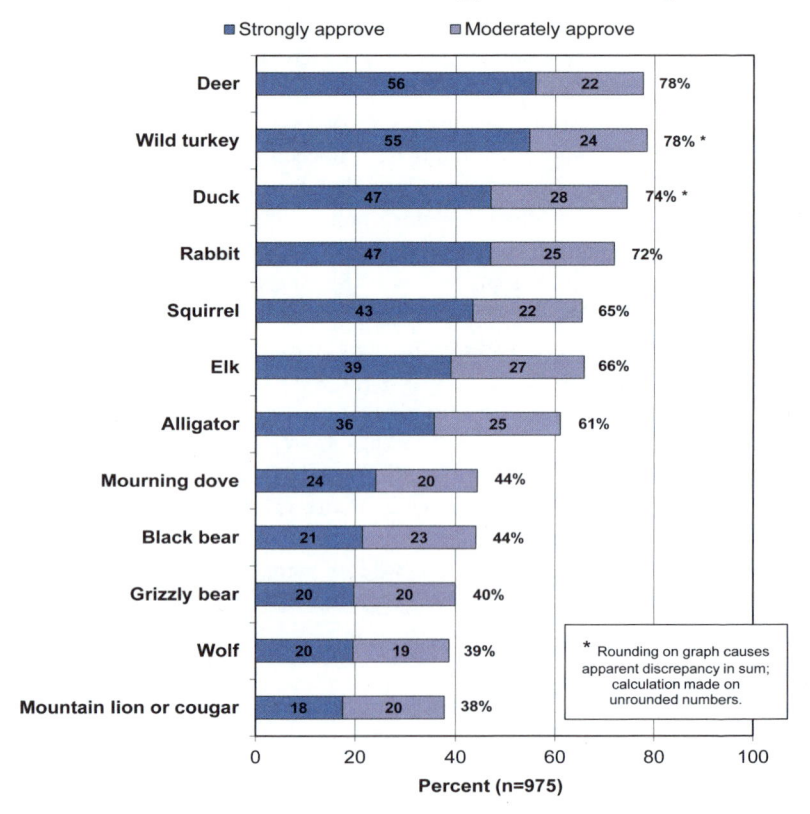

■ Strongly approve   ■ Moderately approve

| Species | Strongly approve | Moderately approve | Total |
|---|---|---|---|
| Deer | 56 | 22 | 78% |
| Wild turkey | 55 | 24 | 78% * |
| Duck | 47 | 28 | 74% * |
| Rabbit | 47 | 25 | 72% |
| Squirrel | 43 | 22 | 65% |
| Elk | 39 | 27 | 66% |
| Alligator | 36 | 25 | 61% |
| Mourning dove | 24 | 20 | 44% |
| Black bear | 21 | 23 | 44% |
| Grizzly bear | 20 | 20 | 40% |
| Wolf | 20 | 19 | 39% |
| Mountain lion or cougar | 18 | 20 | 38% |

Percent (n=975)

* Rounding on graph causes apparent discrepancy in sum; calculation made on unrounded numbers.

*Source: Responsive Management.*[121]

## Approval of Hunting by Method

The method of hunting also affects approval. A survey exploring attitudes toward various hunting methods and techniques found that while a large majority of Americans approve of hunting with a bow and arrow, less than half approve of hunting in high-fence preserves, hunting over bait, and hunting using high-tech gear.[122] Research suggests that opposition to these latter practices is often rooted in the belief that they violate the concept of fair chase, meaning hunters are perceived as having an unfair advantage over the animal.[123]

**Percent of Americans who approve of...**

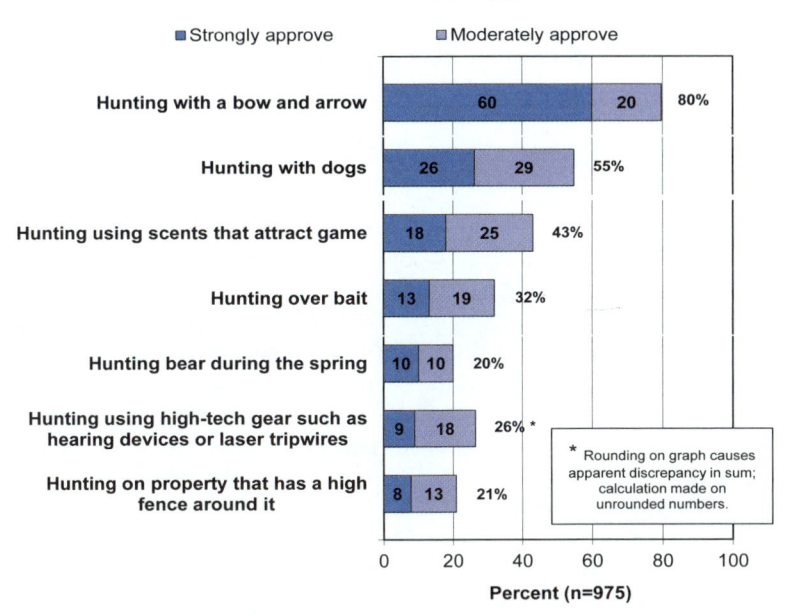

| Method | Strongly approve | Moderately approve | Total |
|---|---|---|---|
| Hunting with a bow and arrow | 60 | 20 | 80% |
| Hunting with dogs | 26 | 29 | 55% |
| Hunting using scents that attract game | 18 | 25 | 43% |
| Hunting over bait | 13 | 19 | 32% |
| Hunting bear during the spring | 10 | 10 | 20% |
| Hunting using high-tech gear such as hearing devices or laser tripwires | 9 | 18 | 26%* |
| Hunting on property that has a high fence around it | 8 | 13 | 21% |

Percent (n=975)

*Rounding on graph causes apparent discrepancy in sum; calculation made on unrounded numbers.

Source: *Responsive Management.*[124]

## Approval of Hunting by Motivation

Finally, approval of hunting fluctuates based on the reason or motivation for the hunting, with utilitarian reasons having the highest rates of approval. For example, large majorities of Americans approve of hunting to protect humans from harm, hunting for meat (including local and organic meat), hunting for wildlife management, and hunting to protect property. However, much smaller percentages approve of hunting for the sport, hunting for the challenge, and hunting for a trophy.[125]

## Percent of Americans who approve of hunting...

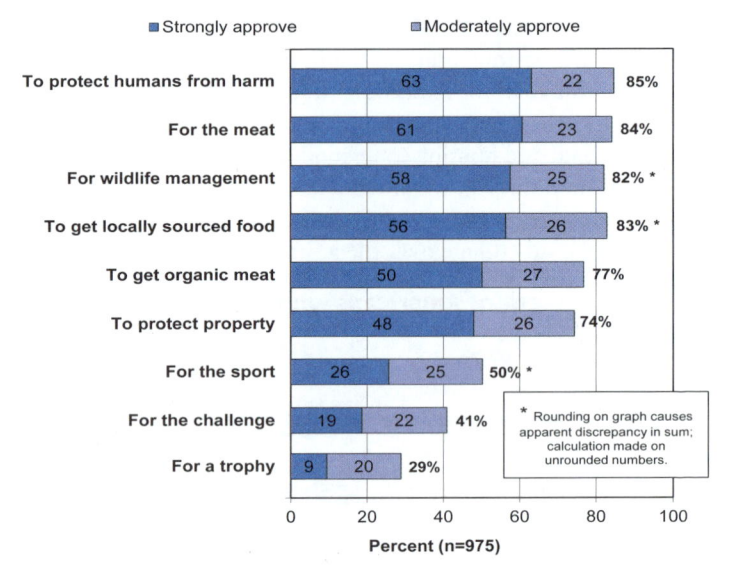

■ Strongly approve ▫ Moderately approve

| Reason | Strongly | Moderately | Total |
|---|---|---|---|
| To protect humans from harm | 63 | 22 | 85% |
| For the meat | 61 | 23 | 84% |
| For wildlife management | 58 | 25 | 82% * |
| To get locally sourced food | 56 | 26 | 83% * |
| To get organic meat | 50 | 27 | 77% |
| To protect property | 48 | 26 | 74% |
| For the sport | 26 | 25 | 50% * |
| For the challenge | 19 | 22 | 41% |
| For a trophy | 9 | 20 | 29% |

\* Rounding on graph causes apparent discrepancy in sum; calculation made on unrounded numbers.

Percent (n=975)

*Source: Responsive Management.*[126]

In general, Americans are more likely to support ecological reasons for hunting than human-centered reasons like recreation. Research has found that, among individuals who are not already strong hunting proponents, approval of hunting tends to be highest when ecological or biological reasons are given. Such reasons include if habitat could be better protected, if the overall health of the ecosystem would be better, if hunting were used to manage wildlife, and if hunting a common species was done to help an endangered species. These motivations for hunting have notably higher levels of support than reasons relating to sport or recreation, or even hunting to reduce property damage experienced by farmers.[127]

In addition to finding majorities of Americans expressing approval of hunting in general similar to preceding Responsive Management surveys, other research bears out the tendency for approval to fluctuate based on the reason for the hunting. And similar to Responsive Management research, for example, research from Cornell University identified higher approval for "community-centric benefits" of hunting like controlling wildlife that damage ecosystems than for "hunter-centric benefits" like being close to nature. Consistent with other research, the Cornell survey also found the lowest level of approval for hunting for a trophy.[128]

ATTITUDES TOWARD HUNTING

> When talking about the benefits of hunting, focus on the benefits of hunting to wildlife rather than the benefits to people. For example, if arguing for hunting in a situation of an overpopulation of deer, focus on how hunting will benefit the deer population and their habitat, rather than on the decreased damage to human property or orchards.

Approval of trophy hunting, while always fairly low, dipped even further following the high-profile killing of an African lion by an American dentist in 2015. As shown in the graph below, approval of trophy hunting decreased from 28 percent in 2006 to 21 percent in 2016 (the year following the African lion incident), before rebounding to 29 percent in 2019.[129]

**Percent who strongly or moderately approve of hunting for the following motivations:**

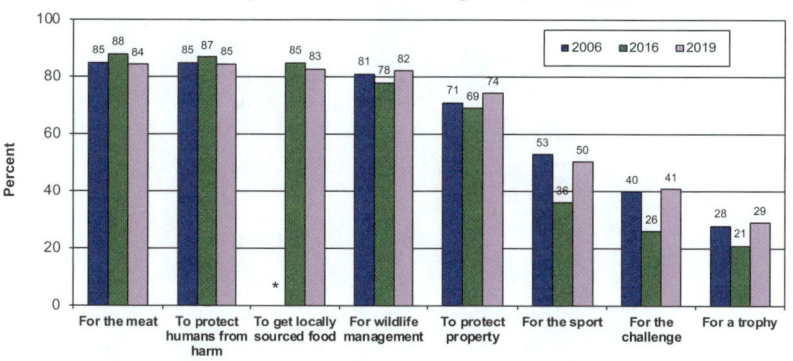

| Motivation | 2006 | 2016 | 2019 |
|---|---|---|---|
| For the meat | 85 | 88 | 84 |
| To protect humans from harm | 85 | 87 | 85 |
| To get locally sourced food | * | 85 | 83 |
| For wildlife management | 81 | 78 | 82 |
| To protect property | 71 | 69 | 74 |
| For the sport | 53 | 36 | 50 |
| For the challenge | 40 | 26 | 41 |
| For a trophy | 28 | 21 | 29 |

*Motivation not asked about in 2006 survey

*Source: Responsive Management.*[129]

Many Americans also respond positively to the idea of hunting as a funding mechanism for wildlife conservation. However, most people do not realize that hunting serves this purpose—it is only when they are

61

informed of it that they express approval of the concept. Survey data indicates that a solid majority of people who are not strong proponents of hunting would nonetheless approve of hunting if they knew it was being used to generate funding for wildlife—which indeed is the case.[130]

It is also worth considering how strongly Americans approve of hunting specifically for the meat. Given that the vast majority of Americans consume meat, it may come as little surprise that hunting as a way to obtain healthy protein is an idea that resonates with many. In considering the concept of hunting for the meat, some people draw a direct comparison with factory farming, believing that hunting represents a far more humane way for humans to use animals for food (i.e., sourcing the meat from animals that roam freely instead of living in confinement). In a focus group held exclusively with people strongly opposed to hunting, one person commented, "If I could end factory farming and people would still be allowed to hunt, I'd be okay with that. It's a greater good kind of thing."[131]

## Untangling and Addressing *Trophy Hunting* When Talking About Hunting

There is a reason why those strongly opposed to hunting intentionally refer to almost all hunting as *trophy hunting*: it is by far the most misinterpreted and emotionally charged phrase when communicating about hunting. Labeling most, if not all, hunting as *trophy hunting* is potentially the most powerful tool an anti-hunter can wield when trying to frame hunting in a negative light.

The trophy hunting label is an effective one because the phrase sounds deceptively simple, promoting a commonly held misconception among the general public. Unfortunately, hunters often unknowingly compound the problematic perception of trophy hunting by using the term without realizing it is being misconstrued and misinterpreted.

---

> There is a reason why those strongly opposed to hunting intentionally refer to almost all hunting as trophy hunting: it is by far the most misinterpreted and emotionally charged phrase when communicating about hunting. Labeling hunting as trophy hunting is potentially the most powerful tool an anti-hunter can wield when trying to frame hunting in a negative light.

⊕

---

The modern concept of trophy hunting is rooted in the late 19th century, connected in large part to Rowland Ward, a British taxidermist and book publisher who started in 1892 the publication, *Horn Measurements and Weights of the Great Game of the World*. The publication became the *Records of Big Game* series of books containing measurements of game animals harvested around the world—still being published.[132]

Today, however, much of the public's perception of trophy hunting is summed up by the following comment: "Trophy hunting is just a waste of the animal. If all you're going to do is kill the animal, cut the head off, and put it on your wall, and throw the rest in the trash, I think that's wrong."[133] This image of trophy hunting in the minds of many is, of course, not accurate.

Wildlife conservation writer and lecturer Shane Mahoney notes that most hunters would reasonably qualify as "trophy hunters," given that most hunters mark the achievement and memory of a hunt by bringing back a memento or keepsake (the "trophy" may be antlers, horns, or merely a photograph). But, Mahoney writes, trophy hunting in the traditional sense of the term involves targeting "mature animals that have already contributed to the genetic pool of the species." Mahoney further observes that such animals are "of an age where death is a pressing reality and likelihood, and animals that, because of their physical size and attributes, will uniquely attract international hunters and thus provide badly needed income to support local human communities and wider conservation campaigns."[134]

As with almost all hunting, the meat from trophy hunts is usually consumed. Additionally, regardless of whether the hunt is for a trophy, for food, or for some other purpose, the revenue generated by the hunter's license and equipment purchases is used to support conservation. Thus, the concept of "trophy hunting" is multifaceted and nuanced. Reducing all hunting simply because of opposition to trophy hunting does a disservice by ignoring other important purposes, motivations, and outcomes. While hunters intuitively know this, the general public does not.

In no other case in the hunting/anti-hunting debate is Frank Luntz's phrase more appropriate—"It's not what you say, it's what people hear."[135] Advocates of hunting must understand the extent to which the term "trophy hunting" is freighted with assumptions and misperceptions, as this will be the difference between successful and unsuccessful communications about hunting overall.

## ATTITUDES TOWARD TROPHY HUNTING

The latest research indicates that three quarters of U.S. adults disapprove of hunting for a trophy. Here it is again worth noting that hunting for a trophy is the least popular answer given by U.S. hunters when they are asked about their single most important reason for hunting.[136]

Research suggests that those who oppose trophy hunting view the practice as wasteful or immoral, in the sense that they perceive the killing of an animal for a trophy to be unnecessary (there appears to be little awareness that most trophy hunters make use of the meat from their harvest). Opposition to trophy hunting is highest among Hispanic people, black people, females, and people with advanced degrees (several of the same groups with the highest opposition to hunting in general).[137]

The relative lack of support for trophy hunting among Americans means that an effective anti-hunting communications strategy is to continually define hunting in general as *trophy hunting* specifically. Repeated enough, this strategy can be effective. When asked to describe their feelings about legal hunting in general, some Americans respond by commenting specifically about trophy hunting. This suggests that, for many people, trophy hunting has overshadowed hunting in general to the point where it has come to define it almost completely.

---

Disapproval of hunting is largely rooted in concern over the well-being of individual animals and the concept of fair chase. This helps to explain the relatively high opposition to hunting that is perceived as unnecessary, hunting using methods perceived as giving an unfair advantage over wildlife, and hunting that does not appear to serve a legitimate purpose.

⊕

---

The tendency for attitudes toward hunting to vary based on species, method, and motivation is consistent with the most common reasons for approving or disapproving of hunting. Approval of hunting is often rooted in the belief that hunting constitutes a natural connection between humans, wildlife, and nature that has persisted throughout history. Americans are therefore largely approving of hunting scenarios in line with this premise: that is, the hunting of plentiful species for their meat or for wildlife management purposes, using methods that allow for fair chase.

Disapproval of hunting, meanwhile, is largely rooted in concern over the well-being of individual animals and the concept of fair chase. This helps to explain the relatively high opposition to hunting when it is perceived as unnecessary, hunting using methods perceived as giving an unfair advantage over wildlife, and hunting that does not appear to serve a legitimate purpose.

## RECREATIONAL HUNTING IN CONTRAST TO TROPHY HUNTING

Most recreational hunting is *not* trophy hunting as some Americans imagine it. The concept of *sport hunting* emerged during the early 20th century, when Teddy Roosevelt established a series of programs and services to conserve and protect our nation's natural resources. The term, *sport hunting*, was coined during this era to distinguish ethical, recreational hunting from unregulated *market* hunting that lacked fair chase, wasted the meat, or focused solely on killing. Sport or recreational hunting in the U.S. meant hunting productively but also ethically, maintaining respect for the resource. Roosevelt established the Boone and Crockett Club in 1887 to promote these ideals of sport hunting and to unite the activity with conservation efforts.[138]

## WHY THE COMMON MISPERCEPTIONS AND INACCURATE STEREOTYPES OF TROPHY HUNTING CREATE THE PERFECT VILLAIN FOR ANTI-HUNTING ARGUMENTS

Trophy hunting amounts to the perfect villain or straw man argument for opponents of hunting because so many in their target audience fail to differentiate between the perceived worst aspects of trophy hunting and the more palatable aspects of legal, recreational hunting in the U.S.

First and foremost, opponents of hunting focus on trophy hunting as if the trophy is the *sole* reason for the hunt—this allows them to easily paint the picture of the privileged hunter traveling to a remote location to kill a large or striking animal, take its antlers or horns, and waste the rest of the animal. Trophy parts from the harvested animal are then shown off to impress family and friends. The perception is that the trophy is not just a memento of the hunt but a status symbol of wealth and physical prowess. It is an easy yet effective image to paint, one that angers and offends by suggesting that hunting is done only for fun and without benefit to wildlife. This depiction, although inaccurate, is the perfect way to present hunting as a dominionistic activity in which the hunter's mastery or control over wildlife is the only real objective. This dominionistic image harms the reputation of hunting by suggesting that hunters are wholly unconcerned with the pain, suffering, and general well-being of wildlife (see Chapter 5 for more discussion on this topic).

Another misperception typically associated with trophy hunting is the idea that trophy hunting decimates wildlife populations, allows for the harvest of endangered species, and results in wasted meat and other usable parts of the animal. Trophy hunting is also often presented as "canned" hunting, meaning the animals are held in a confinement of some kind to guarantee hunter success.

Modern sport hunting has not caused the extinction of any animal species. In fact, since the early 1900s, many of the most popular game species in the United States have become more abundant, thanks to the curtailing of market hunting, the development of scientific wildlife management to determine seasons and limits, and help from revenues generated by the sales of hunting licenses and ammunition that have been used for habitat protection and restoration.[139]

—*James Swan*

⊕

Inflammatory misperceptions of trophy hunting conveniently ignore the conservation, economic, and food supply benefits of these types of hunts, both in America as well as abroad. Anti-hunting arguments simply conflate the perceived negative aspects of trophy hunting with all types of regulated hunting. For example, anti-hunters can paint the average U.S. hunter of deer or big game as an unethical trophy hunter simply by conjuring images of mounted deer heads and photos of impressive bucks (again, ignoring the likelihood that such items are merely kept as reminders of the hunt and that the deer harvested is being consumed and fully utilized). Depicting all regulated hunting as trophy hunting is also fairly easy to do because most non-hunters have never actually observed a hunt: with a blank canvas to work with, the anti-hunter can skillfully paint in bold shades of exaggeration and falsehood regarding the specifics of how animals are hunted.

The rise of social media has also strengthened opposition to perceived trophy hunting by facilitating the rapid spread of images that appear to celebrate "trophy harvests"—the lack of backstory and context for such photos is an asset for anti-hunters and a liability for ethical sportsmen and women. Furthermore, recreational hunters often unwittingly play into the stereotype by posting photos of harvested animals but not the hunt itself (i.e., the setting and scenery of the hunt). This can reinforce the view of hunting as nothing more than an activity of killing and exercising control over wildlife. What other impression is a non-hunter left with? Celebratory photographs that appear to portray a dominionistic attitude and lack of respect for wildlife are crucial pieces of "evidence" for the anti-hunter in demonstrating the evils of hunting.

## THE MISPERCEPTIONS AND INACCURACIES OF APPLYING TROPHY HUNTING TO RECREATIONAL HUNTING IN THE U.S.

Recreational hunting is not the same activity depicted by opponents of hunting when they use the negative misperception of trophy hunting to argue that hunting in general is unethical. Sport or recreational hunting as practiced in the U.S. is characterized by ethical standards of fair chase, meat utilization, and conservation of the resource. Furthermore, recreational hunting is regulated by state fish and wildlife agencies to ensure the conservation of the wildlife populations and other resources on which the wildlife depend. Additionally, all states have strict laws against wanton waste of game (thus invalidating one of the most common objections to trophy hunting—that it results in the waste of the animal).

---

Ninety-five percent of all U.S. hunters eat the meat from their harvest. Just 1 percent of all U.S. hunters say that the trophy is their most important reason for hunting.

---

Most U.S. hunters do not identify as trophy hunters. In a 2017 nationwide survey, 39 percent of U.S. hunters said that the meat was their most important reason for hunting. And while the remaining hunters cited reasons of recreation, being close to nature, and/or spending time with friends and family, the fact remains that, regardless of their top reason for hunting, 95 percent of all hunters eat the meat from their harvest. For perspective, just 1 percent of all U.S. hunters say that the trophy is their most important reason for hunting.[140]

## WHAT OPPONENTS OF HUNTING WANT YOU TO THINK ABOUT RECREATIONAL HUNTING

- Recreational hunting in the U.S. is the same as the common misperceptions of trophy hunting.

- Recreational hunters possess dominionistic qualities in which the mastery or control of animals is the goal.
- Recreational hunting does not contribute to wildlife management or conservation.
- Recreational hunting is not for the meat, or the meat is wasted.

## HOW TO RESPOND WITH FACTS ABOUT RECREATIONAL HUNTING IN THE UNITED STATES

- **Challenge anti-hunters to define "trophy hunting," and be ready to instruct them on what trophy hunting is and is not.** Do not allow anti-hunters to get away with blatant and inaccurate misrepresentations of what trophy hunting is.
- **Recreational hunting in the U.S. is not the same as the common misperceptions of trophy hunting.** Recreational hunters appreciate the recreation and the challenge but also hunt within the regulations set up to protect and manage wildlife populations. They also utilize the meat from their harvest and contribute financially—about $1.6 billion per year—to wildlife conservation and management.
- **The North American Model of Wildlife Conservation practiced in the U.S. is designed for recreational hunting to help protect and manage wildlife populations.** When they hunt, hunters help manage the size of the population for optimal health with respect to food availability, habitat, and disease control. Hunting helps prevent starvation and disease among wildlife. If not for recreational hunting, fish and wildlife management agencies would be employing sharpshooters and other means of lethal methods to control population sizes and health, as well as to prevent human-wildlife conflicts in urban areas. Hunters also spend money on licenses and equipment that goes back to help manage and conserve wildlife in their state.
- **Recreational hunters value the wildlife that they harvest and utilize as much of the animal as possible—and, most importantly, the meat is consumed.** Recreational hunters do not waste the resource; if they have more meat than necessary to feed their family, they share it with friends or donate it to organizations that will distribute it to those in need of food, such as Hunters for the Hungry, which has provided over 28.8 million servings of meat from hunters' donations since its inception in 1991.[141]

- Conservation and ethics are extremely important to recreational hunters, who hunt within the ethical standards of fair chase, utilization of the harvest, and conservation of the resource. Recreational hunters enjoy the recreation and challenge of hunting, which would not be present without engaging in fair chase, so they are careful to hunt ethically and legally. As mentioned previously, the vast majority eat the meat from their harvest while others donate it. Finally, hunting is integral to our wildlife management system because it helps maintain populations, health, and funding for conservation.

## Attitudes Toward Hunters

Americans' attitudes toward *hunters* are slightly different than their attitudes toward *hunting*, with some notable inconsistencies in their beliefs. For example, surveys show that people assume hunters to be knowledgeable about wildlife and the environment, to care about other people, and to hold strong family values. Yet at the same time, many Americans believe that hunters practice unsafe behavior, drink alcohol, and violate hunting laws.[142] More than half of U.S. residents feel that hunting is a dangerous sport, despite the fact that hunting has far fewer injuries per 100 participants than football, skateboarding, basketball, soccer, and other mainstream activities.[143] What's more, nearly half of Americans erroneously believe that regulated hunting, as practiced today in the United States, causes some species to become endangered.[144]

Regardless of the persistence of some negative stereotypes about hunters among some people, there remains no credible research linking hunting with anti-social behavior.[145] Inaccurate assumptions about hunters therefore reflect the need for hunters to act as grassroots ambassadors of the activity at every opportunity. Additionally, all legal hunting in the United States is regulated precisely so that wildlife populations remain healthy and thriving—the belief that legal hunting can result in diminished populations suggests that many Americans confuse legal hunting with poaching.

## Attitudes Toward the Enforcement of Hunting Laws and Hunter Safety Instruction

Hunting in America is regulated primarily by state fish and wildlife agencies, which employ conservation law enforcement officers to enforce hunting regulations and wildlife-related laws. (Primary regulation is at the state level; there is regulatory oversight by the federal government of migratory bird hunting.) Just as Americans show strong support for legal hunting, there is widespread recognition of the importance of these conservation law enforcement efforts.

Asked to rate the importance of conservation law enforcement work to their state, Americans give an average rating of 8.61 on a 0 to 10 scale of importance, suggesting high importance. The same study asked U.S. residents to rate the importance of twenty-seven different conservation law enforcement areas, from enforcing boating laws and regulations to responding to nuisance wildlife issues. The top tier based on the average ratings of importance includes several areas directly related to hunting, including enforcing laws to protect fish and wildlife from being taken illegally, enforcing hunting laws and regulations, and enforcing laws regarding the illegal use of equipment to hunt or fish. Finally, more than half of Americans would like to see *more* conservation law enforcement officers in their state, as opposed to fewer or the same amount.[146]

There is also a good deal of support among Americans for hunter safety instruction. The latest research indicates that a solid majority of Americans agree that hunter safety instruction should be taught in schools, either in general or as an elective (this is apart from the hunter safety courses offered through state fish and wildlife agencies and various nonprofit organizations).[147]

In recent years, hunter safety programs have expanded to include online-only or online-mostly offerings; such alternatives to traditional classroom courses have helped to address demand for hunter education, particularly in areas of the country where the infrastructure necessary for on-site hunter safety courses (e.g., classrooms, shooting ranges, qualified instructors) may be limited.

One such program is the National Rifle Association's online hunter education course. Having developed America's first hunter education program in 1949, the NRA now offers an online course with the most encompassing curriculum of any online hunter education course. The NRA online hunter education course content has been developed to meet the standards of each state fish and wildlife agency, and the course is offered to students free of charge.[148]

## Talk About Hunting

The strongest socio-demographic variable related to support of hunting is knowing a hunter. This strong and direct relationship has been found in studies of adults and youth.[149] This has important implications in increasing support for hunting.

Hunters need to talk about hunting. Hunters need to talk to non-hunters about their experiences—the natural beauty that they see in the field, the sunrises and sunsets, the camaraderie that is formed among hunting associates, and the steroid-free healthy meat and meals that are the result of a successful hunt.

Responsive Management research over the years has found that many adults and youth do not talk about hunting because of a fear of being misunderstood or ostracized. But done in a thoughtful and gentle manner, emphasizing the benefits of hunting as outlined in this book will have positive benefits for the overall long-term cultural acceptance of hunting.

---

"Hunting gave my life spiritual meaning. It taught me about the habits of animals and their interrelationships with the environment. It showed me the value of wildlife and the necessity for protecting it. Hunting gave the woods a "sense of place" for me. I care about that patch of bobwhite quail cover, and about that wetland filled with nesting ducks. I will fight to protect it. I care about that farm opening where turkey broods and deer go to feed...and so too the great horned owl. Those need protection too."[149]

—David E. Samuel

from *Know Hunting: Truth, Lies & Myths*

## Youth Attitudes Toward Hunting

Youth attitudes toward hunting are largely consistent with the attitudes of Americans as a whole, with three out of four young people between the ages of eight and seventeen approving of hunting when it is legal to do so. Similarly, nine out of ten young people agree that, regardless of their personal opinion, other people should be allowed to hunt.[150]

At the same time, only a little more than one third of young people say they hold a positive opinion of hunting, while almost half hold a negative opinion. As with adults, negative attitudes toward hunting among youth are typically based on general opposition to the idea of killing or causing pain to animals. (In a focus group with youth participants, one individual explained his interest in target shooting but not hunting as follows: "I like shooting but not killing."[151])

Young people also have some of the same misperceptions about hunting that are common among adults. For example, majorities of young people agree that, compared to other sports, hunting is a dangerous sport; that most hunters do not obey all hunting laws; and that legal hunting as practiced today in the United States causes some species to become endangered. On the other hand, most young people also agree that hunting wild animals such as turkey or deer for food is okay, and that, in general, people who hunt care about wildlife.[152]

As with Americans overall, one of the most important factors influencing youth attitudes toward hunting is simply exposure to the activity. Research indicates that young people who personally know a hunter are more likely to approve of hunting, more likely to try hunting, and more likely to encourage their friends to participate as well.[153]

## Key Takeaways

- Use the full term, "legal, regulated hunting," not just "hunting." Clarify the extent to which legal hunting is regulated.

- Define hunting as a food source and a wildlife management tool.

- Separate hunting from poaching. Many Americans confuse hunting with poaching. The public needs to be assured that legal, regulated hunting is the opposite of poaching. Hunters must assure people that legal, regulated hunting does not endanger wildlife populations.

- When talking about hunting, focus on the benefits of hunting to wildlife rather than the benefits of hunting to people.

- Don't be afraid to talk about hunting. For many people, hunting must be demystified. Hunters should seize on opportunities to explain why they hunt and the benefits hunting provides.

- Don't forget that peer influence matters. People who personally know a hunter are far more likely to support and participate in hunting. This reinforces an important point: people need to talk about hunting so that the public is more aware of it and more familiar with hunters themselves.

- Make the point that almost all hunters eat what they harvest.

- Focus on the benefits of hunting, not the fallacies of anti-hunters.

- Be aware of the lack of support for "trophy hunting" and all the nuances involved with the term.

- When necessary, challenge your debate opponent to define "trophy hunting." Do not allow anti-hunters to get away with blatant and inaccurate misrepresentations of what trophy hunting is.

- Emphasize hunter ethics in programs and messaging to hunters. Always practice ethical hunting in the field. An unethical hunter is an anti-hunter's best friend.

- Communicate hunting as a safe activity.

- Build on support for firearms and hunting safety instruction in schools.

# CHAPTER 5

# *Attitudes Toward Animal Rights, Animal Welfare, and Dominionism*

**THIS CHAPTER COVERS AMERICANS' ATTITUDES** *toward the use of animals, which fall on a continuum of acceptability: one extreme end is defined by the animal rights mindset (the belief that animals have rights like humans and should not be used by humans in any way), while the other extreme end marks the dominionistic mindset (the belief that animals may be used by humans regardless of the animal's welfare or rights). Most Americans fall in the middle of the continuum, being proponents of animal welfare—the idea that animals may be used by humans as long as the animals do not experience undue pain and suffering. Absent these definitions, many Americans claim to support animal rights; provided the definitions, however, most Americans say they are supporters of animal welfare, not animal rights (consider that meat consumption and the use of animal products are ubiquitous with Americans).*

## The Continuum of Acceptability Regarding the Use of Animals

Americans' attitudes toward the use of animals exist on a continuum of acceptability. At one end of the continuum is the *animal rights* mindset, which is the belief that animals have rights like humans and should not be used in any way. At the opposite end is the *dominionistic* mindset, or the belief that animals can be used by humans regardless of the animal's welfare or rights. The middle of the continuum represents *animal welfare*—the idea that animals can be used by humans, as long as the animal does not experience undue pain and suffering.

Each mindset is accompanied by various beliefs and behaviors concerning the extent to which animals may be used by humans, as shown in the visualization of the continuum below.

## Understanding Public Acceptance of the Use of Animals

| Animal Rights | Animal Welfare | Dominionism |
|---|---|---|
| • Opposing all utilization and management of animals | • Utilizing animals while working to minimize their pain and suffering | • Utilizing animals without regard for their pain and suffering |
| • Not consuming meat | • Practicing legal, regulated, ethical hunting | • Wounding of animals when hunting due to negligence or improper technique |
| • Not wearing leather shoes or clothing | • When hunting, ensuring quick kills to minimize pain and suffering | • Perception of hunting done solely for a trophy (i.e., wasting the rest of the animal) |
| • Not having pets | • Honoring and respecting the animal (e.g., praying for or giving thanks to the animal) | |
| • Opposing the use of animals for any research purposes | • Ensuring sustainable wildlife populations | • "Factory" farming |
| | • Hunting selectively, not indiscriminately, in accordance with regulations to maintain healthy populations | • Using irreverent or inflammatory language when talking about hunting (e.g., "If it flies, it dies") |
| • Using only vegan and cruelty-free-labeled products | | • Posting images of bloody trophy kills on social media |
| | • Using organic, local meat and cage-free products | |

*Source: Responsive Management, 2019*[154]

## ATTITUDES TOWARD ANIMAL RIGHTS, ANIMAL WELARE, AND DOMINIONISM

Most Americans identify as proponents of animal welfare—the middle of the continuum. When given definitions of animal rights, animal welfare, and dominionism and asked to select the one that best describes their beliefs, 82 percent of Americans choose animal welfare, compared to 14 percent who select animal rights and just 4 percent who identify as proponents of dominionism.[154] (Other research, while not using the exact same terminology, has found essentially the same patterns in the beliefs of Americans regarding the qualified use of animals by humans.[155])

**For the following three statements, please choose the one that best describes your beliefs.**

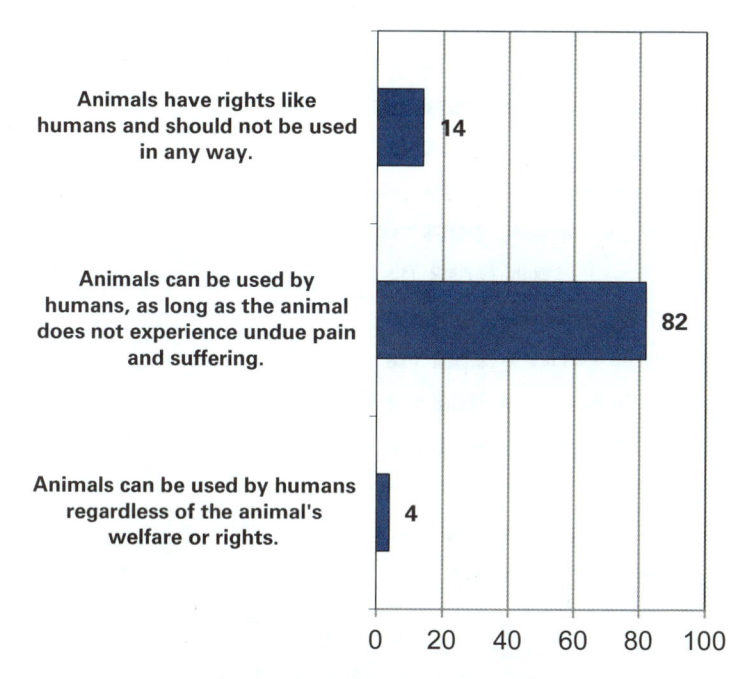

| Statement | Percent |
|---|---|
| Animals have rights like humans and should not be used in any way. | 14 |
| Animals can be used by humans, as long as the animal does not experience undue pain and suffering. | 82 |
| Animals can be used by humans regardless of the animal's welfare or rights. | 4 |

*Source: Responsive Management.*[156]

Just as approval of hunting varies by audience, individuals in certain demographic groups are more likely to identify as animal rights proponents. These groups include Hispanic people, black people, those with a high school education or less, and females.[157]

## Percent who believe animals have rights like humans and should not be used in any way:

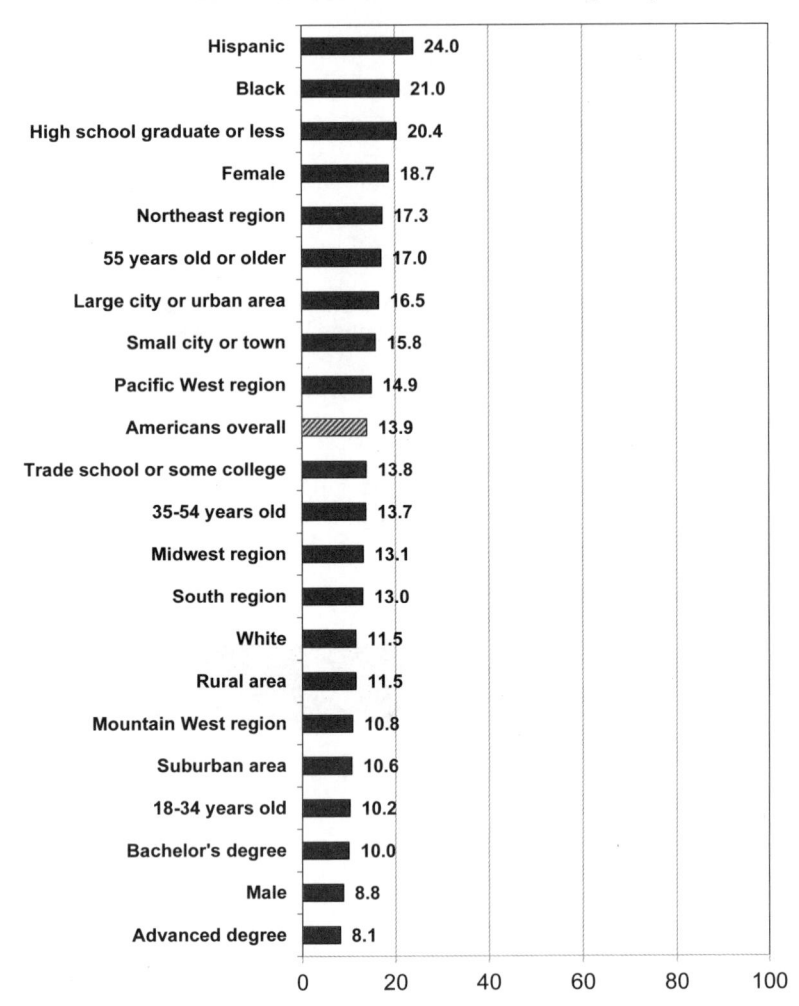

| Category | Percent |
|---|---|
| Hispanic | 24.0 |
| Black | 21.0 |
| High school graduate or less | 20.4 |
| Female | 18.7 |
| Northeast region | 17.3 |
| 55 years old or older | 17.0 |
| Large city or urban area | 16.5 |
| Small city or town | 15.8 |
| Pacific West region | 14.9 |
| Americans overall | 13.9 |
| Trade school or some college | 13.8 |
| 35-54 years old | 13.7 |
| Midwest region | 13.1 |
| South region | 13.0 |
| White | 11.5 |
| Rural area | 11.5 |
| Mountain West region | 10.8 |
| Suburban area | 10.6 |
| 18-34 years old | 10.2 |
| Bachelor's degree | 10.0 |
| Male | 8.8 |
| Advanced degree | 8.1 |

Source: Responsive Management.[158]

By itself, the term "animal rights" is frequently misinterpreted by the public as referring to animal welfare. When simply asked outright whether they support animal rights (i.e., based on the term alone, before hearing any definition), eight out of ten Americans say that they do.[159]

## Do you consider yourself a supporter of animal rights?

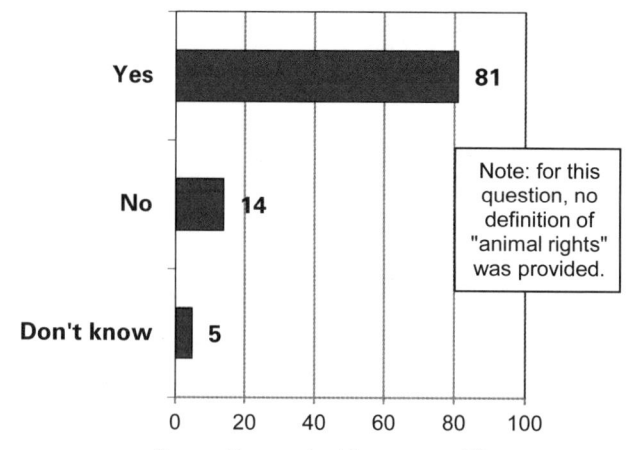

- Yes: 81
- No: 14
- Don't know: 5

Note: for this question, no definition of "animal rights" was provided.

*Source: Responsive Management.*[160]

Another two thirds of Americans say they have family members or friends who are supporters of animal rights (again, this high percentage appears to be due to a misunderstanding of the terminology, given that most Americans are actually supporters of animal welfare).[161] Survey findings that are based on the respondent's *perception* of a term rather than an understood *definition* of it (as in these examples with the term "animal rights") can lead to inaccurate conclusions about how the American public feels about the use of animals. Animal rights organizations, in turn, may enthusiastically report such findings to imply that the animal rights movement has more support from the public than it actually does.

---

Animal rights groups misleadingly use the concept of animal welfare to promote and fund an animal rights agenda.

⊕

---

The fact that so many Americans claim to support "animal rights" (at least based on the term alone) might suggest that most people do indeed believe that animals have certain rights—those entitling them to reasonable and humane treatment by humans. Of course, the actual commonly held definition of "animal rights" dictates no use of animals by humans whatsoever, and this is not something most Americans agree with: the overwhelming majority identify more with animal *welfare* after hearing the definitions of the terms.

> Survey findings that are based on the respondent's perception of a term rather than an understood definition of it (as in these examples with the term "animal rights") can lead to inaccurate conclusions about how the American public feels about the use of animals. Animal rights organizations, in turn, may enthusiastically report such findings to imply that the animal rights movement has more support from the public than it actually does.

This distinction is important, as many animal rights groups misleadingly use the concept of animal welfare to promote and fund an animal rights agenda. Commercials, advertisements, and solicitations for donations from animal rights groups may imply that support is needed to ensure the humane treatment of animals in various unethical and emotionally charged situations; in actuality, the missions of such groups typically discourage the use of animals altogether, whether for food, medical research, or other purposes.[162]

The implication is that, insofar as terminology is concerned, "animal rights," "animal welfare," and "dominionism" are essentially meaningless to most people outside of specialized areas of interest—people tend to think they are supporters of animal rights when in fact they are supporters of animal welfare. However, the meaning behind these labels remains

> Proponents of hunting should not cede the middle ground—the belief that animals can be used by humans provided they are treated humanely—to proponents of animal rights. As the vast majority of hunters are ethical and care about the humane treatment of wildlife, legal hunting is consistent with animal welfare. Despite animal rights claims to the contrary, legal and ethical hunting is not a dominionistic activity.

important, and proponents of hunting should not cede the middle ground—the belief that animals can be used by humans provided they are treated humanely—to proponents of animal rights. As the vast majority of hunters are ethical and care about the humane treatment of wildlife, legal hunting is consistent with animal welfare. Despite animal rights claims to the contrary, legal and ethical hunting is not a dominionistic activity.

## Americans' Attitudes and Behaviors Regarding the Use of Animals

Most Americans hold attitudes consistent with animal welfare, not animal rights. For example, pet ownership and meat consumption hold little controversy for most Americans: nine out of ten approve of owning a dog or cat and the same number consume meat.[163] At the same time, Americans are less approving of practices perceived as being potentially inhumane: only about half of U.S. residents approve of consuming veal or wearing fur.[164]

Three out of four Americans think it is acceptable to use animals in research, as long as it does not harm or kill any animals, while less than half of all Americans approve of using animals in research *even if it may harm or kill some of them*.[165] Still, this is a share of the U.S. population notably larger than the percentage who self-identify as having a dominionistic belief, meaning many people in the animal welfare category value the potential gains in medical research enough to accept the loss of some animals to achieve these gains. Along these lines, only three percent of Americans think *all* animal use should be banned (a percentage that more accurately reflects the actual size of the population of animal rights proponents in the U.S.).[166]

Beyond their stated beliefs, Americans' lifestyle choices reflect a predominantly animal welfare mindset. More than nine out of ten Americans consume meat, and approximately three out of four wear leather shoes, gloves, or other clothing. Among all Americans, only two percent do not eat meat *or* wear leather.[167]

What's more, just 1 percent of Americans actually follow a strict animal rights lifestyle by not consuming meat or wearing leather (while 13 percent hold the animal rights position yet eat meat and/or wear leather).[168] It also bears repeating that an overwhelming majority of Americans express support for the term "animal rights" (i.e., without a definition) while also eating meat and using leather—activities that are philosophically inconsistent with the animal rights belief.

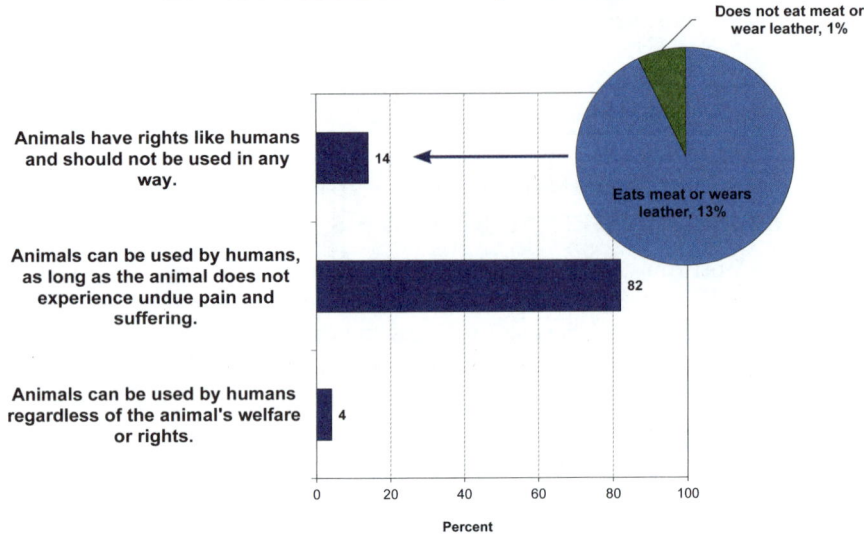

**For the following three statements, please choose the one that best describes your beliefs.**

- Animals have rights like humans and should not be used in any way. — 14
- Animals can be used by humans, as long as the animal does not experience undue pain and suffering. — 82
- Animals can be used by humans regardless of the animal's welfare or rights. — 4

Percent

Pie chart:
- Does not eat meat or wear leather, 1%
- Eats meat or wears leather, 13%

*Source: Responsive Management.*[169]

## Perceptions of Animals by Species and Purpose

Many people, consciously or not, perceive animals in terms of a hierarchy, from those species of which they feel favorable and even protective to those that inspire more neutral or even dismissive feelings. Generally speaking, the most concern is for pets, followed by animals that are perceived as charismatic, having humanlike traits, or rare or endangered; of least concern are game species that are thought of as common or plentiful.[170]

An example of this hierarchy can be seen in how differently the public views the hunting of various species: most Americans approve of hunting turkey, deer, and duck, but well less than half approve of hunting bear, mountain lion, or wolf.[171]

The hierarchical view also emerges in focus group discussions about animals. For example, many people think that dogs, cats, and other pets should be protected, whereas cows, pigs, chickens, and fish are deemed acceptable to eat. Regarding animals used in medical research, some people allow for the use of rats or mice while opposing the use of monkeys or other primates.[172]

Some Americans also strongly disapprove of the use of animals for entertainment purposes such as circuses and rodeos; zoos and aquariums have also been described as problematic in terms of the humane treatment of animals.[173]

### How Americans Talk About the Use of Animals:

"I wouldn't say a farm animal has more rights or less rights than a forest animal, but I think I'm okay with the use of animals for the welfare of society."

"I don't think a cockroach or a gerbil has the same rights as I do. When you get a certain animal, of course you think differently. But you have to draw the line somewhere."

"[It's okay to use animals] for food, and then for work, but not when you go to the circus and they're whipping a tiger. ...They [animals] can be used, but I think they should be treated well."

"To me, research where it's about curing disease or understanding anatomy or things like that, it's [the use of animals] justified. If it's adding value to further mankind, from a health standpoint, maybe saving people's lives down the road, then I'm a little bit okay with it."

"I have venison in my freezer. I'd feel better about eating that than if I were to go to a grocery store and get cheap ground beef, because I know that animal [that was hunted] lived a happier life than the very short and probably miserable life that any factory farm animal lives."

*Source: Responsive Management.*[174]

## Americans' Changing Views of Animals

In general, people become attached to animals at an early age for a variety of reasons: by having pets, through visits to zoos, or through movies, television, and other entertainment that includes anthropomorphized animal characters.

Over the past few decades, Americans have moved from having primarily *traditionalist* views about wildlife (the idea that wildlife should be managed by humans) to more *mutualistic* views (the idea that wildlife and humans ought to coexist). Researchers at Colorado State University and the Ohio State University[175] have identified the modernization of America as the primary cause of this shift, with modernization encompassing the urbanization of the country as well as increasing levels of income and education. Urbanization, in particular, means that people are increasingly less likely to interact with wildlife in their day-to-day lives.

As a result, Americans may come to view wildlife in idealized terms and feel more protective of various species. Given current and anticipated demographic trends in the United States, it is likely that Americans will continue to shift toward predominantly mutualistic views of wildlife in the years to come.[176]

One example of the shift away from a traditionalist view of wildlife can be seen in the fact that nearly twice as many Americans think that fish and wildlife populations should be managed primarily for the benefit of the fish and wildlife themselves, compared to those who think such management should primarily benefit humans.[177]

Animal rights and animal welfare issues are prominent in the media. About half of all Americans say they have seen or heard something about either animal rights or animal welfare in the past few years, and the examples named typically relate to cruelty or mistreatment: animal shelters; abuses in the food industry or at factory farms; whaling and whales in captivity; big game poaching; the ivory trade; pet neglect; overharvesting of fisheries; and endangered species.[178] Surveys also show that images of trophy kills posted on Facebook and other social media are particularly unpopular with the public.[179] These findings suggest that concern for animals in various contexts is a common sentiment among many Americans.

## Hunting in the Context of Animal Welfare and Animal Rights

As discussed in Chapter 4, eight out of ten Americans approve of hunting in general, hunting for the meat, hunting to protect humans from harm, and hunting for wildlife management—all forms of the activity perceived as being consistent with an animal welfare philosophy.[180]

At the same time, only about one third of Americans approve of trophy hunting (i.e., hunting that is perceived as being done solely for the trophy).[181] Research suggests that many opponents of trophy hunting view it as needless killing—in their eyes, an example of a dominionistic treatment of wildlife.

Also relevant to animal welfare and animal rights considerations is the question of where the meat that Americans eat comes from. While proponents of animal rights tend to strongly oppose the consumption of animal meat as a matter of principle, some allow for a "lesser of two evils" distinction by deeming the legal hunting of certain game species to be preferable to a reliance on industrialized farms for animal protein—this preference for hunting over factory farming is based on the perceived suffering (or lack thereof) of the animals in each respective scenario.[182]

## Youth Attitudes Toward Animals

Research shows that youth attitudes toward animals tend to evolve as youth themselves progress in their cognitive development. Communications about hunting and the use of animals directed at youth must proceed from a basic understanding of the stages of youth development: communications that do not account for these stages will be doomed to fail, in the same way that attempting to teach a second grader calculus would be futile—the information must be relevant and comprehensible to the intended recipient.

The influential Swiss psychologist Jean Piaget identified four primary stages of youth development.[183] During the sensorimotor stage from birth to around two years of age, children learn immediate cause and effect and gain understanding of the existence of objects that are not visible. The preoperational stage that follows sees children adopting a "literal" view of the world in which dreams are considered real, objects can be alive, and differences in appearance are understood to mean that the altered item has truly transformed. During the concrete operational stage between ages seven and eleven, youth gain problem-solving skills and sharpen the ability to categorize things; for example, Labrador retriever and beagle are understood as breeds of the same overall species. Finally, the formal operational stage is characterized by the development of abstract problem-solving skills.

Researchers later applied Piaget's theories to the stages in which youth develop an understanding of wildlife and the natural world.[184] Specifically, between second and fifth grade, children develop affective and emotional concern for animals; between fifth and eighth grade, youth develop cognitive and factual understanding of animals. The last stage of development occurs during the middle school and high school years, as young people begin to foster ethical and ecological appreciation of wildlife and gain interest in wildlife-related outdoor recreation.

Comments from young people in focus groups validate these general tendencies.[185] For example, fourth graders typically communicate emphatic interest in and affection toward animals, sometimes objecting to the use of animals to make products for humans. In line with this concern, fourth graders may be especially resistant to the concept of hunting, preferring instead that meat be purchased in grocery stores. Youth at this age also may hold moralistic opinions about wildlife, having definitive ideas about the right and wrong treatment of animals. Finally, being unaware of regulations, fourth graders may believe that legal hunting has the potential to endanger wildlife or cause them to go extinct.

By contrast, middle schoolers and high schoolers are generally less likely to question using animals to make human products. They may also be more likely to express tolerance for things in which they do not believe or do not personally participate, such as hunting. Older youth may conceive of circumstances in which human needs may take priority over the needs of wildlife. Finally, middle schoolers and high schoolers may recognize that a person's views regarding the use of animals may be especially influenced by region or circumstance.

---

Talking about the use of animals, including through hunting, is not a matter of changing Americans' values but of affirming them.

---

## Developing Communications About the Use of Animals

Communications about the use of animals must be based on what Americans actually think and how they behave. This means that the most effective communications will embody the animal welfare philosophy, consistent with the beliefs and behaviors of most Americans.

Characterizing the American public through labels alone, absent context or definition, can be misleading. For example, it would be incorrect to conclude that most Americans are supporters of "animal rights"—rather than accurately describe the opinion of most people with regard to the use of animals, this conclusion instead simply reflects widespread misunderstanding of the term "animal rights."

What matters is the meaning behind these labels and whether people actually live according to the underlying philosophies. In this way, talking about the use of animals, including through hunting, is not a matter of *changing* Americans' values but of *affirming* them.

ATTITUDES TOWARD ANIMAL RIGHTS, ANIMAL WELARE, AND DOMINIONISM

## Percent of Americans who...

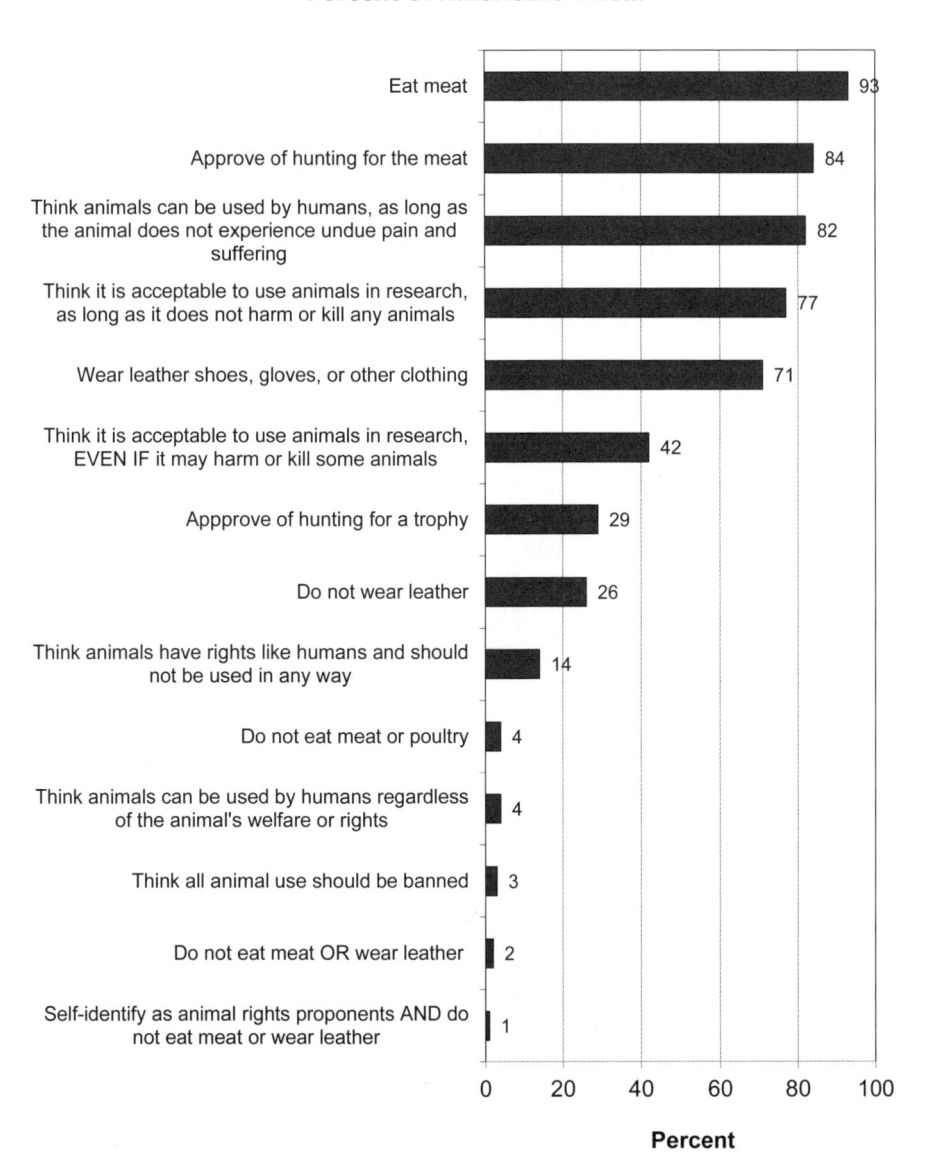

| Category | Percent |
|---|---|
| Eat meat | 93 |
| Approve of hunting for the meat | 84 |
| Think animals can be used by humans, as long as the animal does not experience undue pain and suffering | 82 |
| Think it is acceptable to use animals in research, as long as it does not harm or kill any animals | 77 |
| Wear leather shoes, gloves, or other clothing | 71 |
| Think it is acceptable to use animals in research, EVEN IF it may harm or kill some animals | 42 |
| Appprove of hunting for a trophy | 29 |
| Do not wear leather | 26 |
| Think animals have rights like humans and should not be used in any way | 14 |
| Do not eat meat or poultry | 4 |
| Think animals can be used by humans regardless of the animal's welfare or rights | 4 |
| Think all animal use should be banned | 3 |
| Do not eat meat OR wear leather | 2 |
| Self-identify as animal rights proponents AND do not eat meat or wear leather | 1 |

*Source: Responsive Management.*[186]

87

## Key Takeaways

- Americans' attitudes toward the use of animals exist on a continuum of acceptability. At one end of the continuum is the animal rights mindset, which is the belief that animals have rights like humans and should not be used in any way. At the opposite end is the dominionistic mindset, or the belief that animals can be used by humans regardless of the animal's welfare or rights. The middle of the continuum represents animal welfare—the idea that animals can be used by humans, as long as the animal does not experience undue pain and suffering.

- Most Americans are not proponents of the animal rights philosophy—Americans do not favor banning the use of animals altogether. The animal rights mindset is incompatible with the beliefs and behaviors of most Americans.

- All communications about hunting must be viewed through the prism of the continuum of acceptability regarding animal rights, animal welfare, and dominionism. Communications that appear to be aligned with the dominionistic side of the continuum will be rejected; messages built around animal welfare, on the other hand, are more likely to be accepted.

- Hunters must communicate respect for animals. This is especially important when posting pictures of harvested animals on social media. Non-hunters, typically without the context to appreciate or understand such photos, may find them objectionable and even egregious.

- While irreverent comments from hunters may seem harmless, non-hunters may interpret them as disrespectful toward wildlife. Foul language and phrases like, "if it flies, it dies," and, "if it's brown, it's down," are dominionistic and will likely turn people away from hunting.

- Hunters should strive to show people they care by demonstrating empathy and concern for the humane treatment of animals.

- Hunters should share their game meat with others while highlighting the quality of the game meat. Hunting animals for meat is consistent with animal welfare—remember that most Americans eat meat, and many people view hunting for meat as more humane than obtaining meat through factory farming.

# CHAPTER 6

# *Arguing for Hunting: What Works and What Doesn't*

**THIS CHAPTER EXPLAINS THE MOST** *effective arguments in support of hunting. The chapter covers the results of scientific research that assessed the effectiveness of numerous arguments for and against hunting. The chapter looks at both the most effective individual arguments as well as the themes and concepts on which these arguments are based.*

## The Most Effective Arguments in Support of Hunting

Based on NRA Hunters' Leadership Forum-sponsored research[187] that tested the effectiveness of 51 pro-hunting arguments, the themes that work the best in support of hunting are:

- Hunting as a food source.
- Hunting as conservation (i.e., hunting as a form of wildlife management that produces ecological benefits to both game and non-game species).
- Hunting as a right.

The assessments of the pro-hunting arguments in the study showed that these themes are the most effective when talking about support of hunting. After more than 15,000 Americans rated the various messages, the themes of food, conservation (wildlife management), and rights emerged as the most effective.

Specifically, the top five most effective arguments in support of hunting in the study were as follows:

- Hunting for food does not cause any more animal suffering than slaughtering livestock for food.
- Those who do not hunt or do not approve of hunting don't have to hunt, but they should respect the right of others to hunt.
- Hunting specifically helps control the deer population, which is overabundant and has no natural predators in many areas.
- Hunting controls wildlife populations and helps with species management.
- Hunting is properly regulated, and there are rules and regulations in place to ensure fair and moral hunting that also protects wildlife populations as a whole.

The full results of the study are shown later in this chapter.

## Arguments Against Hunting That Must Be Countered

This same study cited above also tested 31 anti-hunting arguments, and the themes that garner the most opposition to hunting are as follows:

- Hunting as a violation of fair chase.
- Hunting being linked to trophy hunting.
- Hunting results in diminished wildlife populations.

With some rare exceptions, such as fenced hunting (which many hunters oppose[188]), hunting in the U.S. embodies the concept of fair chase. Talk to people about your hunting and emphasize the fair chase that is involved.

While hunters certainly are thrilled with trophy-sized game, this is rarely the primary reason that hunters hunt. Hunting for food, to be with family and friends, and to be out in nature are all more important reasons to hunt among hunters than is hunting for a trophy. Counter the trophy hunting argument with these reasons for your hunting. Another argument is that you hunt to help with wildlife management, which brings us to the third theme against hunting that resonated.

> Hunting for food, to be with family and friends, and to be out in nature are all more important reasons to hunt among hunters than is hunting for a trophy.

⊕

Some anti-hunters may argue that hunting results in diminished wildlife populations. In reality, the opposite is the case. Hunting and hunters have benefited and still benefit species—even non-game species. Emphasize that hunting helps with species management and that funding from hunters pays for the conservation of habitat and the species themselves. (Chapter 1 details some of the species that were brought back from near extinction to healthy levels by hunters and the funding they provide.)

## Effective Arguments in Support of Hunting Among Those Who Do Not Currently Support Hunting

Americans who are the most disapproving of hunting still respond to the themes of hunting for food and the ecological benefits of hunting through wildlife management. Specifically, the five most effective arguments among this group were:

- Wild animals experience a better life than do farm animals raised for food.
- Hunting for food does not cause any more animal suffering than slaughtering livestock for food.
- Humans are a natural part of the food chain and cycle of life.
- The vast majority of hunters hunt safely.
- Hunting controls wildlife populations and helps with species management.

## Hunting Does Not Cause Species to Become Endangered or Extinct

### Populations of key species.

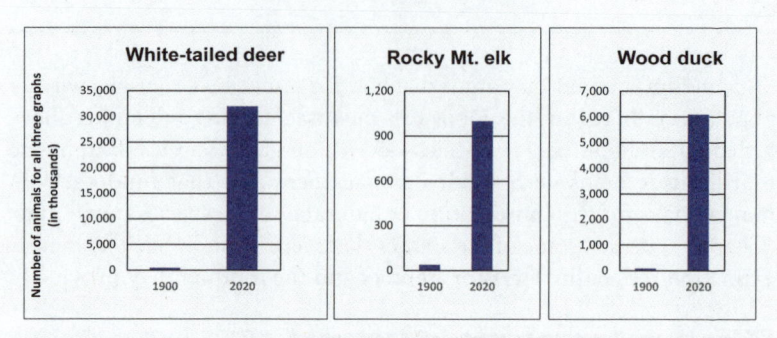

| White-tailed deer | Rocky Mt. elk | Wood duck |
|---|---|---|
| 1900: <500; 2020: ~32,000 | 1900: 40; 2020: ~1,000 | 1900: very low; 2020: ~6,000 |

(Number of animals for all three graphs in thousands)

*In 1900, there were fewer than 500,000 white-tailed deer, compared to 32 million today. The Rocky Mountain elk population has increased from 40,000 in 1900 to 1 million today. And the wood duck, once extremely rare, now has a population of 6 million.*

One of the most distressing survey findings regarding public attitudes toward hunting is that 46 percent of Americans feel that hunting as practiced in the United States today can cause species to become endangered.[189] In fact, more Americans agree with this erroneous statement (46 percent) than disagree (40 percent) with it. This false narrative is also the basis for one of the most effective anti-hunting arguments.

This of course is not true; in fact, the exact opposite is true. No species has become extinct in the era of modern wildlife management because of regulated hunting. This is the reason that there are so many laws and regulations on seasons, limits, and methods of hunting.

Yes, in the old days, unregulated hunting—especially market hunting—caused the endangerment and even the demise of some species. But modern hunting in America is totally different. It is important to understand the major differences between hunting before modern wildlife management and hunting after regulations were instituted in each of the states in the first half of the 1900s.

Making sure that non-hunters know that regulated hunting in the U.S. does *not* cause species to become endangered is one of the most important messages to get across when talking about hunting.

## Countering Arguments Against Hunting Among Those Who Do Not Currently Support Hunting

The anti-hunting statements that did well among those most disapproving of the sport linked hunting to lack of fair chase, the suffering of animals, and the benefits of watching wildlife over hunting. The statements are shown below, with ways to counter these arguments following the list.

- Canned hunts, such as when animals are kept in a confined area, are extremely unethical and violate the concept of fair chase.
- Animals have a nervous system and feel pain. It is morally wrong to inflict pain and suffering on any living thing.
- Pictures of smiling hunters and dead animals are disturbing and painful for many anti-hunters and animal lovers.
- Because hunters sometimes wound but do not kill animals, many animals are left to suffer and die slowly.
- An animal can be watched thousands of times but can be killed only once. For this reason, watching wildlife is more economically beneficial to communities than hunting.

To counter the lack of fair chase argument, do not let hunting as a whole be colored by canned hunting. That type of hunting is the exception, and most hunters have not done such hunting themselves. In fact, most do not support canned hunting.[190]

Emphasize the ethics of hunting (and hunt ethically yourself as an example) that limits the pain and suffering of the animal. Ethical hunters seek clean kills and track wounded game to ensure that animals do not unduly suffer.

Hunters should be seen as honoring the wildlife that they hunt. Some people, of course, will always be uncomfortable with photos of hunters posing with their kills. However, be respectful of the wildlife—including in photos. Lighthearted or silly poses, while entertaining in the moment, do not translate well to non-hunters and imply a callous attitude.

Right now, very little of open land preserved for habitat and for wild species, has been paid for by wildlife watchers. It has been hunters (and anglers) who have been at the forefront of the conservation of lands for habitat and wildlife. Talk about the ecological benefits provided by hunters and hunting dollars that in some cases have provided the very opportunities to watch wildlife in the first place. Wildlife watching also is

**How to Talk About Hunting** ⊕ *Research-Based Communications Strategies*

*Since 1934, all U.S. waterfowl hunters have been required to purchase a Federal Migratory Bird Hunting and Conservation Stamp (commonly known as a Duck Stamp), with the proceeds used to preserve wetlands and other habitat through the National Wildlife Refuge System.*

benefited from hunting because of the wildlife management that hunting provides for both game and non-game species.

## Full Results of the Study

The following is only for those interested in the specific methods used in this scientific study that tested 82 pro- and anti-hunting arguments. The messages that were tested in a survey of more than 15,000 Americans were compiled through a comprehensive review of television, streaming, and print media messages about hunting—both for and against it. The researchers also reviewed campaign and promotional materials produced by both pro- and anti-hunting organizations, as well as editorials and articles about hunting.

Note that the researchers did not address the validity of any of the statements—they only looked at how the arguments would be perceived, regardless of what the messages actually said. There were 51 pro-hunting arguments and 31 anti-hunting arguments that were tested.

Each argument was rated by survey respondents using a 1 to 10 scale, with 1 meaning a very weak argument and 10 meaning a very strong argument. Mean scores were then run of each argument's effectiveness.

Because a single respondent could not feasibly rate all 82 arguments, each respondent was given a random subset of the arguments. Additionally, to lessen possible confusion in the survey, each respondent was given only pro-hunting arguments or only anti-hunting arguments. Nobody was given both pro- and anti-hunting arguments.

In the analysis, each of the arguments was categorized by theme—so that top themes could be identified as well as top individual statements. The eight themes that the arguments fell into were behavior, conservation, economic, ethics, morality and rights, pain/suffering, safety, and social. Each of the themes had some arguments in support (color coded green in the tables) and some arguments against (color coded red in the tables) hunting. The themes are shown below:

| Categorization System for Arguments | |
|---|---|
| In support | Behavior - hunters are good |
| Against | Behavior - hunters behave badly |
| In support | Conservation - benefits conservation / ecology |
| Against | Conservation - harms conservation / ecology |
| In support | Economic - good for economy |
| Against | Economic - not good for econ / other acts. better |

| | |
|---|---|
| In support | **Ethics** - hunting is honorable and natural |
| Against | **Ethics** - not fair chase / not fair to animal |
| In support | **Morality and rights** - hunter rights |
| Against | **Morality and rights** - animal rights / hunting immoral |
| In support | **Pain / suffering** - does not increase animal suffering |
| Against | **Pain / suffering** - increases or causes animal suffering |
| In support | **Safety** - makes humans safer / hunting is not unsafe |
| Against | **Safety** - more danger to humans |
| In support | **Social** - has social benefits |
| Against | **Social** - harms society |

The table that follows shows the full results among Americans as a whole. See where your arguments rank.

| All Arguments Ranked by Mean Rating | Mean | Category |
|---|---|---|
| Canned hunts, such as when animals are kept in a confined area, are extremely unethical and violate the concept of fair chase. | 7.28 | Ethics - not fair chase / not fair to animal |
| Hunting for food does not cause any more animal suffering than slaughtering livestock for food. | 7.17 | Pain / suffering - does not increase animal suffering |
| Those who do not hunt or do not approve of hunting don't have to hunt, but they should respect the right of others to hunt. | 7.11 | Morality and rights - hunter rights |
| Hunting specifically helps control the deer population, which is overabundant and has no natural predators in many areas. | 7.09 | Conservation - benefits conservation / ecology |
| Hunting controls wildlife populations and helps with species management. | 6.98 | Conservation - benefits conservation / ecology |
| Hunting is properly regulated, and there are rules and regulations in place to ensure fair and moral hunting that also protects wildlife populations as a whole. | 6.89 | Behavior - hunters are good |
| The vast majority of hunters hunt safely. | 6.81 | Behavior - hunters are good |
| Hunting is human nature, having been part of human survival and culture since mankind has existed. | 6.79 | Ethics - hunting is honorable and natural |
| Hunting provides meat for hunters and their families. | 6.73 | Social - has social benefits |
| Hunting is critical to conservation. Ethical, regulated hunting is the driving force that maintains abundant wildlife. | 6.71 | Conservation - benefits conservation / ecology |
| The vast majority of hunters hunt legally and ethically. | 6.66 | Behavior - hunters are good |

## ARGUING FOR HUNTING: WHAT WORKS AND WHAT DOESN'T

| All Arguments Ranked by Mean Rating | Mean | Category |
|---|---|---|
| Hunting prevents wildlife overpopulation that leads to starvation and suffering. | 6.63 | Conservation - benefits conservation / ecology AND Pain / suffering - does not increase animal suffering |
| Hunting and hunters are responsible for the restoration of specific species (e.g., Canada goose, elk, wolf). | 6.55 | Conservation - benefits conservation / ecology |
| Humans are a natural part of the food chain and cycle of life. | 6.48 | Ethics - hunting is honorable and natural |
| Although hunting strictly for a trophy is not condoned, when the whole animal is used (e.g., meat, pelt) it is acceptable to save an unusable part as a reminder of the hunt. | 6.48 | Ethics - hunting is honorable and natural |
| The vast majority of hunters are not trophy hunters. | 6.47 | Behavior - hunters are good |
| Hunting is a good way to get youth out in nature and away from electronics. | 6.46 | Social - has social benefits |
| The vast majority of hunters use hunting methods that do not cause undue suffering. | 6.44 | Pain / suffering - does not increase animal suffering |
| Hunters and non-hunters are not so different: most oppose habitat destruction, want healthy wildlife populations, prefer that wildlife do not suffer, and enjoy eating meat. | 6.42 | Behavior - hunters are good |
| Hunting is the primary source of funds (through hunting licenses) for fish and wildlife agencies responsible for the successful management of wildlife and habitat. | 6.38 | Conservation - benefits conservation / ecology |
| Hunters provide the primary source of funds for conservation organizations such as the Rocky Mountain Elk Foundation, the National Wild Turkey Federation, & Ducks Unlimited. | 6.36 | Conservation - benefits conservation / ecology |
| Hunting provides population and nuisance wildlife control at no cost to the taxpayer (i.e., hunting is less expensive than sharpshooters and immunocontraceptives). | 6.33 | Conservation - benefits conservation / ecology |
| Hunters have a higher regard for wildlife and the health of wildlife than many other people, and hunters are concerned with the health and management of wildlife populations. | 6.31 | Behavior - hunters are good |
| Hunting promotes biodiversity and balances the ecosystem. | 6.27 | Conservation - benefits conservation / ecology |

**How to Talk About Hunting** ⊕ *Research-Based Communications Strategies*

| All Arguments Ranked by Mean Rating | Mean | Category |
|---|---|---|
| Hunters can be a source of education and information for those who are unable, unwilling, or uninterested in getting involved in important wildlife-related efforts. | 6.27 | Conservation - benefits conservation / ecology |
| Hunting is a cultural, social, and evolutionary tradition. | 6.26 | Ethics - hunting is honorable and natural |
| Hunting controls nuisance and invasive species. | 6.26 | Conservation - benefits conservation / ecology |
| Most scientists and non-governmental agencies agree that hunting is important to conservation. | 6.24 | Conservation - benefits conservation / ecology |
| Hunting helps humans develop an understanding of, respect for, and connection with nature. | 6.24 | Social - has social benefits |
| The hunting community wants hunting to coexist with other forms of ecotourism. | 6.24 | Economic - good for economy |
| Hunting and hunters provide the most funding for conservation efforts for game species, non-game species, habitat, game lands, wetlands, parks, and more. | 6.21 | Conservation - benefits conservation / ecology |
| Hunting assists farmers and landowners by reducing property damage and financial loss, with meat being consumed rather than wasted. | 6.19 | Social - has social benefits |
| Hunters purchase Duck Stamps, the proceeds from which are used for habitat and conservation efforts. | 6.18 | Conservation - benefits conservation / ecology |
| Most Americans approve of hunting. | 6.12 | Ethics - hunting is honorable and natural |
| Those who consume meat should not oppose hunting. Those who oppose hunting need to understand that not eating meat does not exempt them from wildlife-related consumerism. | 6.12 | Morality and rights - hunter rights |
| Wild animals experience a better life than do farm animals raised for food. | 6.12 | Pain / suffering - does not increase animal suffering |
| Hunting contributes substantially to the overall economy—globally, nationally, and locally. | 6.10 | Economic - good for economy |
| Hunting reduces wildlife-vehicle collisions, minimizing wildlife suffering, human fatalities, property damage, and costs associated with vehicular accidents. | 6.00 | Social - has social benefits AND Pain / suffering - does not increase animal suffering |
| Many game species have diminished populations, and scientists have advised against hunting them; yet these remain some of the most popular species hunted by trophy hunters. | 5.99 | Conservation - harms conservation / ecology |

| All Arguments Ranked by Mean Rating | Mean | Category |
|---|---|---|
| Hunting provides an organic source of meat, while farm animals raised in an industrial setting for food do not. | 5.92 | Social - has social benefits |
| Hunting is an important activity for spending time with friends and family. | 5.79 | Social - has social benefits |
| Hunting is less dangerous and results in fewer injuries than many other activities. | 5.78 | Safety - makes humans safer / hunting not unsafe |
| Hunting provides jobs and income. | 5.77 | Economic - good for economy |
| Hunting prevents the spread of disease, such as tick-borne diseases. | 5.65 | Safety - makes humans safer / hunting not unsafe |
| Trophy hunters do not hunt for food; they hunt only for sport. Hunting for a trophy or sport is immoral. | 5.51 | Morality and rights - animal rights / hunting immoral |
| Hunting is a bigger economic contributor than other ecotourism activities like wildlife photography. | 5.46 | Economic - good for economy |
| Hunters donate large amounts of meat to feed the hungry. | 5.45 | Social - has social benefits |
| Hunters use all parts of the animals they harvest. | 5.44 | Ethics - hunting is honorable and natural |
| Baiting, trapping, hunting with dogs, and technology are often used in hunting, and these techniques violate the concept of fair chase. | 5.36 | Ethics - not fair chase / not fair to animal |
| Hunting provides exercise. | 5.28 | Social - has social benefits |
| Humans have dominion over animals, and animals are here for our sustenance and use. | 5.21 | Morality and rights - hunter rights |
| Hunting helps humans develop survival skills. | 5.19 | Social - has social benefits |
| Hunters do not protect non-game species, but instead focus their "conservation" efforts only on game species that they can hunt. | 5.16 | Conservation - harms conservation / ecology |
| Hunters are not properly educated. They often target animals they should not be hunting, use incorrect or unsafe procedures, and pass on bad behavior to others. | 5.08 | Behavior - hunters behave badly |
| Animals have a nervous system and feel pain. It is morally wrong to inflict pain and suffering on any living thing. | 5.04 | Morality and rights - animal rights / hunting immoral AND Pain / suffering - increases or causes animal suffering |
| According to the Bible, man has dominion over animals; therefore, it is acceptable to hunt, harvest, and use animals for food. | 4.99 | Morality and rights - hunter rights |

**How to Talk About Hunting** ⊕ *Research-Based Communications Strategies*

| All Arguments Ranked by Mean Rating | Mean | Category |
|---|---|---|
| Animals deserve the same basic right to life as humans. | 4.93 | Morality and rights - animal rights / hunting immoral |
| An animal can be watched thousands of times but can be killed only once. For this reason, watching wildlife is more economically beneficial to communities than hunting. | 4.76 | Economic - not good for econ / other acts. better |
| Pictures of smiling hunters and dead animals are disturbing and painful for many anti-hunters and animal lovers. | 4.72 | Pain / suffering - increases or causes animal suffering |
| Because hunters sometimes wound but do not kill animals, many animals are left to suffer and die slowly. | 4.64 | Pain / suffering - increases or causes animal suffering |
| Animals cannot possess rights because they lack an innate morality. | 4.57 | Morality and rights - hunter rights |
| Hunting is not the best approach to wildlife population control because wildlife still experience pain and suffering when shot. | 4.41 | Pain / suffering - increases or causes animal suffering |
| Hunting does not contribute as much to the economy as hunters claim. | 4.37 | Economic - not good for econ / other acts. better |
| When wildlife has no commercial value, it doesn't pay to protect it. Successful conservation depends on wildlife having value. | 4.32 | Conservation - benefits conservation / ecology |
| Hunting is disruptive: hunters may litter, damage property, or behave rudely, and loud gunshots may be frustrating to those living in or near areas where hunting takes place. | 4.16 | Behavior - hunters behave badly |
| Hunting can never be fair chase because hunters are at a distinct technological advantage; also, wildlife often do not realize they are being hunted. | 4.09 | Ethics - not fair chase / not fair to animal |
| Hunting hurts wildlife populations because hunters target the strongest and healthiest animals. | 3.94 | Conservation - harms conservation / ecology |
| Hunting leads to more species becoming threatened, endangered, and even extinct. | 3.93 | Conservation - harms conservation / ecology |
| Hunting today is no longer necessary and is done only for sport. There are plenty of other food sources available. | 3.90 | Morality and rights - animal rights / hunting immoral |
| Hunters have pushed nuisance species into more populated regions & neighborhoods. | 3.90 | Conservation - harms conservation / ecology |
| Hunting may increase the spread of wildlife disease because healthy animals with natural immunity are killed. | 3.86 | Conservation - harms conservation / ecology |
| Having the choice to hunt or not means we have an obligation not to hunt: wildlife must hunt other animals to survive, but humans do not need to. | 3.85 | Morality and rights - animal rights / hunting immoral |

| All Arguments Ranked by Mean Rating | Mean | Category |
|---|---|---|
| Humans, pets, and wildlife can be injured or killed by stray bullets or arrows from hunters. Hunting is dangerous and increases the chance of a fatal accident. | 3.82 | Safety - more danger to humans |
| Hunters can't be trusted to follow rules, such as bag limits or season guidelines. | 3.80 | Behavior - hunters behave badly |
| Hunting costs taxpayers: lands managed for hunting are sometimes purchased and maintained through general tax funds, and most taxpayers do not hunt. | 3.72 | Economic - not good for econ / other acts. better |
| Hunters disrupt the ecosystem. Nature will take care of itself and animals that are meant to flourish will do so without hunting being used as a management tool. | 3.71 | Conservation - harms conservation / ecology |
| Hunting is not a sustainable model. Eventually, populations of hunted species will decline and no longer flourish. | 3.41 | Conservation - harms conservation / ecology |
| Hunting actually causes overpopulation because wildlife populations are managed specifically so that there are more animals to hunt. | 3.36 | Conservation - harms conservation / ecology |
| Hunters are inclined toward violence and such violence can lead to sociopathic tendencies. Hunting & hurting animals lead to other abusive or violent actions against humans. | 3.36 | Social - harms society |
| Hunting is not necessary because there are non-lethal, humane methods of wildlife population control such as immunocontraceptives. | 3.29 | Morality and rights - animal rights / hunting immoral |
| Hunting is cost-prohibitive to some and is therefore an activity that only the wealthy can afford. | 3.28 | Social - harms society |
| Hunting pushes wildlife onto roads, increasing vehicle collisions. | 3.24 | Conservation - harms conservation / ecology |

 The results above pertain to the individual arguments. As noted, the themes of the arguments were also examined. In the table that follows, the first data row shows the total number of messages in that theme. The second data row shows the number of messages in that theme that were in the top half of the ranking (i.e., that did well). The bottom data row shows the percentage of the messages in that theme that were in the top of the ranking.

 As an example of how to read the table, look at the theme that did the best—conservation. There were 15 total pro-hunting messages in the conservation theme (in the "Conservation, for" column), and 11 of them were in the top half of the ranking, which is 73 percent of the arguments for hunting.

|  | Safety | | Economic | | Morality and rights | | Behavior | | Conservation | | Social | | Pain/suffering | | Ethics | |
|---|---|---|---|---|---|---|---|---|---|---|---|---|---|---|---|---|
|  | For | Ag. | For | Ag. | For | Ag. | For | Ag. | For | Ag. | For | Ag. | For | Ag. | For | Ag. |
| Total messages | 2 | 1 | 4 | 3 | 5 | 6 | 6 | 3 | 15 | 10 | 10 | 2 | 5 | 4 | 6 | 3 |
| Top half | 0 | 0 | 1 | 2 | 1 | 3 | 4 | 1 | 11 | 4 | 3 | 1 | 3 | 1 | 3 | 3 |
| Percent | 0 | 0 | 25 | 67 | 20 | 50 | 67 | 33 | 73 | 40 | 30 | 50 | 60 | 25 | 50 | 100 |

Total messages = number of messages of that theme.
Top half = number of messages in the top half of the ranking.
Percent = percent of the messages of that theme in the top half of the ranking.
"For" = For; "Ag." = Against.

## Other Arguments and How to Rebut Them

Several arguments outside of those that were addressed in the study cited above have been put forward by opponents of hunting. Four of them are refuted in this section. The first argument contends that hunters do *not* fund a large portion of wildlife conservation; in fact, they do. The second argument is that non-lethal methods can be used to control populations of animals such as deer; the reality is that they are not effective enough and are quite costly. The third argument is that hunting older, larger animals—which some hunters attempt to do—negatively affects the genetic makeup of the species; these effects are actually overestimated. Finally, the fourth argument suggests that hunting leads to sociopathic behavior; research shows that this purported link is entirely erroneous.

### ANTI-HUNTING ARGUMENT: HUNTERS DO NOT FUND A LARGE PORTION OF CONSERVATION

Some anti-hunters claim that very little of the funding for conservation through federal and state agencies comes from hunters. Setting aside the question of whether it matters if *most* of the funding or just a *substantial portion* of the funding comes from hunters, some of the claims make assumptions that are suspect. For instance, one study[191] examined the amount of funding from hunters and non-hunters in conservation programs, but its assumptions on what constitutes a conservation program were not accurate. In particular, the authors took a very broad look at agency budgets but were much more surgical and specific when it came to segmenting taxes from different types of firearms and ammunition to reduce the Pittman-Robertson contribution.

The report asserts that "non-human predators (wolves, mountain lions, coyotes, ravens and others) are disfavored by wildlife managers at all levels" but does not offer any substantiation of this statement. But today's wildlife managers in state fish and wildlife agencies seek to have a healthy habitat for all species, recognizing that no single species can be managed in isolation.[192] This wildlife management includes ensuring that the population sizes of various species do not overwhelm a habitat.

The inaccurate assumption discussed above did not directly pertain to the purpose of the study, which was to gain a better understanding of how much wildlife management is funded by hunters; rather, the inaccurate assumption merely tips the reader of the biases of those researchers. Specifically, the study compared all conservation to the portion of conservation attributable to hunters. It did this by two comparisons: one looked at budgets of agencies and organizations, and the second looked at acreage of land being managed.

To conduct their analysis, those researchers first looked at the eight "largest federally funded wildlife programs" but included the U.S. Bureau of Land Management (BLM) as a "conservation program." However, many activities of the BLM are not for conservation, such as its administration of grazing rights or mineral rights, as well as providing such things as off-highway vehicle recreation. In fact, the BLM will spend $139.2 million[193] on its oil and gas programs—showing that the BLM's efforts are not strictly for conservation. Labeling all BLM funding as conservation funding and then saying that hunting contributes very little to that funding is a false narrative. A quick review of BLM activities would show that it would be improper to categorize its entire spending as conservation funding.

Likewise, this same report listed the budget of the National Park System—all $3.65 billion of it—as conservation funding. Again, while some conservation is carried out by the National Park Service, many of its activities could hardly be called conservation. Among its activities is providing camping opportunities and maintenance of campgrounds. While this is an important effort of the National Park Service, it does not qualify as conservation.

The study did not include state funding because, said the authors, "most state wildlife agency funding flows from the federal government," thereby making a look at state funding moot because its funding is folded into the look at federal funding in the report. This excludes all the state money from the sale of hunting licenses—a considerable sum to those states. In other words, the analysis in that report excluded the largest source of hunting dollars that go into helping run the agency. This state funding multiplied by 50 states becomes a huge amount of money from hunting that was not even considered in the analysis.

The authors also downplay the funding contributions of hunters through the study's analysis of items taxable through the Pittman-Robertson Act. For this component, the study separates firearms and ammunition calibers commonly used for hunting from firearms and calibers generally *not* used for hunting, thereby distinguishing presumed revenues from hunters versus revenues potentially provided by non-hunting sport shooters. Yet this careful parsing of individual items is the opposite approach the authors employ in their broad look at overall federal agency budgets (i.e., the latter component does not distinguish individual conservation and non-conservation programs within the agencies).

The aforementioned study also looked at the amount of land that various government agencies control and then compared that amount to the land purchased by hunters for conservation. Included in this comparison is the total amount of land controlled by the BLM and the total amount of purchases funded by hunters—it being relatively small compared to all BLM land. Again, this is a false narrative. Nearly all the land that the BLM controls was part of the extensive tracts that the federal government owned outright when the BLM was created. To compare these lands—many of them owned by the federal government by default because they were undevelopable and undesirable for private owners rather than because they were in need of being conserved—to the amount purchased using hunter dollars creates an inaccurate impression.

This examination of the claims shows that many assumptions that have been made to make the argument that hunters contribute very little to conservation are incorrect. But even if one were to suggest that *most* of the funding for conservation does not come from hunters (and this is far from settled), it would still be true that a *substantial amount* comes from hunters and that, lacking those hunter dollars, much less habitat would be conserved today if it were not for hunters.

## ANTI-HUNTING ARGUMENT: NON-LETHAL METHODS CAN REPLACE HUNTING AS A WAY TO CONTROL WILDLIFE POPULATIONS

Some anti-hunters claim that hunting is not necessary to control animal populations because the use of contraceptives or sterilization is a better, non-lethal way to achieve the same goal. However, attempts to use contraceptives and sterilization, as well as studies on their feasibility for use in population control, have demonstrated that these methods are not practical for widescale use, and not feasibly possible on open (i.e., non-fenced) populations where other wildlife can migrate into the area.

Starting the discussion with sterilization, a wildlife management study at Cornell University on the utility of sterilization to reduce deer populations on its campus and adjacent lands found that, "Despite our efforts during the first five years of this study, it became clear that we could not reduce deer numbers on Cornell lands to a level that alleviated negative impacts, such as deer-vehicle collisions and overbrowsing."[194]

The Cornell study also looked at previous research and, more importantly, the way other communities had approached the problem and the results those communities had obtained. The study concluded that sterilization "in practice...has resulted in inconclusive results or failed in open deer populations in suburban landscapes." Subsequently, Cornell University gave up the sterilization effort in favor of various hunting programs.

An alternative to sterilization is the use of immunocontraceptive vaccines, but they have proven less effective than sterilization; as the Cornell study states, "our own experience suggests that culling is the most cost-effective management option." One problem with immunocontraceptives is that they often require annual booster shots.

In either method—sterilization or immunocontraceptives—"modeling studies have suggested that a high percentage (80 percent or more) of female deer must be treated to have measurable effects (either population stabilization or decline) over a period of 5 to 10 years. Male deer are not sterilized because a single buck can mate with dozens of female deer, and capturing all male deer in an open population is extremely difficult."

The facts about the utility of sterilization as a game management tool are that:

- Surgical sterilization of female deer is very expensive and limited by scale.
- Sterilization requires that more than 90 percent of the female deer be treated—an extremely high rate to achieve in the field.
- "The entire procedure costs about $1,000 per animal, on average.[195] However, this cost per deer is not constant because the easy-to-capture deer are treated first with little effort ($700–800 per deer). Yet much greater effort is needed to catch the last remaining individuals to reach target sterilization levels. This greatly increases treatment costs per deer. Once 85 percent or more of the females have been sterilized, it may cost >$3,000 per animal to treat the last 10 to 15 percent of remaining females." [The study had previously pointed out that a rate of 95 percent was thought to be the necessary threshold.]
- Once the initial sterilization goal was reached, there would be ongoing annual costs in treating immigrating untreated females.

Regarding immunocontraceptives:

- The Cornell study stated: "Due to the high cost, this will only be feasible in affluent communities, or with help of donors."
- They require that more than 90 percent of the female deer be treated—an extremely high rate to achieve in the field. Furthermore, booster shots are often required.
- Field experiments found difficulty in keeping free-ranging deer on a booster schedule. In particular, "after deer have been trapped and tagged, experienced deer become bait shy, and may be difficult to approach within dart range (15–25 yards), even in a suburban setting."[196]
- Another community's attempt at immunocontraceptives proved difficult: in its third year of the program, biologists had vaccinated only 48 deer, estimated to be less than half the population, and far less than was necessary for the program to be effective.[197] In yet another community, two biologists hired to treat deer with immunocontraceptives, after a full week of work, were able to treat only a single deer.[198]
- In Silver Spring, Maryland, near Baltimore, a field experiment with immunocontraceptives demonstrated the difficulty in treating enough deer to be effective. The biologist overseeing the study for the U.S.

Department of Agriculture, Kevin Sullivan, stated: "You need a small, controlled area, two or three square miles. [Otherwise] you won't be able to dart and vaccinate enough animals in a wide-open space to make a difference."[199] As the researchers in this study pointed out, "Even if it was 100 percent effective, immunizing every deer is a slow, costly way to manage the population. It's not pixie dust that can be applied everywhere. It's a tool we look forward to using, but it will never replace hunting...."

- There is some evidence that an immunocontraceptive can alter deer behavior in ways that harm the deer.[200] The female deer can have a longer estrus period (the time when hormones are released that attract male deer), meaning that it could be chased by bucks for months instead of only days. It is unknown but probable that this extra energy use could lead to stress and weight loss, which in turn would lead to more mortality in the winter. In simple words, it could harm female deer, causing much suffering by them, as well as higher mortality.
- Steroidal drugs persist in deer carcasses, so that they can impact other species (e.g., humans or scavengers) after meat consumption.

Cornell indicated that communities considering, or being forced into, a deer sterilization program by opponents of deer removal "should be prepared to only achieve small reductions in deer numbers." In fact, communities that tried sterilization only have subsequently changed to lethal deer management, "or allowed deer populations to persist at undesirable levels." Neither sterilization nor immunocontraceptives have proven effective at achieving desired deer population reductions in wild, free-ranging deer populations. And Cornell advised that nonlethal methods "have not shown promise in areas where deer can move freely on the landscape." Another study reached the same conclusion: "Contraception tends to work poorly to control open populations.... In highly promiscuous breeders [i.e., those in which one male mates with multiple females], achieving population goals through contraception may not be feasible."[201]

The Cornell study also looked at translocation. The study found that deer have a high mortality rate after translocation (conjectured to be caused by the stress of the process), so much so that some wildlife managers consider the method a *lethal* method because of the high proportion that die. Furthermore, translocation is costly, opens up a vector for disease transmission, and suffers from a lack of places that will accept the animals. Many wildlife management agencies prohibit this technique for population control.

## ANTI-HUNTING ARGUMENT: HUNTING OLDER, LARGER ANIMALS DAMAGES THE GENETIC POOL OF THE POPULATION

One argument sometimes posited by anti-hunters is that the genetic composition of an animal population, such as deer, is negatively affected when the larger trophy animals are taken. This argument says that a herd could be evolutionarily affected by the selective harvest of older, larger animals. For instance, this hypothesis says that horn size on bighorn sheep would get smaller over time through evolutionary selection as the older, larger sheep are culled through hunting (because sheep with large horns would be selected against). However, studies do not support this argument.

For instance, one extensive study of 72 hunt areas across the United States concluded that "changes in horn growth patterns are an unlikely consequence of harvest across most of North America."[202] This report indicated that changes in average horn size were caused by factors other than a change in the genetic makeup of the herd, such as a change in age-sex structure of the herds caused by hunting and changes in the environment/habitat, rather than an evolutionary change in the genetic pool caused by the selective harvest of older, larger animals. Another researcher noted that other factors were more important, saying that "horn and antler growth are influenced by nutrition, which can override selective effects of harvest."[203]

Even though it is not clear whether selective harvest would greatly alter the evolutionary makeup of a population, researchers examined whether such an effect would be detectible. In doing so, researchers found that the inflow of animals from outside of areas of selective harvest would counteract any slight change to the genetic pool caused by selective harvest of bigger, older animals. Specifically, the researchers said that "a few animals moving from parks into hunted areas and surviving to breed would be more than adequate to swamp any selective effect."[204]

A study that did find the possibility that selective hunting of older, larger animals could cause an evolutionary change in a population indicated that such a change would be too small to match other studies that had allegedly found such change happening. In essence, this study found that other studies reporting evolutionary changes in populations could not be accurate because "the fastest rates of phenotypic change attributable to trophy hunting via evolution that are theoretically possible under standard assumptions of quantitative genetics are 1–2 orders of magnitude slower than the fastest rates of phenotypic change reported from statistical analyses."[205] This calls into question studies that reportedly find that hunting of older, larger animals have caused evolutionary changes to the population.

Another study that found a diminishing of antler and horn sizes in some populations could not definitively say it was caused by an evolutionary change caused by selective harvest of older, larger animals. It noted that a "genetic change imposed by selective harvest may be less likely to occur in free-ranging populations when other factors, such as age and nutrition, can override genetic potential for size."[206]

All of this makes sense because hunting of older, larger animals means that hunters are taking "mature animals that have already contributed to the genetic pool of the species."[207] All of these older, larger animals will have already bred, typically many times. It is not without irony that many of these studies suggest that any evolutionary change in populations that occurs from selective hunting would be offset by other factors—such as nutrition and habitat—and it is those other factors that the funding from hunting dollars has improved.

## ANTI-HUNTING ARGUMENT: HUNTING LEADS TO SOCIOPATHIC BEHAVIOR

A final anti-hunting argument concerns the idea that hunting leads to sociopathic behavior, or that hunting itself constitutes sociopathy. For example, People for the Ethical Treatment of Animals (PETA) president and co-founder Ingrid Newkirk equated hunting with serial killing, described imagery in hunting magazines as "fueling violent fantasies," and compared trophy hunters who keep horns or antlers to murderers who take souvenirs from their victims.[208]

To justify this argument, anti-hunters may point to research by Dr. Stephen Kellert and Dr. Alan Felthous that established a link between childhood acts of animal cruelty and subsequent aggressive criminal behavior during adulthood.[209] In this study, individuals classified as aggressive violent criminals were substantially more likely than moderately aggressive criminals and nonaggressive criminals to have committed acts of animal cruelty as children, with the acts ranging from tearing the wings off bugs to skinning animals alive or beating them to death. Motivations for such behavior included the urge to control animals, the desire to retaliate against animals, displaced hostility from a person to an animal, shocking people for amusement, and general sadism.

Proceeding from the idea that it is morally wrong to inflict pain on any living thing, anti-hunters may use the core findings of Kellert-Felthous research to argue that hunting constitutes animal cruelty. They might further contend that hunting results in at least some amount of animal suffering because of instances in which hunters wound animals but fail to kill them quickly.

There are two major flaws with the "hunting as sociopathy" argument. First, the Kellert-Felthous research concerns only aggressive criminals, not law-abiding licensed hunters. Simply conflating legal, regulated hunting with sadistic acts of animal abuse among violent offenders is to commit a gross and completely erroneous fallacy. The anti-hunting argument asserts a connection that, in reality, does not exist. As noted by botanist and zoologist Ann Causey, "no studies have shown that people who engage in sport hunting are more likely to commit violent crimes or display excessive aggression than are non-hunters."[210] There simply is no link between hunting and sociopathy.

Secondly, in attempting to equate accidental wounding of wildlife with intentional animal abuse, anti-hunters ignore the fact that wounding by hunters is the exception and not the rule—though accidental wounding does sometimes occur, ethical hunters never set out to *intentionally* wound animals. The reality is that ethical hunters strive to hunt in a way that limits the pain and suffering of the animal—ethical hunters seek clean, humane kills and track wounded game to ensure that animals do not unduly suffer (ethical hunters do not allow wounded animals to suffer and die slowly). In fact, these aspects of hunting are covered extensively in the hunter education courses that new hunters are required to complete.

The "hunting as sociopathy" argument rests entirely on a fallacious, nonexistent connection between animal abuse and legal, regulated, ethical hunting.

## *Key Takeaways*

- The argument themes that work the best in support of hunting are hunting as a food source, hunting as conservation (i.e., hunting as a form of wildlife management that produces ecological benefits to both game and non-game species), and hunting as a right.

- The argument themes that garner the most *opposition* to hunting are hunting as a violation of fair chase, hunting being linked to trophy hunting, and hunting resulting in diminished wildlife populations. These concepts can be easily rebutted.

- Link hunting to food; it was the most effective theme in pro-hunting messages.

- Talk about the locavore appeal of hunting. (Locavore refers to a diet that is produced from local sources—for some dedicated locavores not more than 30 miles from home—which is considered more ecologically friendly because of the reduced energy for producing and getting the food to the table. Hunting and fishing together can be an integral part of a locavore diet.)

- Talk about the wildlife management benefits that hunting provides, including the benefits to the ecological habitat as a whole and to many non-game species.

- You can talk about hunting as a basic right—particularly the right of people to feed their families—but generally to a lesser degree than talking about the themes of food and wildlife management. (Those most disapproving of hunting responded best to the themes of food and wildlife management rather than hunting as a right. Those on the fence, however, did respond to the rights argument.)

- Don't let hunting be defined as canned hunting—fair chase is extremely important to people.

- Talk about ethical hunting that minimizes the pain and suffering of animals. After the hunt, show that you respect the wildlife.

## CHAPTER 7

# Participation in Sport Shooting

**A SKILLED COMMUNICATOR DEFENDING HUNTING** *must understand sport shooting participation in America, as sport shooting participation is often a gateway to hunting participation. Additionally, even sport shooters who do not hunt help to fund wildlife conservation through their purchase of firearms and ammunition (as these items are subject to Pittman-Robertson Act excise taxes). Because so much hunting is done with a firearm, and because of the overlap of hunting and sport shooting, it is useful to look at sport shooting participation on its own. This chapter takes a look at sport shooting participation, both within the context of hunting as well as outside of it. Increasing support for hunting can often begin with increasing support for sport shooting. The place to start is demonstrating that firearm ownership is widespread and that sport shooting is an increasingly popular, and socially diverse, activity—as evidenced by the numbers.*

## Households With Firearms

Gun ownership and sport shooting participation is prevalent in American society. More than four in ten households in America contain a firearm, according to surveys by Gallup[211] and the Pew Research Center,[212] two of the most prominent survey research organizations in the world. Similarly, a Responsive Management study in 2017 found that 45 percent of households have a firearm.[213] The same Responsive Management study found that approximately 25 million people own a firearm but have not gone sport shooting in the previous 5 years. And each year, more than 50 million Americans engage in various types of recreational shooting.[214]

## Sport Shooting Participation Rates and Numbers of Shooters

Overall participation in sport shooting is on the rise. A series of studies conducted by Responsive Management and the NSSF[215] finds that shooting participation has been increasing over the past decade, rising from 15 percent of adult Americans to 22 percent of them, which is roughly 34 million sport shooters in 2009 to 52 million in 2018. Additionally, with the exception of 3-gun shooting, participation in every sport shooting activity has risen. (Note that the term, *sport shooting*, as used throughout this chapter encompasses target shooting as well as the various other shooting activities.)

*More than 40 percent of households in the United States have a firearm.*

## PARTICIPATION IN SPORT SHOOTING

Sport shooting participation is often a gateway to hunting participation. As well, sport shooters who do not hunt help to fund wildlife conservation through their purchase of firearms and ammunition.

⊕

The most dramatic rise is in target shooting with a handgun, increasing from 10 percent of Americans to 16 percent of them, and target shooting with a modern sporting rifle, going from 4 percent of Americans to 8 percent. In terms of participants, target shooting with a handgun went from 22 million to 38 million individuals—making it the most popular of the sport shooting activities. Meanwhile, modern sporting rifle shooting went from 9 million shooters to 18 million shooters. The table below shows the number of participants in the five study years that surveys were conducted.

**Numbers of Participants in Various Shooting Activities**

| Activity | Estimated Total Participants* | | | | |
|---|---|---|---|---|---|
| | 2009 | 2012 | 2014 | 2016 | 2018 |
| Any target or sport shooting | 34,382,566 | 40,779,651 | 51,226,765 | 49,361,637 | 52,073,224 |
| Target shooting with a handgun | 22,169,700 | 28,209,283 | 34,221,107 | 33,276,976 | 38,182,610 |
| Target shooting with a rifle | 24,045,795 | 26,822,425 | 31,764,116 | 27,949,753 | 32,169,412 |
| Skeet shooting | 6,979,680 | 12,090,346 | 12,596,361 | 8,626,450 | 11,563,358 |
| Target shooting with a modern sporting rifle | 8,868,085 | 11,976,702 | 16,267,924 | 13,986,528 | 18,327,314 |
| Trap shooting | 7,582,479 | 10,116,684 | 11,227,278 | 7,855,875 | 10,227,286 |
| Sporting clays | 8,399,989 | 8,789,340 | 13,033,633 | 10,545,394 | 13,174,752 |
| Target shooting at outdoor range | no data available | 24,818,394 | 28,075,842 | 26,148,339 | 29,636,581 |
| Target shooting at indoor range | no data available | 9,756,514 | 14,007,982 | 15,306,421 | 17,912,845 |

*Ages 18 years old and older

Source: Responsive Management.[216]

## Firearm Ownership Is Hard to Measure

*"Hello. I'm from the federal government—we'd like to know how many firearms you have in your household."*

Firearm ownership is hard to measure and is likely underreported. There are a few primary reasons for this. One is that many firearm owners are reluctant to say that they have a firearm or that they participate in sport shooting. One study by Zogby Analytics[217] asked current firearm owners, "If a national pollster asked you if you owned a firearm, would you determine to tell him or her the truth, or would you feel it was none of their business?" In response, 35 percent said it was "none of the pollster's business."

There is also evidence that some firearm ownership numbers may be subject to personal or political influence. For example, one of the coordinators of a major survey regarding Americans' attitudes toward a variety of current issues was once quoted as saying that a large drop in firearm ownership would "make it easier for politicians to do the right thing on guns."[218] The bottom line is that firearm ownership is increasingly difficult to measure, and there are many people who will not indicate in surveys that they own a firearm or are involved with firearms, resulting in lower reported firearm ownership and sport shooting participation rates.

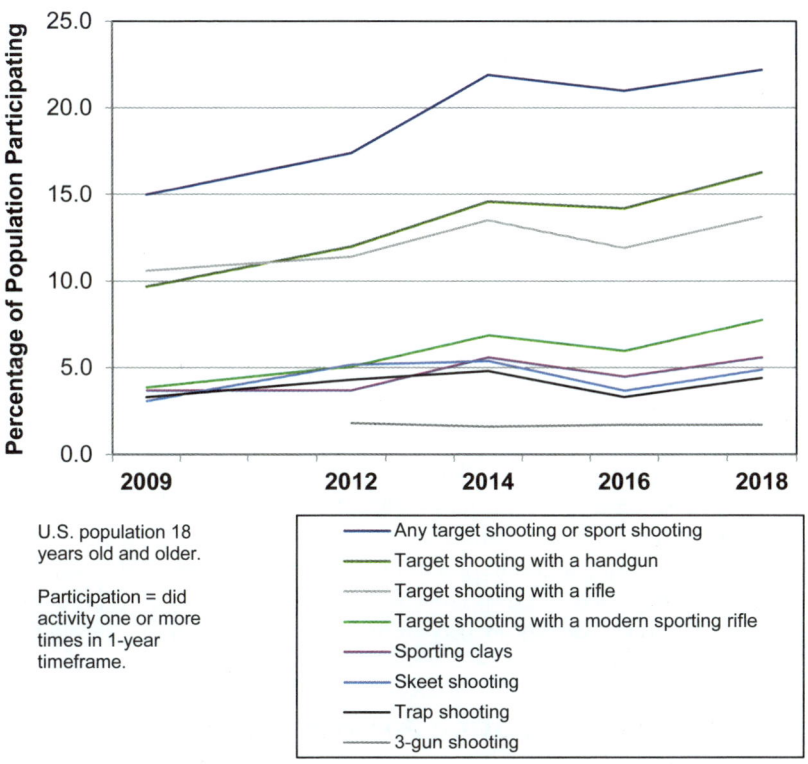

## Annual Participation Rates of Several Shooting Activities Over Time.

U.S. population 18 years old and older.

Participation = did activity one or more times in 1-year timeframe.

Legend:
- Any target shooting or sport shooting
- Target shooting with a handgun
- Target shooting with a rifle
- Target shooting with a modern sporting rifle
- Sporting clays
- Skeet shooting
- Trap shooting
- 3-gun shooting

Source: *Responsive Management.*[219]

Target shooting at both outdoor and indoor ranges rose over the years from 2012 to 2018, also shown in the table on a previous page and graphically shown on the following page. Outdoor ranges are more popular than indoor ranges, with 30 million outdoor shooters, compared to 18 million indoor shooters, in 2018. However, indoor ranges have shown a greater increase in popularity: outdoor ranges have just under 5 million more sport shooters in 2018 compared to 2012, while indoor ranges have slightly more than 8 million more sport shooters.

**Annual Number of Range Users Over Time.**

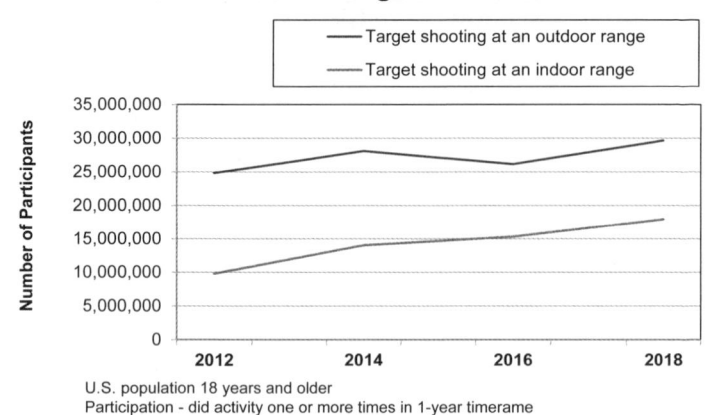

— Target shooting at an outdoor range
— Target shooting at an indoor range

U.S. population 18 years and older
Participation - did activity one or more times in 1-year timerame

*Source: Responsive Management.*[220]

The Responsive Management/NSSF studies are not the only ones to find increases in sport shooting participation. Studies by the Sports & Fitness Industry Association have found overall increases over the past decade in target shooting with a handgun, target shooting with a rifle, sporting clays, and trap/skeet shooting.[221] Studies by the National Sporting Goods Association also found a rise in overall target shooting in the past decade, as well.[222]

## Days of Sport Shooting Participation

Most participants go sport shooting anywhere from 10 days to 15 days a year—with modern sporting rifle shooters being the most avid.

| Activity | Mean Days Spent on Activity, 2018 | Median Days Spent on Activity, 2018 |
|---|---|---|
| Target shooting with a traditional rifle | 11.3 | 5 |
| Target shooting with a modern sporting rifle | 15.3 | 5 |
| Target shooting with a handgun | 12.4 | 5 |
| Trap shooting | 11.0 | 3 |
| Skeet shooting | 9.8 | 4 |
| Sporting clays | 14.8 | 3 |
| Shooting at a range | 10.0 | 4 |

*Source: Responsive Management.*[223]

## PARTICIPATION IN SPORT SHOOTING

Days of participation vary greatly from person to person, as illustrated by the graph below showing days of target shooting with a rifle and with a handgun. While the majority of rifle and handgun shooters went sport shooting no more than 5 days, there were some who shot for many more days, including about one in ten rifle shooters and one in eight handgun shooters who did so for more than 20 days in 2018.

**How many days did you target shoot with a [traditional rifle, in other words a rifle with bolt or lever action, / handgun] in 2018?**
(Asked of those who went target shooting with a [traditional rifle / handgun] in 2018.)

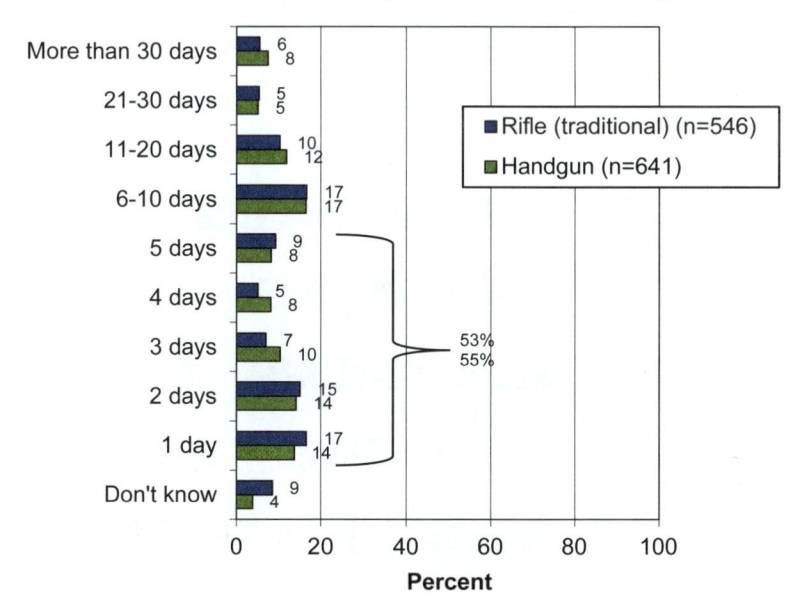

| Days | Rifle (traditional) (n=546) | Handgun (n=641) |
|---|---|---|
| More than 30 days | 6 | 8 |
| 21-30 days | 5 | 5 |
| 11-20 days | 10 | 12 |
| 6-10 days | 17 | 17 |
| 5 days | 9 | 8 |
| 4 days | 5 | 8 |
| 3 days | 7 | 10 |
| 2 days | 15 | 14 |
| 1 day | 17 | 14 |
| Don't know | 4 | 9 |

53% / 55% (sum of 1-5 days)

*Source: Responsive Management.*[224]

## Types of Firearms Used in Sport Shooting

Handguns are the most popular type of firearm for sport shooting, and they have been the most popular since 2012 when this series of surveys started asking about the types of firearms used in sport shooting. The 2018 survey[225] found that 71 percent of sport shooters used a handgun, 59 percent used a traditional rifle, 53 percent used a shotgun, 34 percent used a modern sporting rifle, and 12 percent used a black powder firearm. (The sum is more than 100 percent because some sport shooters use more than one type of firearm.)

## Motivations for Sport Shooting

Being with family and friends tops the list of reasons that people go sport shooting, markedly more important than any other reason: 71 percent of sport shooters said to be with family and friends was very important as a reason to go shooting. In a second tier are for self-defense (59 percent said it is very important) and for the sport and recreation (57 percent).

**Percent of target shooters who indicated each of the following was at the given level of importance to them as a reason to go target shooting.**

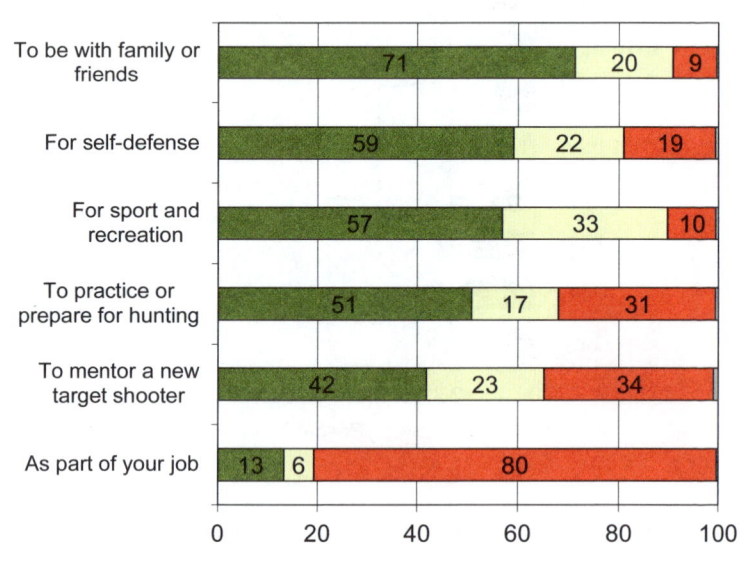

Legend: ■ Very important  □ Somewhat important  ■ Not at all important  □ Don't know

| Reason | Very important | Somewhat important | Not at all important |
|---|---|---|---|
| To be with family or friends | 71 | 20 | 9 |
| For self-defense | 59 | 22 | 19 |
| For sport and recreation | 57 | 33 | 10 |
| To practice or prepare for hunting | 51 | 17 | 31 |
| To mentor a new target shooter | 42 | 23 | 34 |
| As part of your job | 13 | 6 | 80 |

*Source: Responsive Management.*[226]

Self-defense as a reason to shoot is markedly more important in the South than in other regions, as a regional analysis of the data in the table above found. Two thirds of sport shooters from the South (66 percent) said that self-defense was a very important reason for their shooting participation, compared to no more than 58 percent of sport shooters from any other region.

## Overlap of Sport Shooting and Hunting

Many sport shooters also hunt. In looking at the pool of people who sport shoot or hunt (or do both)—nearly half of sport shooters/hunters participated in hunting (47 percent did so in 2018, as shown in the graph below—the sum of the 12 percent who hunted but did not sport shoot and the 35 percent who hunted and went sport shooting). However, the hunter portion of this breakdown has been declining over the past decade in favor of those who sport shoot but who do not hunt—those who solely sport shoot made up 39 percent of the total pool in 2012, but they now make up more than half of the total pool—53 percent. In short, many new sport shooters added over the past decade are non-hunters. This is the result of fewer Americans hunting and more of them sport shooting without hunting.

**Breakdown of those who went target shooting or hunting.**

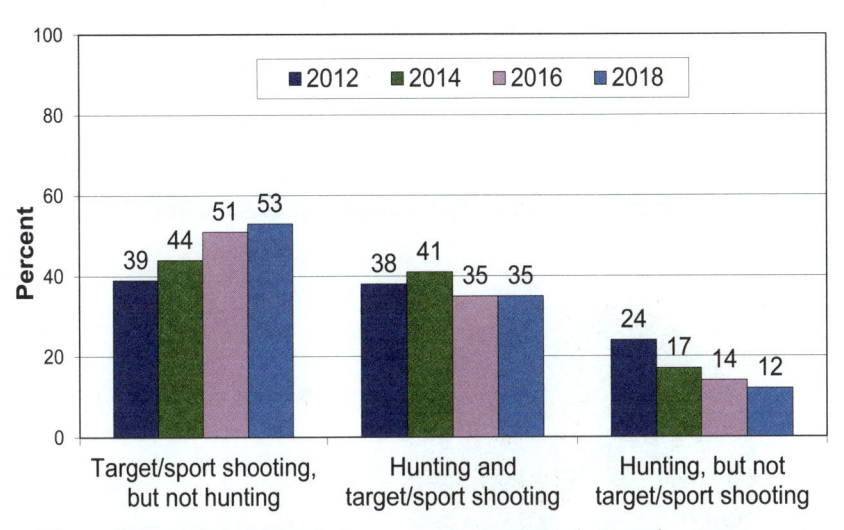

| | 2012 | 2014 | 2016 | 2018 |
|---|---|---|---|---|
| Target/sport shooting, but not hunting | 39 | 44 | 51 | 53 |
| Hunting and target/sport shooting | 38 | 41 | 35 | 35 |
| Hunting, but not target/sport shooting | 24 | 17 | 14 | 12 |

The pool of people in this analysis encompasses anyone who went hunting or went target/sport shooting in 2018, including those who just hunted, hunted and shot, or just shot.

*Source: Responsive Management.*[227]

## Demographic Characteristics of Sport Shooters

Participation in target and sport shooting is correlated with hunting participation, being male, being 18 to 34 years old, and being on the rural side of the urban-rural continuum—these are the groups who are more likely to sport shoot. Note that, although rural people are *more likely* to go shooting than are urban people, more sport shooters come from a large city/urban area or suburban area (41 percent do) than from a rural area (30 percent do) (see graph below). This is because of the sheer number of Americans living in large cities/urban areas and suburban areas is so much greater than the number living in rural areas, so even with a lower *rate* of ownership in those more urbanized settings, there are more gun owners there in absolute numbers.

It is also important to know that the sport shooting community is multi-cultural, representing a cross section of America. While older, rural, white men are perceived as the typical shooters, they are not the only shooters. Among active sport shooters in 2018, more than a quarter were women, more than half were younger than 45 years old, and, as discussed previously, about two thirds were *non*-rural. Additionally, minorities make up a substantial portion of new shooters, further discussed in the next section of this chapter.

**Residence breakdown of sport shooting participants 2018.**

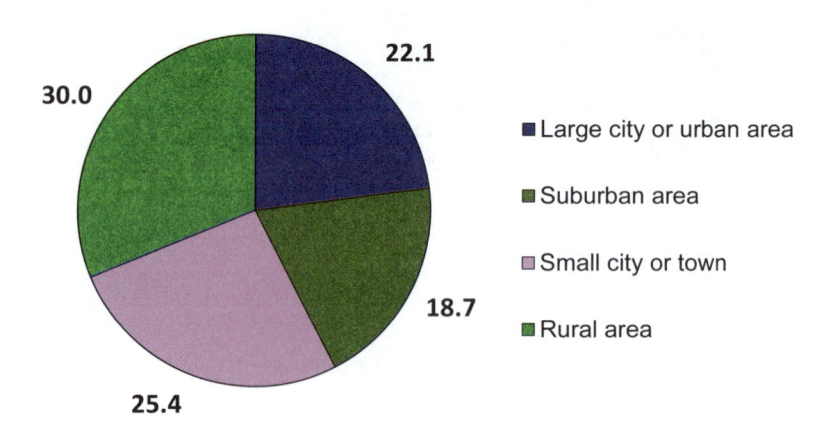

- Large city or urban area: 22.1
- Suburban area: 18.7
- Small city or town: 25.4
- Rural area: 30.0

*Source: Responsive Management.*[228]

PARTICIPATION IN SPORT SHOOTING

*Sport shooting participation is increasing. New shooters are more likely than traditional shooters to be younger, urban or suburban, female, and people of color.*

## *The Importance of Accessible Shooting Ranges*

The farther away sport shooters are to shooting ranges, the more likely they are to drop out of the sport. Sport shooters typically travel no more than 30 minutes to get to their shooting range, and additional travel distance results in some shooters leaving the sport. Ex-shooters typically had to travel farther to go target shooting (when they went target shooting in the past) than do active target shooters (when they go shooting now). As shown in the graph below, ex-shooters' travel time was a quarter hour greater than the travel time of current shooters. This demonstrates the need for sport shooters to have close, local, easily accessible shooting ranges. Fortunately, the Federal Aid in Wildlife Restoration Act is helping to make this happen, allowing the funds from the Act to be used for the construction and operation of public target ranges.[229]

**Mean travel time to go shooting.**

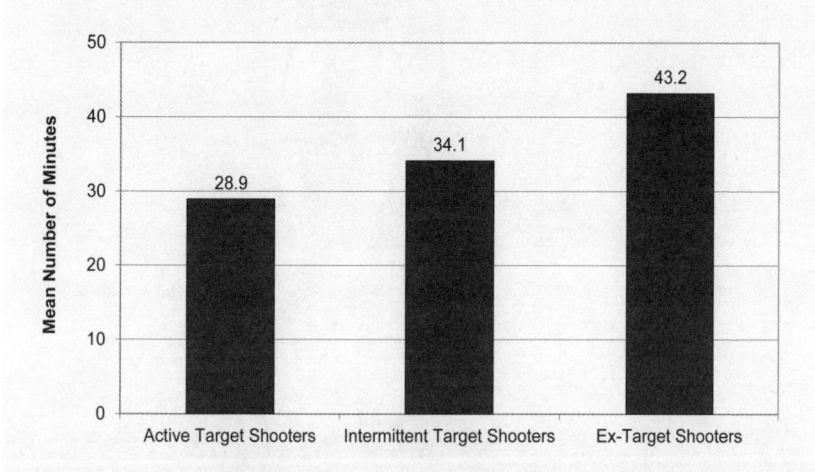

| Category | Mean Number of Minutes |
|---|---|
| Active Target Shooters | 28.9 |
| Intermittent Target Shooters | 34.1 |
| Ex-Target Shooters | 43.2 |

*Source: Responsive Management.*[230]

## New Shooters

As sport shooting participation increases, it is also becoming more diverse. About one in seven sport shooters in 2018 were new shooters (defined here as someone who started shooting within the previous 5 years).

New sport shooters tend to be demographically different than established sport shooters. They are more likely to live in urban areas, more likely to be female, non-white, and younger, and less likely to hunt. These new shooters are also more likely to shoot handguns and go to indoor ranges.

The implications regarding hunting are that new sport shooters are not as likely as established sport shooters to have come to the activity in the traditional way—through hunting—and they are less likely to consider themselves hunters. While they have a stake in hunting and wildlife conservation because of the Federal Aid in Wildlife Restoration Taxes they are paying on their firearms and ammunition (see Chapter 1), it should not be taken for granted that they are supportive of hunting. Talking about hunting in a positive way to them is important.

## Non-Shooting Firearm Owners

A substantial number of people in the U.S.—more than 25 million—own a firearm but do not go shooting or hunting.[231] This is an important segment of society that should be reached to increase their participation in shooting and perhaps ultimately hunting. While increasing actual sport shooting participation among this group is important from a shooting and hunting participation standpoint, the most important reason to get these people shooting and practicing is from a safety perspective. Owning a firearm requires frequent practice to ensure that the firearm can be safely handled.

The majority of non-shooting firearm owners are men (61 percent), while 39 percent are women. However, this percentage of females is higher than in the active shooting population, meaning women make up a greater proportion of non-shooting firearm owners than they do active sport shooters.

One could conjecture that non-shooting firearm owners might be older men dropping out of the sport (age and health are often cited as reasons for reduced hunting and shooting participation, as well as reasons for quitting these sports entirely[232]). However, a breakdown of the ages shows them to include a substantial percentage of younger people: one third are younger than 35 years old. Additionally, three quarters of them are *not* retired.

Access to shooting ranges plays a part in lack of sport shooting participation. Nearly three quarters of non-shooting firearm owners live in a large city/urban area or a suburban area—places where shooting in one's yard is nearly always prohibited. Only 16 percent live in a rural area.

An overall lack of information is a major constraint; this includes not knowing where to go, not knowing how to legally transport a firearm to a shooting location, and not knowing how to maintain a firearm. Many non-shooting firearm owners lack confidence—in part an outgrowth of their lack of knowledge—and feel that they may be critiqued by others.[233]

Industry is not seen as welcoming, and staff at shooting ranges are often perceived as impatient or dismissive when asked basic questions.[234]

But perhaps the most important lesson that has been learned over the past several decades is that people will go shooting if asked by a friend or family member. In fact, by far the best way to get someone involved—either someone who has a firearm but has not used it in a while or even someone who has not gone shooting—is to invite him or her to go with you.[235] A simple invitation is perhaps one of the most important things a hunter or sport shooter can do to increase someone's interest in and support of sport shooting, as well as their possible participation in and support of hunting.

## In Summary

Shooting participation often leads to hunting participation. Therefore, increasing participation in shooting can increase participation in hunting. This, in turn, leads to increased support for hunting because more people will know a hunter (research shows that the most important variable in support of hunting is knowing a hunter) and there will be more people to safeguard hunting itself.

Additionally, shooters have a direct connection to hunting through their funding of a substantial portion of wildlife conservation programs. These programs include the provision of hunting opportunities. Every hunter has a stake in firearms and shooting participation, and every sport shooter *should* have a stake in hunting and wildlife conservation.

## Key Takeaways

- More than 40 percent of households have a firearm.

- A little more than one in five adult Americans participate in sport shooting in a given year, which represents about 52 million adults.

- Sport shooting participation is on the rise. In particular, target shooting with a handgun is increasing in popularity, having the largest rise in number of participants since 2009.

- Handguns are the most popular type of firearm for shooting, followed by a traditional rifle, shotgun, and modern sporting rifle.

- Being with family and friends is an important reason that people go sport shooting. Self-defense is also important.

- The pool of sport shooters and hunters (those who did either or both) is increasingly made up of non-hunting shooters. That proportion of hunters and shooters who *only* sport shoot but do not hunt went from 39 percent in 2012 to 53 percent in 2018.

- New sport shooters tend to be different than established sport shooters. They are more likely to live in urban areas, be female, be people of color, and be younger, and they are less likely to hunt.

# CHAPTER 8
# Attitudes Toward Sport Shooting

**THIS CHAPTER DISCUSSES AMERICANS' OVERALL** *attitudes toward sport shooting, specifically approval and acceptance of recreational sport shooting. The discussion includes the characteristics of those who approve of sport shooting, as well as some general statistics on firearm ownership and exposure to firearms.*

## Public Approval of Recreational Sport Shooting

A strong majority of Americans support recreational target and sport shooting. Support/opposition or approval/disapproval of the shooting sports are not caught up in animal welfare and animal rights issues, which makes the shooting sports somewhat less controversial than hunting. Nonetheless, there are some characteristics and demographics more strongly associated with approval of recreational sport shooting, such as participation in hunting and shooting, gender, and race. The majority of adult Americans have had some type of exposure to firearms, either through personal ownership or knowing someone who owns a firearm.

Most Americans approve of recreational sport shooting: 81 percent of Americans today approve of legal recreational shooting, and most of that is strong approval. In contrast, only 12 percent disapprove. Furthermore, approval of recreational shooting has remained relatively stable from 2006 to 2019, with only a notable decline in 2011.[236]

## Do you approve or disapprove of legal recreational shooting?

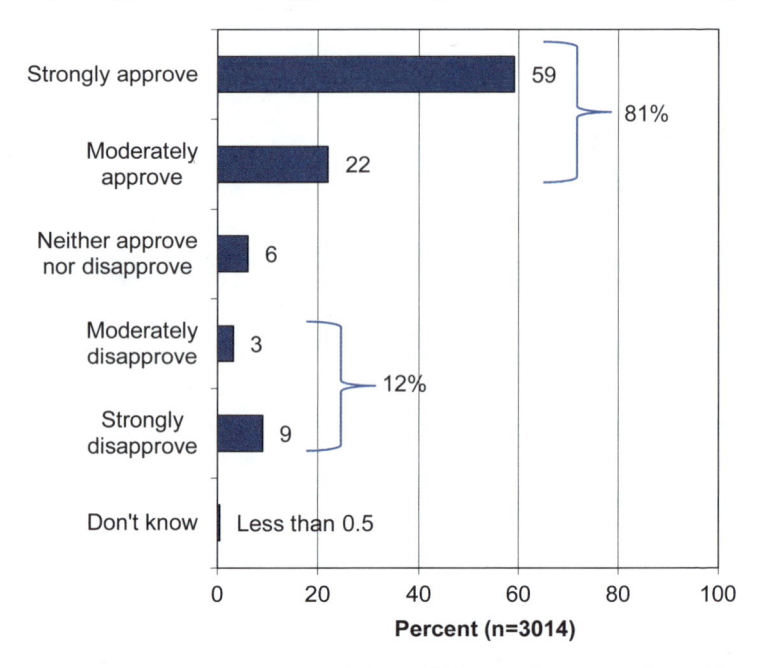

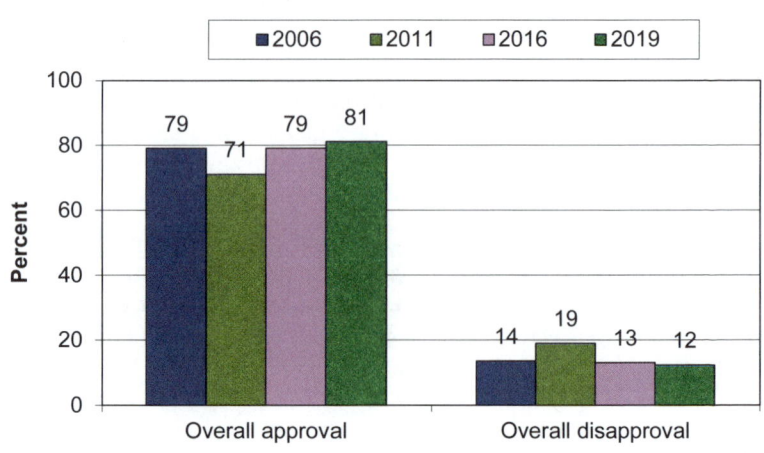

| Response | Percent |
|---|---|
| Strongly approve | 59 |
| Moderately approve | 22 |
| Neither approve nor disapprove | 6 |
| Moderately disapprove | 3 |
| Strongly disapprove | 9 |
| Don't know | Less than 0.5 |

Strongly approve + Moderately approve = 81%
Moderately disapprove + Strongly disapprove = 12%

Percent (n=3014)

*Source: Responsive Management / National Shooting Sports Foundation.[237]*

## Do you approve or disapprove of legal recreational shooting?

| | 2006 | 2011 | 2016 | 2019 |
|---|---|---|---|---|
| Overall approval | 79 | 71 | 79 | 81 |
| Overall disapproval | 14 | 19 | 13 | 12 |

*Source: Responsive Management / National Shooting Sports Foundation.[238]*

The 2019 study also asked survey respondents to select a statement from three options that best reflects their opinion of recreational shooting sports. A majority (65 percent) selected "Shooting sports are perfectly acceptable," an opinion that has remained relatively steady since 2001. Another 23 percent indicated, "Shooting sports are OK, but maybe a little inappropriate now."

**Which of the following statements best describes your opinion of recreational shooting sports?**

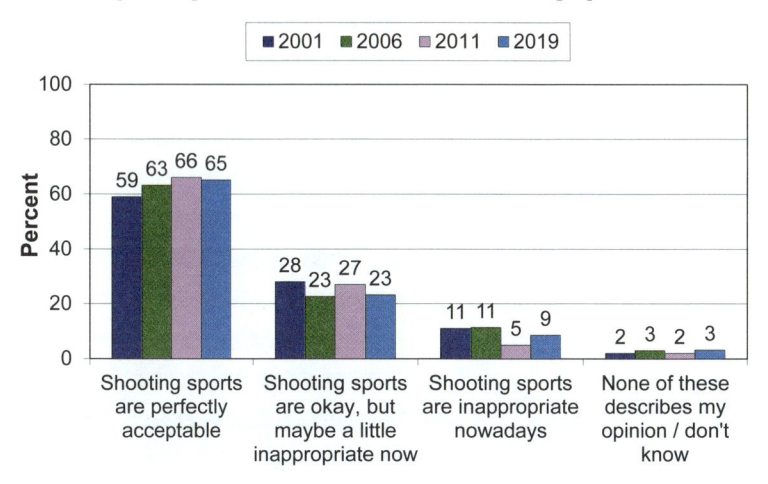

■ 2001   ■ 2006   ■ 2011   ■ 2019

| | 2001 | 2006 | 2011 | 2019 |
|---|---|---|---|---|
| Shooting sports are perfectly acceptable | 59 | 63 | 66 | 65 |
| Shooting sports are okay, but maybe a little inappropriate now | 28 | 23 | 27 | 23 |
| Shooting sports are inappropriate nowadays | 11 | 11 | 5 | 9 |
| None of these describes my opinion / don't know | 2 | 3 | 2 | 3 |

*Source: Responsive Management / National Shooting Sports Foundation.*[239]

Furthermore, most Americans approve of recreational sport shooting, even if they do not actually participate themselves. While 81 percent of the U.S. adult population approves of recreational shooting, only about 22 percent of Americans age 18 or older participated in any type of target or sport shooting in 2018, which is about 52.1 million adults.[240]

## Characteristics Associated With Approval of Sport Shooting

The characteristics and demographics associated with approval of recreational sport shooting were examined in the 2019 study discussed above. Groups most commonly associated with approval of recreational sport shooting are hunters and anglers, those who grew up with a family that owned firearms, those who live in rural areas, white residents, and male residents. At the opposite end, the groups most commonly associated

**How to Talk About Hunting** ⊕ *Research-Based Communications Strategies*

with disapproval of shooting are black residents, those who did not grow up with a family that owned firearms, Northeast region residents, Hispanic residents, and female residents.[241]

**Percent of each of the following groups who approve of legal recreational shooting:**

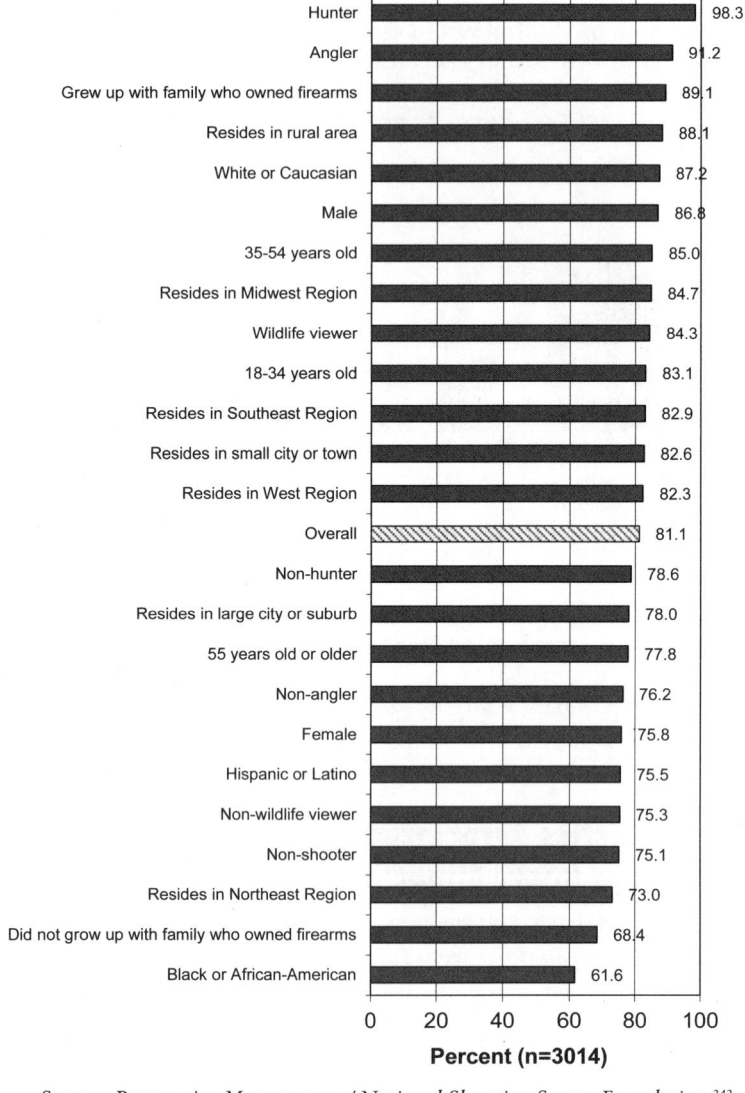

| Group | Percent |
|---|---|
| Hunter | 98.3 |
| Angler | 91.2 |
| Grew up with family who owned firearms | 89.1 |
| Resides in rural area | 88.1 |
| White or Caucasian | 87.2 |
| Male | 86.8 |
| 35-54 years old | 85.0 |
| Resides in Midwest Region | 84.7 |
| Wildlife viewer | 84.3 |
| 18-34 years old | 83.1 |
| Resides in Southeast Region | 82.9 |
| Resides in small city or town | 82.6 |
| Resides in West Region | 82.3 |
| Overall | 81.1 |
| Non-hunter | 78.6 |
| Resides in large city or suburb | 78.0 |
| 55 years old or older | 77.8 |
| Non-angler | 76.2 |
| Female | 75.8 |
| Hispanic or Latino | 75.5 |
| Non-wildlife viewer | 75.3 |
| Non-shooter | 75.1 |
| Resides in Northeast Region | 73.0 |
| Did not grow up with family who owned firearms | 68.4 |
| Black or African-American | 61.6 |

**Percent (n=3014)**

*Source: Responsive Management / National Shooting Sports Foundation.*[242]

A study conducted by Pew Research Center in 2017 examined characteristics associated with gun and firearm ownership.[243] While the results do not necessarily apply directly to approval, it is worth noting that this study also found that white males are more likely than any other demographic group to be associated with firearms. Specifically, the study found that white males are more likely to own firearms. Moreover, males who own a firearm are more engaged in what the study refers to as the *gun culture*, such as hunting participation, visiting related websites, watching related television programs, and many other activities related to firearms.

Although only 22 percent of Americans participated in recreational sport shooting in 2018,[244] the Pew study also found that many more Americans have still had exposure to firearms, whether they personally own one or not.[245] According to Pew Research, at least two thirds of adult Americans have lived in a household with a firearm at some point in their lives. Both Pew and Gallup[246] found that 30 percent of Americans currently own a firearm, and another 11 percent to 13 percent do not own a firearm but live in a household with one. Another 36 percent told Pew that while they don't own one now, they might be open to owning a firearm in the future.

Finally, the Pew study also found that 48 percent of Americans grew up in a household with a firearm, 59 percent say at least some of their friends own a firearm, and 72 percent have shot a gun at some point in their lives.

**Percent of adult Americans who...**

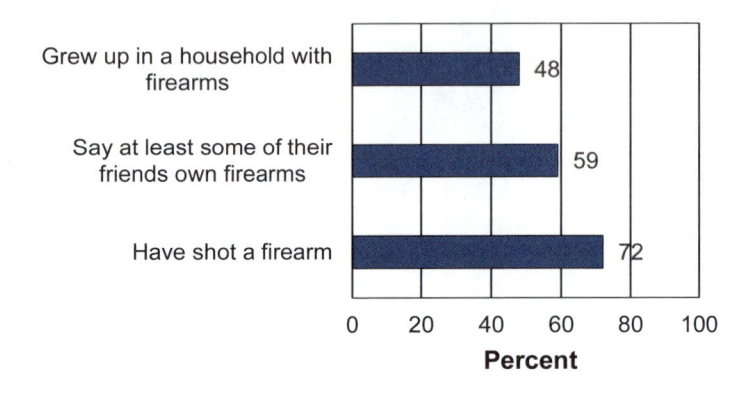

| | Percent |
|---|---|
| Grew up in a household with firearms | 48 |
| Say at least some of their friends own firearms | 59 |
| Have shot a firearm | 72 |

*Source: Pew Research Center.*

---

Most Americans approve of recreational sport shooting: 81 percent of Americans today approve of legal recreational shooting, and most of that is strong approval. In contrast, only, 12 percent disapprove.

---

While the Pew study did not measure approval of recreational sport shooting and, therefore, did not examine the data for a direct correlation between exposure to firearms and such approval, the widespread exposure to firearms described in the study suggests that it is possible the high approval rate of recreational sport shooting may be related more to exposure to firearms than to direct participation in sport shooting, If so, this relationship would be similar to the research indicating that the most important variable related to support for hunting is knowing a hunter (see Chapter 4, *Attitudes Toward Hunting*).

## Key Takeaways

- Most Americans (81 percent) approve of legal, recreational sport shooting.

- A majority of Americans say, "Shooting sports are perfectly acceptable."

- Most Americans approve of recreational sport shooting, even if they do not actually participate themselves: 81 percent approve but only 22 percent participated in any type of target or sport shooting in 2018.

- Groups most commonly associated with *approval* of sport shooting are hunters and anglers, those who grew up with a family that owned firearms, those who live in rural areas, white residents, and male residents.

- Groups most commonly associated with *disapproval* of sport shooting are black residents, those who did not grow up with a family that owned firearms, Northeast region residents, Hispanic residents, and female residents.

- Many Americans have had exposure to firearms, whether they personally own one or not and whether they participate in recreational shooting activities or not.
    - At least two thirds of adult Americans have lived in a household with a firearm at some point in their lives.
    - Nearly half of Americans (48 percent) grew up in a household with a firearm.
    - 59 percent of Americans say at least some of their friends own a firearm.
    - 72 percent have shot a gun at some point in their lives.

# CHAPTER 9

# *Debating About Hunting*

**WHILE MOST DISCUSSION ABOUT HUNTING** *occurs in casual or informal settings, arguments for and against hunting are sometimes put forth in formal debates. Making an effective case for hunting in a debate requires training and practice in the use of proven rhetorical strategies and tactics, such as framing the discussion to establish the need for hunting, making strong offensive arguments that explain why hunting is a logical solution, and rebutting damaging claims from the other side using well-reasoned defensive arguments. Above all, debaters must be knowledgeable about the most effective arguments both for and against hunting.*

## Why Debates Matter

Attitudes toward hunting are shaped mostly through everyday discussions with friends, family, and colleagues, as well as information received through the media. However, formal debates about hunting, especially those available to the public, can be important opportunities to build support from a wider audience. At the same time, structured debates can be risky propositions if the pro-hunting side is unprepared or overmatched by formidable communicators on the anti-hunting side, or if those on the pro-hunting side are simply more comfortable outdoors than onstage. Failing to make a decisive and convincing case for hunting in a debate means sacrificing an opportunity to explain why hunting matters. Unsuccessful debates can also put hunters on the defensive by casting doubt over the legitimacy of hunting. Fortunately, though, hunting advocates can win debates by crafting strong arguments and delivering them in compelling ways.

## What to Accomplish in a Debate

First, those who debate on behalf of hunting must be adaptable, as certain arguments will persuade some audiences but not others (and some arguments may fall on deaf ears altogether). While there is no script of talking points to use to win a debate every time, advocates of hunting must remember that most of the American public already holds a pro-hunting mindset (most Americans approve of hunting to obtain meat and to control wildlife populations, and most Americans consume meat and use products derived from animals).

The survey data outlined in Chapter 6 identifies both the pro-hunting themes and individual arguments that Americans generally find most compelling. The themes that work the best in support of hunting are:

- Hunting as a food source.
- Hunting as conservation (i.e., hunting as a form of wildlife management that produces ecological benefits to both game and non-game species).
- Hunting as a right.

The specific arguments include the following:

- Hunting for food does not cause any more animal suffering than slaughtering livestock for food.
- Those who do not hunt or do not approve of hunting don't have to hunt, but they should respect the right of others to hunt.
- Hunting specifically helps control the deer population, which is overabundant and has no natural predators in many areas.
- Hunting controls wildlife populations and helps with species management.
- Hunting is properly regulated, and there are rules and regulations in place to ensure fair and moral hunting that also protects wildlife populations as a whole.

Apart from being knowledgeable about these arguments and the points that support them, pro-hunting debaters must work to frame the debate in their favor. Framing means setting the terms of the discussion by defining a reference point or common goal. A good way to do this in a debate is to convince the audience of the need to manage and maintain wildlife in the first place; if an audience is receptive to this need, hunting can then be shown as a logical way to go about doing this. The debater can point to America's thriving wildlife populations as evidence of the effectiveness of hunting as a management tool.[247] The key is to establish hunting as the best way to achieve the goal. Hunting is conservation not just because it provides revenue to support programs but also because hunting itself is a part of active wildlife management. To accomplish this, pro-hunting debaters may need to refute (even preemptively) the idea that nature requires no human intervention—discrediting this belief is a prerequisite to building support for hunting (i.e., it is not a question of *whether* people should intervene in nature, but *how*).[248]

It is worth noting here that nine out of ten Americans agree that fish, wildlife, and their habitat require active management to ensure healthy populations (most *strongly* agree with this). Further, roughly four out of five Americans agree that their state fish and wildlife agency plays an important role in managing fish and wildlife and their habitat.[249]

Depending on the focus of the debate (or the exact wording of the debate motion), another useful framing strategy may be to focus on the need for healthy food—hunting can then be positioned as an ethical choice in sourcing meat, consistent with the right to obtain one's own food.

Pro-hunting speakers also need to win the credibility debate by offering the most convincing solution to the problem. They must communicate that hunting, being supported by every agency tasked with maintaining healthy populations of game and nongame species, is consistent with scientific wildlife management. As described later in this chapter, demonstrating why hunting is the *best choice* is different than defending hunting as something that is merely *not that bad*.

Finally, those debating on behalf of hunting must remember the implications of the animal rights-animal welfare-dominionism continuum covered in Chapter 5: if hunting is framed by the opposition as being a dominionistic activity (i.e., using animals without regard for their welfare or rights), it is likely to be rejected. If hunting is instead shown to be consistent with animal welfare (i.e., using animals in a way that does not cause undue pain and suffering), it is much more likely to be understood and accepted.

## Debate Strategies and Tactics

Just as it is important to know the right words and arguments to use when debating hunting, it is also crucial to have a firm grasp on strategies and tactics for making points.[250]

### ANALYZING THE AUDIENCE

Debates about hunting might occur everywhere from classrooms to brightly lit stages before live audiences. Before any debate about hunting, though, one must analyze the audience in question and consider whether basic adjustments in tone or approach need to be made. Debaters should take the time to consider the audience, including what the debate setting might indicate about the audience: does it include people who may have some familiarity with hunting, or is it more likely to be mostly non-hunters? Is it a highly educated academic group or closer to a mix of general population residents? Such considerations will help to ensure that the pro-hunting points put forth in the debate connect as intended. The important point is to establish a connection to the audience.

### INCORPORATING *ETHOS*, *PATHOS*, AND *LOGOS*

The most resonant arguments will incorporate all three of Aristotle's elements of persuasion: *ethos*, *pathos*, and *logos*.[251]

*Ethos* is credibility—debates about hunting will only be won if the audience is convinced that the person arguing for hunting is trustworthy. One way to quickly establish credibility is to connect to a real-world concern shared by the audience. It is also useful to keep in mind that fish and wildlife agency personnel, especially uniformed staff like game wardens and biologists, are viewed as some of the most credible sources on wildlife and hunting.[252]

*Pathos* is an emotional connection—without this, people are unlikely to be persuaded. This does not mean that arguments must rest entirely or even primarily on emotion. Rather, it underscores the importance of communicating basic emotional information, such as the fact that hunters care about the well-being of wildlife.

*Logos* is logic—arguments need to be fundamentally logical if they are to persuade. Persuasive arguments have both internal and external validity. Internal validity means that an argument does not appear to contradict itself. For example, an anti-hunter might challenge a hunter to explain why it is not contradictory to both care about wildlife and enjoy hunting. (The hunter might respond that care for wildlife is precisely what motivates them to actively participate in wildlife management through hunting.) External validity means that an argument does not appear to contradict what is generally understood about the real world. For example, the argument that no one should eat meat from animals would seem to lack external validity, given the fact that the vast majority of Americans eat meat.

*Extremely rare in 1900, there are now an estimated 6 million wood ducks in North America.*

## STRUCTURING POINTS AND ARGUMENTS

Debaters should use a structure to organize their thoughts and make points. There are different ways to do this. Philosopher Stephen Toulmin's approach entails the "claim-warrant-data" structure: the claim is the thesis or anchor point; the warrant is the justification of why the claim is true; and the data is the evidence supporting both.[253] Claims without a warrant shift the burden of explanation to the other party, such as when an anti-hunter describes hunting as animal cruelty without justifying the claim (it is then left to the pro-hunting side to explain why this perspective is wrong).

Another structure is the "problem-cause-answer-net benefit" (P.C.A.N.) model, which was developed by G. Richard Shell and Mario Moussa, directors of the Wharton School's Strategic Persuasion Workshop.254

Similar to a sales technique, the structure entails identifying a problem to be solved (e.g., wildlife must be managed) and then explaining the cause of the problem. The answer (legal, regulated hunting) and net benefits (thriving wildlife populations, funding for conservation, humanely harvested meat, etc.) follow.

The "identify-beat-mean" (I.B.M.) structure, developed by A-Game Speech and Debate Consulting, is a useful way to organize rebuttals or responses to earlier points.[255] The debater first identifies the point to which they will respond, beats the opposing side's best argument on that point, and explains the implications—in other words, what the argument means and why it matters. Proceeding to the opposition's best argument, even if it has not yet been put forth, is a way to neutralize the argument before the opposing side has a chance to build it up.

## STRUCTURING ARGUMENTS FOR MAXIMUM IMPACT

Debates consist of offensive and defensive arguments. Offensive arguments communicate why it is good to do something. Defensive arguments explain why it is *not that bad* to do something.[256] Arguing for hunting entirely from a defensive position is unlikely to win a formal debate—hunters must put forth strong offensive arguments explaining why hunting is a humane way to source meat and a wildlife management tool that promotes conservation and biodiversity.

Hunting advocates should enter debates anticipating the best arguments from the other side, ideally expecting which may be used offensively and which will be used defensively. Research shows that the most effective anti-hunting arguments in general emphasize hunting as a violation of fair chase, hunting being inextricably linked with trophy hunting, and hunting being a danger to wildlife populations.257 (See Chapter 6 for a breakdown of different ways to counter these anti-hunting arguments.)

Debates about hunting sometimes come down to anti-hunters being allowed to make offensive arguments that claim the moral high ground; in response, the pro-hunting side must argue from a defensive position why hunting is not that bad. The pro-hunting side should instead try to begin with offensive arguments showing why hunting is indeed the ethical thing to do.

Defensive arguments are useful in mitigating damaging claims from the other side (for example, the claim that hunting is dangerous might invite a defensive argument citing accident statistics or the hunter safety education requirement). The key is to put forth the best offensive arguments while having defensive arguments in the ready. Remember that one of the best pro-hunting offensive arguments frames hunting as a fundamental right (by contrast, the corresponding defensive anti-hunting argument would deny the right to hunt).

## MAKING EFFECTIVE COUNTERARGUMENTS

Effective counterarguments may take the form of *link turns*, which communicate the idea, "the thing you think we cause, we actually prevent," or *impact turns*, which communicate the idea, "the thing you think we decrease, we actually increase."[258]

For example, an anti-hunter might argue that hunters cause injuries and accidental deaths during hunting. As a link turn, the pro-hunter could respond that hunters actually reduce injuries and accidental deaths through state-mandated safety courses—without hunters supporting and completing these courses, there would be far more hunting accidents. Similarly, an impact turn might follow the claim that hunting endangers wildlife populations: the pro-hunter could reply that hunters actually fund wildlife conservation and ensure the sustainability of game and nongame species, and have a long documented history of doing so.[259]

## STAYING ON POINT

Debate opponents may employ red herrings, which are points or arguments purposely designed to derail the discussion or distract from the original point. Red herrings are traps to be avoided; to sidestep a red herring, a debater might say, "That's an interesting issue but that's not what we're here to debate today."[260]

## THINKING IN THE MOMENT

Speakers in debates will inevitably encounter arguments or points they are less prepared to respond to than others. Unable to provide a direct and meaningful response to a point, debaters should fall back on the concepts with which they are most comfortable and familiar—they should identify the point to which they want to respond, restate the point as necessary, and then address it.[261] This is essentially the same thing as reframing the discussion by acknowledging the original issue or argument and then pointing out that the *real* issue is the one addressed in the forthcoming response (e.g., the basic right of people to hunt, hunting as a way to obtain food, or hunting as a wildlife management tool).

## FALLING BACK ON RELIABLE EXAMPLES

Debaters will inevitably sometimes fall back on data or examples that they consider to be particularly effective in illustrating points. Selectively picking strong examples, if not done excessively, can set up arguments that are difficult for opponents to refute or respond to. As an example, the overpopulation of feral pigs in certain areas of the southeastern United States has resulted in considerable property damage—those familiar with the situation might find it difficult to argue against legal, regulated hunting as a viable population control measure.[262] Another highly relatable example may be the potential for overpopulations of deer to contribute to vehicular accidents in many areas of the country.

## LEVERAGING THE STRENGTHS OF THE HUNTING COMMUNITY

It is sometimes possible in a debate to gain an advantage by invoking or appealing to a credible scholarly source. In debates about hunting, such figures might include respected conservationists like Aldo Leopold or Theodore Roosevelt, or a highly regarded cultural figure like Ernest Hemingway. Scholarly figures and other acknowledged subject matter experts can be difficult to attack, and their support for hunting reinforces the fact that it is intertwined in the roots of the conservation movement. Other unique strengths of the hunting community relate to the social and biological benefits hunting offers (e.g., the role of hunting in ethical meat procurement and wildlife population control).[263]

## FINDING COMMON GROUND

In any debate, the pro-hunting side should attempt to acknowledge the contribution of the opposition, especially by recognizing shared motivations and values (e.g., "Clearly we both care deeply about the future of wildlife"), noting particular points that resonate (e.g., "Something you mentioned really strikes a chord with me and I'm glad you brought it up"), or simply thanking those on the opposing side for their passion and contribution to the discussion.[264] By sincerely and respectfully trying to connect with an idea or aspect from the opposition, hunting advocates will demonstrate good faith participation in the discourse. Above all, debaters should maintain the moral high ground by responding to the argument instead of the person—personal attacks and unfair generalizations will not help to advance the hunting message.

## USING CRITICAL LISTENING

Critical listening during debates will help speakers identify the frames being used by the other side. For example, pro-hunting speakers should listen for the opposing side's framing of hunting as animal cruelty, or hunting being an insufficient way to fund conservation. Listening critically will help identify the philosophical perspectives and justifications of the other side, making it easier to construct sound counterarguments.[265] Critical listening even extends to taking notes during the debate, allowing the debater to track the structure of the opposing side's arguments and respond to specific claims.

## MAINTAINING CONSISTENCY

Changing an argument or conceding an important point mid-debate can suggest uncertainty or a lack of conviction. By contrast, some debates are won when a debater simply holds onto an argument and refuses to let it go.[266] Prior to any debate, hunting advocates should identify the positions and arguments that they believe are defensible no matter what—this will avoid the need to reverse course later on to potentially damaging effect.

## DELIVERING CONCLUDING REMARKS

Debaters usually have an opportunity at the end to clarify points or put forth any final arguments. Concluding remarks can also be used to reassert the desired framing of the discussion: anti-hunters may attempt to bring the discussion back to animal rights, whereas pro-hunters may return to the fundamental right of people to hunt or the centrality of hunting to conservation and wildlife management. Whatever the focus, the pro-hunting side must not let the anti-hunting side decide for the audience which arguments matter most.[267]

The pro-hunting side can also use the debate conclusion to reinforce hunting as an activity that has long been part of the mainstream of society (i.e., humans have hunted for more than a million years and millions of Americans continue to hunt each year; also, sizable majorities of Americans consume meat and approve of hunting). Finally, concluding remarks can remind the audience that hunters are ethical, responsible, and hold values that are similar to most people's (e.g., concern for the environment, love of wildlife, and care about the ethical treatment of animals).

## Case Study: 2016 Intelligence Squared Debate

A live debate held in 2016 featured pro- and anti-hunting speakers debating the motion that hunters conserve wildlife (the debate was sponsored by Intelligence Squared U.S., a nonprofit organization promoting public discourse). According to an audience poll, the pro-hunting side lost the debate: only a third of viewers beforehand said they were *against* the assertion that hunters conserve wildlife; after hearing arguments from the two sides in the debate, two thirds of viewers said they were against the motion.

This debate is notable for the practical lessons it offers on argumentation and persuasive tactics. Following are some of the major takeaways from the debate as determined through analysis by A-Game Speech and Debate Consulting:

- First, the pro-hunting side missed an opportunity early on to use a strong offensive argument sharply distinguishing themselves from the opposition—the pro-hunters made too much of an effort attempting to find common ground with the anti-hunters (the pro-hunting side would have been better off waiting until later in the debate to emphasize any points of agreement with the opposition).
- The anti-hunting side tarnished the image of legal hunting by discussing it alongside dog-fighting and other egregious examples of animal cruelty—this tactic was intended to reframe the debate from conservation to ethics.
- The anti-hunting side attempted to "inoculate" against strong pro-hunting arguments by claiming to allow for a difference between deer hunters hunting for food and wealthy hunters traveling abroad to hunt trophy animals.
- The anti-hunters made references to funding mechanisms for conservation besides hunting (e.g., ecotourism) but did not explain them fully or provide evidence. Yet the pro-hunting side failed to challenge the anti-hunters on this, effectively ceding the point.

- The pro-hunting side also failed to rebut specific claims made by the anti-hunting side about lead ammunition from hunters causing environmental damage, ceding another point.
- The anti-hunting side made numerous claims attacking trophy hunting abroad. On this topic, the pro-hunting side should have challenged the anti-hunters to define trophy hunting specifically; they should have then put trophy hunting in perspective and shifted the discussion back to the more salient topic of regulated hunting in North America.
- The pro-hunting side cited dollar amounts generated through hunting license sales and Pittman-Robertson taxes, but the information came off as dry in comparison to the villainous trophy hunting caricatures offered by the anti-hunting side.
- Speakers on the anti-hunting side were more experienced at debate—they were generally not prone to the tactical errors occasionally committed by the pro-hunters. For example, at one point, a pro-hunting speaker became defensive, even arguing with the moderator—arguments in debates should only be directed at the other side.
- The pro-hunting side failed to adequately convince the audience that hunters care about wildlife—this was another point essentially ceded to the anti-hunters and harmful from the standpoint of hunters' credibility.
- Debates are largely about contrasting worldviews: in this case, what the world looks like *with* hunting versus what it would look like *without* hunting. The pro-hunting side did not adequately establish all of the societal benefits of hunting, especially benefits at the local level. In particular, the pro-hunting side failed to adequately present a contrasting condition of *conservation* without hunting—in other words, what wildlife management would look like without the funding support and other benefits of hunting.

*Source: Intelligence Squared debate held May 4, 2016. Debate accessed online August 28, 2020, via the Intelligence Squared U.S. website. Debate analysis provided by A-Game Speech and Debate Consulting.*

## What to Avoid in a Debate

Advocates of hunting should never ignore strong offensive arguments from the other side, such as assertions about hunters routinely violating hunting laws or wildlife populations being endangered by regulated hunting.[268] The pro-hunting side should be ready to respond to such claims with evidence that most hunters hunt responsibly and that regulated hunting does not pose a risk to wildlife populations.

---

Pro-hunters should also avoid letting anti-hunters dictate the terms of a debate by continually bringing the discussion back to trophy hunting, especially when legal, regulated hunting as practiced in the U.S. is a much more salient topic.

---

Pro-hunters should also avoid letting anti-hunters dictate the terms of a debate by continually bringing the discussion back to trophy hunting, especially when legal, regulated hunting as practiced in the U.S. is a much more salient topic. Data show that support for hunting begins to fade the longer the discussion remains on trophy hunting; on the other hand, approval grows when people learn that hunting is regulated to ensure the sustainability of wildlife populations, and when they believe that hunters themselves care deeply about wildlife.[269]

Pro-hunters must not let anti-hunters exploit public outrage over specific incidents involving celebrity animals—conservation requires a pragmatic focus on wildlife populations as a whole, not unreasonable scrutiny of isolated events. The pro-hunting side should remain focused on the central topic or claim being debated (debates usually consist of arguments for and against a specific motion). It can be easy for anti-hunting debaters to rely on excessive emotion as a shortcut to support, but such feelings are irrelevant in debates about the role of hunting in wildlife management and conservation.[270]

Finally, those advocating for hunting in good faith should avoid entering debates that are impossible to win. They should not engage with sponsors that are bound to an agenda, nor should they participate in events in which the outcome is predetermined—such scenarios are unlikely to generate any new support for hunting.

## *Key Takeaways*

- Pro-hunting debaters must be knowledgeable about the most effective themes and individual arguments for and against hunting, including which ones are offensive arguments (which explain why something is good) and which ones are defensive arguments (which explain why something is not that bad).
- The basic themes that work the best in support of hunting are hunting as a food source, hunting as conservation, and hunting as a right.
- The individual arguments that are most effective in building support for hunting are:
  - Hunting for food does not cause any more animal suffering than slaughtering livestock for food.
  - Those who do not hunt or do not approve of hunting don't have to hunt, but they should respect the right of others to hunt.
  - Hunting specifically helps control the deer population, which is overabundant and has no natural predators in many areas.
  - Hunting controls wildlife populations and helps with species management.
  - Hunting is properly regulated, and there are rules and regulations in place to ensure fair and moral hunting that also protects wildlife populations as a whole.
- The themes that garner the most *opposition* to hunting are hunting as a violation of fair chase, hunting being linked to trophy hunting, and hunting resulting in diminished wildlife populations. These can all be rebutted with strong counterarguments.
- Certain arguments for hunting will persuade some audiences but not others—pro-hunting debaters must therefore be adaptable and ready to analyze the audience. They must find a way to connect with the audience.

## Key Takeaways (continued)

- Pro-hunting debaters should work to frame debates in their favor, such as by establishing the necessity of human management of wildlife.

- The strongest arguments will balance ethos (credibility), pathos (emotion), and logos (logic). Relying on just one of these elements will not be enough to persuade people.

- Using a formal structure in debates, such as the "claim-warrant-data" approach, will help to organize arguments and points.

- Link turns ("the thing you think we cause, we actually prevent") and impact turns ("the thing you think we decrease, we actually increase") are good ways to redirect points made by the opposing side.

- Pro-hunting debaters should avoid red herrings from the other side (points intended to derail the discussion) and be ready to reframe the discussion by returning to the original point or motion.

- Using strong examples and appealing to scholarly sources or noted authority figures can provide some advantages in a debate.

- Pro-hunting debaters should listen critically to the opposition to keep track of points and arguments. In their own arguments, they should maintain consistency and avoid flip-flopping. Pro-hunting debaters should also use concluding remarks to reassert the desired framing of the discussion.

- Advocates of hunting should never ignore strong offensive arguments from the other side, nor should they allow anti-hunters to dictate the terms of a debate by constantly returning to trophy hunting. (See Chapter 4 for a full discussion of how to address trophy hunting.)

- Tell stories. Non-hunters may gain a better understanding of hunting through firsthand stories from hunters that emphasize knowledge and love of wildlife and nature.

## CHAPTER 10

# Developing Formal Communications Programs in Support of Hunting

BEYOND EVERYDAY INTERPERSONAL COMMUNICATION ABOUT *hunting, agencies and sportsperson/conservation organizations sometimes develop formal communications programs on hunting. In the future, the need for such programs may grow as hunting in America continues to be challenged by anti-hunters. This chapter addresses the best ways to develop these types of programs. Also included in the chapter are case studies and real-world examples of effective formal communications programs that focus on building cultural support for hunting.*

## Some Important Considerations in Planning

While attitudes about hunting are shaped largely through interpersonal contact and direct experience, formal communications programs in support of hunting have the ability to potentially reach large numbers of people. However, it is important to distinguish such programs from efforts designed specifically to recruit, retain, and reactivate hunters. Communications programs intended to solidify Americans' cultural acceptance of hunting have a wider, more encompassing goal: they seek to protect and strengthen the very foundation on which recruitment, retention, and reactivation initiatives rest. Hunters make up only a small percentage of the population. From a sheer numbers perspective, a population that approves of hunting is, in many ways, just as important to the future of hunting as hunters themselves.

The research presented in the previous chapters demonstrates that attitudes toward hunting are affected by a variety of factors—both demographic factors such as gender and age, and social factors, such as baseline wildlife values and such things as whether one grows up in a family of hunters or whether one knows a hunter. It is not possible to have only one message for one audience—there is no such thing as a homogeneous general public. Instead, varying groups of Americans have different information and outreach needs. Messaging that works with one group of people may not work with another group. By targeting specific groups with customized messages, communication and outreach efforts in support of hunting will become more effective, and their outcomes can be better measured.

## Step 1. Identify Issues Related to the Cultural Acceptance of Hunting

The first step is to identify and prioritize the issues or concepts related to the cultural acceptance of hunting on which the communications program will focus. Communications programs focused on building cultural support for hunting should not be confused with efforts to recruit new hunters or to retain or reactivate existing hunters. To be clear, it is not possible to increase participation in hunting without broad societal support for hunting in the first place—cultural acceptance of hunting is a necessary condition for any subsequent R3 efforts.

One way to determine the initial issues and concepts of interest is to identify common information gaps, misperceptions, or beliefs about hunting that need to be corrected; find the information that people need to know to make them more supportive of hunting.

For instance, one issue regarding the cultural acceptance of hunting is that some people think that hunting causes species to become endangered or extinct. Then, for this reason, they do not support hunting. The issue being identified in this case is the belief or misinformation about hunting's effect on wildlife population levels.

There are many other facets of hunting that can guide the focus of individual communications initiatives. Consider the following examples, each relating to a specific aspect of the cultural acceptance of hunting:

- Increasing knowledge of the Pittman-Robertson funding mechanism.

- Building awareness of the various ways in which hunters contribute to conservation.
- Increasing understanding of hunter education requirements that ensure safety in the field and promote the ethical harvest of wildlife.
- Raising awareness of hunting as a way to obtain organic, healthy meat.
- Educating non-hunters about the selective culling of herds through hunting (i.e., informing people that hunters do not hunt indiscriminately).

It is vital that program coordinators take the time to initially identify specific issues to address in communications programs. Programs without a clear focus run the risk of being too general or diffuse in their aims: it is difficult to design an effective program that seeks to simply "increase support for hunting among the general public," as such a goal is too vaguely defined to be achievable.

---

*Programs without a clear focus run the risk of being too general or diffuse in their aims: it is difficult to design an effective program that seeks to simply "increase support for hunting among the general public."*

⊕

---

## Step 2. Identify and Prioritize Information and Outreach Issues

The next step is to identify the information and outreach goals and priorities of the organization itself. What important issues related to cultural support for hunting is the organization uniquely suited to address or promote in its communications? For example, an organization that typically focuses on hunter ethics may be well positioned to spearhead a new communications campaign that targets non-hunters with information about the ethical behaviors of hunters. An organization that is involved firsthand in conservation projects funded through hunter dollars may be especially qualified to develop an effective campaign explaining the purpose and impact of such conservation projects. Identifying and prioritizing issues specific to the organization will assist the communications team in identifying outreach-related needs; it will also increase organizational acceptance and buy-in and support partnerships between outreach specialists, administrators, and other staff. It is vital to know the internal issues, strengths, and needs of the organization from the inside-out before outreach efforts move forward—this will ensure that the organization as a whole is on board about which issues will be addressed in the communications programs.

## Step 3. Define Goals and Set Measurable Objectives

Next in the process is to define goals and to set measurable objectives for the communications program. Goals define the intended results within which objectives are pursued. Goals are broad and lofty statements about the desired communications outcomes. Goals should be clearly defined and committed to paper before initiation of the communications program. It is also important for the general goals of communications programs to be consistent with widely held societal values, or to show how the current behaviors of the target audience may be incompatible with their desired or purported values.[271]

In some cases, goals will entail specific measurable increases in support or awareness. For example, a goal might be to increase approval of hunting among Hispanic people or among black people. Another goal might be to increase awareness of the Pittman-Robertson Act among state general population residents.

Objectives are directed toward the accomplishment of the goals and are specific, measurable statements of what, when, and how much will be achieved. The specificity of the objectives is important at this point. Vague objectives generally cannot be achieved and certainly cannot be measured. Therefore, objectives need to be clearly defined, with terms that accurately reflect exactly what is meant in the objective (objectives must not be left open to broad interpretation). It is also vital to determine the link between the communications messaging and the objectives. This answers the question, "How will the communications achieve the goal of increasing support for hunting?" or "How will communications increase non-hunters' knowledge level about the important role hunting plays in conservation?"

## Step 4. Identify, Define, and Target Publics

To develop effective and successful communications, organizations need to identify and classify different audiences to discern their socioeconomic and other characteristics, thereby allowing them to be better targeted. There is no such thing as one "general public"; instead, the public is made up of many disparate groups and might better be thought of as plural: general publics. Research indicates that the way people relate to hunting is affected by a variety of factors, including their age, ethnicity, gender, income, level of education, and other variables. A list of applicable "publics" is important in identifying one's place in a particular market. For instance, research previously shown in Chapter 4 found that Hispanic people, black people, women, younger people, and residents of large cities/urban areas all had a higher rate of opposition to hunting, compared to U.S. residents overall. Each of these constitutes a target market (although some markets in certain situations might be combined, such as young women to capture two of the markets).

---

You buy things that look like you.

⊕

---

When developing communications, the differences among groups must be taken into account so that messages can be tailored for specific audiences. One size does not fit all. For example, an image of an older, white, male hunter may not be effective to younger and/or non-white audiences. This is vital. Perhaps the best advice here comes from a black female in a Responsive Management focus group for a study on why members of ethnic minority groups did not fish at the same level as white people. She said, "You like to buy things that look like you."[272]

---

Because there is no such thing as a single, all-encompassing general public, communications will invariably reach only certain audiences. The question, then, is not whether to segment and target but whether this is done deliberately and consciously or haphazardly by default.

---

This part of the communications plan identifies the specific market segment(s). Who are they exactly? What are the demographic characteristics of the market segment? What do they want and what do they need? What are their attitudes and opinions about hunting? There are numerous ways to better understand these markets, including focus group research and quantitative opinion and attitude surveys.

Subdividing a heterogenous public into smaller, more homogenous subsets based on one or more variables is known as market segmentation. Once different audiences are understood, communications can be developed and tailored to each group. This is known as target marketing.

Because there is no such thing as a single, all-encompassing general public, communications will invariably reach only certain audiences. The question, then, is not whether to segment and target but whether this is done deliberately and consciously or haphazardly by default.

The key to effective segmenting and targeting is to base communications on real differences and match target markets with the goals and objectives of communications. One way that market segmentation is determined is through the crosstabulation of results from attitude and opinion surveys. Targeting and tailoring communications is essential to their success in accomplishing goals and objectives.

## Step 5. Understand the Audiences

This book has presented a large amount of information on how hunting is viewed and under which conditions it is accepted. The following are some aspects of how people relate to hunting.

Understanding *opinions* on hunting is crucial when developing communications plans. This determines how to approach a particular audience.

*Americans' wildlife values* are also important to understand. A detailed typology is available in other research, notably the pioneering work of Dr. Stephen Kellert of Yale University.[273] The typology that follows, developed by the Human Dimensions in Natural Resources Unit at Colorado State University,[274] is useful for the purposes of communications planning.

The overall typology here comes from a matrix of two scales: the first scale is Mutualism, and the second scale is Utilitarian. People are either low or high on each scale. Those with "strong mutualist tendencies see animals as family or companions" and tend to consider individual animals. Those on the other end of the Mutualist scale tend to consider the species as a whole rather than individual animals. Those with strong Utilitarian tendencies believe in the use of animals, while those on the other end think that animals should not be used by humans.

| Colorado State University Wildlife Typologies | | | |
|---|---|---|---|
| | | \multicolumn{2}{c}{Utilitarian} |
| | | High | Low |
| Mutualism | High | **Pluralist** | **Mutualist** |
| | Low | **Utilitarian** | **Distanced** |

Source: Teel et al.; M. Manfredo.[275]

- Pluralists score high on both scales. They are situational in their viewpoints toward wildlife. Different situations result in different orientations.
- Mutualists score high on the Mutualism scale but low on the Utilitarian scale. They see wildlife as part of their extended social network. They would be the most likely to disapprove of hunting.
- Utilitarians are the most extreme in views that wildlife should be managed to be used by people. They would be the group most likely to approve of hunting.
- Distanced people have low levels of thought about wildlife. They show little interest in wildlife. They may not have a strong opinion about hunting either way.

Understanding that people fall into one of these typologies and incorporating this information into market identification will make communications more effective. These typologies have important implications for the types of messages that can be used to reach them. The values of these groups determine how they will perceive hunting and the messages crafted to garner more support of hunting.

Another model of how people relate to conservation (which can be adapted to hunting) is provided by the model of conservation education developed by Henderson.[276] This model looks at stages spanning no awareness of an issue at the bottom to taking action on the issue at the top.

People go through the stages before they decide to take action about an issue (see the diagram on the next page). A person starts with *Little or No Awareness*—simple information that the issue exists should be the focus of outreach. The next stage is *Awareness*; outreach has informed them, and now it attempts to move them to the next stage, which is *Appreciation*. At this stage, the person now cares enough about the issue to continue learning about it. After this stage, the person enters *Understanding* wherein the outreach to them has now informed them of the nuances of the issue. From this stage, the person moves to *Concern*, wherein they care about the issue enough to want to make changes. The final stage is *Action*, wherein the person takes steps to address the issue.

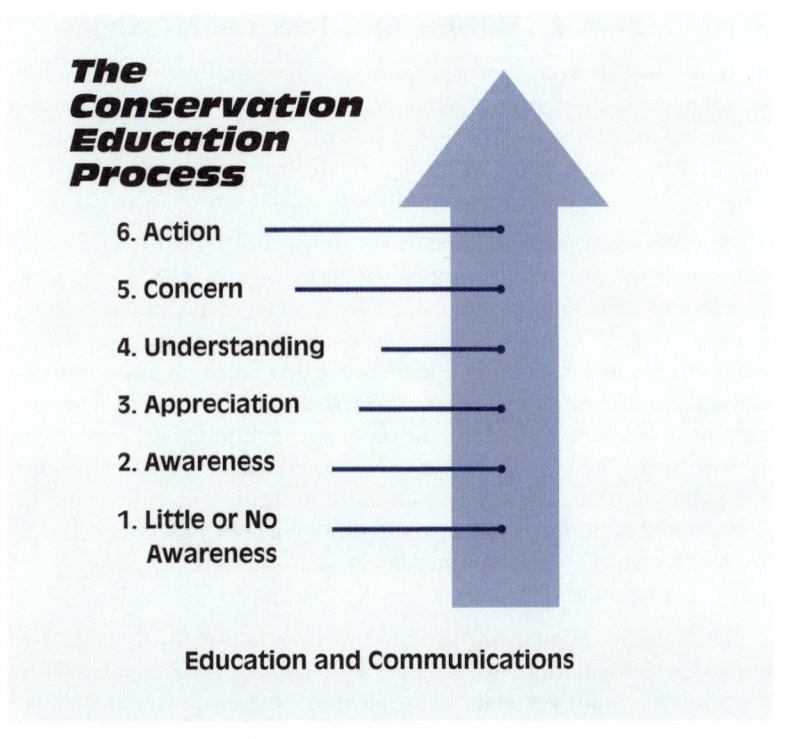

## The Conservation Education Process

6. Action
5. Concern
4. Understanding
3. Appreciation
2. Awareness
1. Little or No Awareness

**Education and Communications**

Where a person falls on this continuum dictates the types of outreach that are most relevant and applicable to them. The outreach to inform a person with no knowledge of an issue is different than outreach that moves them from concern to action.

As an example, outreach for those with no awareness might simply concentrate on the message that hunting is tied to conservation. Outreach for those moving to action would include concrete suggestions on what to do to help ensure that hunting is supported—such as encouraging them to write a letter to the editors of their local newspaper or vote for ballot measures that protect hunting rights (and against ballot measures that restrict hunting rights).

Organizations that coordinate communications programs must decide at the outset whether the intent of the program is simply to increase knowledge or support, or to go a step further by moving people from awareness and understanding to taking action.

## Step 6. Identify, Define, and Test the Messages

It is risky, at best, to develop information and outreach without identifying the messages and communications to be used. Certain messages will resonate with some people but not with others. Decisions must be based on a solid foundation of high-quality research confirming what most resonates with the target audience.

An important consideration is an appeal or motivator or a set of appeals or motivators. An appeal or motivator is what induces the audience to form an opinion or take an action—in this case to become more supportive of hunting in general or to take actions on behalf of hunting, such as voting for ballot measures that protect hunting, posting messages in support of hunting on social media, or even writing letters to the editor of a local newspaper in support of hunting. Basic appeals or motivators include profit, concern about an issue, fear, pleasure, vanity, and guilt. No particular motivator is automatically better than another. For support of hunting, concern over the environment would certainly be one motivator, with the benefit being that hunting supports a great many conservation efforts.

The emotional element also should be mentioned. Appealing to the audience's emotions is necessary to engender their concern. With concern for wildlife populations as the motivator, the potential audience who need to be informed of the benefits of hunting will then be more receptive to the message.

At this stage, it is important that outreach specialists *not* get locked into an unchangeable, specific messaging strategy until research and pretesting prove its utility. Perfecting the messages and strategy may require the abandonment of pet messages and strategies that were initially thought to be useful or effective. Don't be afraid to change course in the development of messages and strategies. It is sometimes the case that communications initiatives to which significant resources have been devoted simply fail to justify their costs—retooling or rethinking these programs will be necessary for the long-term success of the effort.

Another word of caution is to not confuse the audience with too much information or too many messages. Target audiences need time to process the message. An overload at the initial stage of the outreach may cause some people to ignore the entire message. Keep it simple.

The final step is to pre-test the messages and messaging strategy with a small subset of the intended audience. Examples of this are provided in the case studies at the end of this chapter.

Note that Chapter 6 of this book shows some of the national research on message testing. Recall that the chapter discussed themes that resonated: hunting for food, hunting as conservation, and hunting as a right. These are some of the identified themes that have been tested and proven to work well. Also recall in that chapter that five messages that tested well were as follows:

- Hunting for food does not cause any more animal suffering than slaughtering livestock for food.
- Those who do not hunt or do not approve of hunting don't have to hunt, but they should respect the right of others to hunt.
- Hunting specifically helps control the deer population, which is overabundant and has no natural predators in many areas.
- Hunting controls wildlife populations and helps with species management.
- Hunting is properly regulated, and there are rules and regulations in place to ensure fair and moral hunting that also protects wildlife populations as a whole.

Of course, particular messages for particular audiences must be selected and developed. The results above are among Americans overall, but other audiences might have different top messages to which they respond. Pre-testing the messages and matching the message to the audience is extremely important. As an example, a workshop held in Atlanta sponsored by SCI identified more than 140 ideas for getting out messages about hunting.[277] Obviously, without pre-testing and research to winnow down the list, there is no feasible way that all 140 ideas could be used.

## Step 7. Consider Demographic, Social, Economic, and Political Trends

Incorporating data on trends into planning efforts is the next step in developing effective communications programs. Accounting for changing societal factors in communications allows organizations to become proactive, rather than reactive, to external factors. One would not want to develop messages for a society that no longer exists or applies.

Understanding the trends also allows outreach specialists to change the messaging strategy when shifts in demographic, social, economic, and political trends warrant that the messaging strategy be altered. For instance, the world is increasingly moving to a paperless system, but there will still be people, at least for the near future, who are not comfortable in a paperless world. Targeting that specific market, if deemed necessary, will require a different strategy than a market that is comfortable with all or mostly electronic resources.

Another example of how knowledge of trends is important is demonstrated by Americans' changing values regarding wildlife. Years ago, Americans were more utilitarian in their approach to wildlife (as discussed previously in step 5) but are becoming increasingly mutualistic. Messages that would appeal to those who are utilitarian are quite different from messages that would appeal to those who are mutualistic.

## Step 8. Getting the Message Across

The next step in the process is to select the appropriate specific media to transmit the selected message for each potential audience. The decisions should be based on the target groups—where they live, how often they should be reached, and their predisposition regarding hunting. The selection should also be based on budget and costs of media. Costs need to be weighed against the reach of the media.

At this penultimate stage, there are some important internal considerations. One of the most important is to ensure that adequate and appropriate resources are dedicated to the outreach effort. Messages, no matter how well crafted, will not work if they fail to even reach their intended audience.

A strategy must also be given time to work. Communications efforts should not be expected to change opinions or behaviors overnight. Time must be given for the messages to be disseminated and internalized by the recipient. Expecting returns too soon may lead outreach specialists to abandon a good strategy because they did not see the results—because they looked too soon.

Internal organization buyoff on the strategy is also important. All members of the organization need to be on the same page, so to speak, about an outreach strategy. If the organization internally is not on board, the outreach strategy could be undermined (even if not consciously).

A common barrier to effective communications that should be avoided is the fear or boredom of repetition in messaging. People within an organization may be hesitant to repeat the same message because they feel like they have already said it—however, the organization must keep in mind that the communications are not intended for the organization but for the target audience. While a messaging strategy may need to evolve, it should not change until the time is right for the change. Redundancy is important in outreach efforts. Repetition makes messages stick, and being repetitive (up to a certain point) is not a waste of resources.

## Step 9. Evaluations

The final step occurs after the outreach effort has started. The goals that were laid out in the initial steps should be reached, judged by whatever measurements were decided on and taken. For instance, a goal may have been to make a certain target audience more aware of a certain aspect of hunting, and measurements could entail a survey of this group to gauge their awareness of that aspect.

Evaluations will tell outreach specialists whether the messaging strategy is working and whether certain parts of the strategy need to be adjusted. Evaluations will also signal when a messaging strategy needs to move to its next phase.

The National Hunting and Shooting Sports Action Plan developed by the Wildlife Management Institute and the Council to Advance Hunting and the Shooting Sports (which focuses on recruitment, retention, and reactivation but is nonetheless relevant to the guidelines being discussed here) recommends that effective evaluations take into account the acceptable return-on-investment for programs. The Action Plan further recommends that target audiences be surveyed before, during, and after implementation of communications programs—evaluation surveys are useful for identifying the extent to which the program has shifted attitudes, increased knowledge, or effected some other desired change. Finally, the Action Plan notes that the most effective evaluations will result in concrete steps to improve program delivery and content in order to better meet the needs of the target audience.[278]

Other case studies later in this chapter show the communications program planning steps in action. First, however, are some cautionary words on why some outreach efforts fail, as well as some considerations when selecting spokespersons.

## Why Some Communications Plans and Programs Fail

There are a number of key reasons why many formal communications programs do not succeed:[279]

- Appropriate and adequate financial and personnel resources are not allocated.
- A systematic planning process is not employed.
- Organizations often rush to develop messages without implementing the communications process systematically as described above. They assume that they already know the messages and delivery methods that will work without testing them.
- Goals and objectives are not firmly established or put in writing.
- Target audiences are not identified.
- Target audience knowledge levels, opinions, and attitudes toward the specific outreach topic are not adequately researched.
- Messages are not carefully identified and crafted.
- There are too many messages and these messages tend to be too complex.
- Appropriate media are not selected with the specific target audience in mind.
- There is too much emphasis on program *outputs* as opposed to program *outcomes*.
- Efforts and initiatives are not implemented long enough. Spokespersons forget that, by the time they are tired of the message, the audience may just be catching on.
- Efforts are not evaluated quantitatively.

There are myriad reasons why many communications programs are not as successful as they could be. One reason is referred to as the "feel good factor" in which coordinators evaluate a program based solely on visibly obvious outputs (e.g., webpage visits or certifications reflecting the number of participants who have completed a course) rather than on the desired outcomes (e.g., the actual change in attitudes or increase in knowledge on a particular topic). It is important to look at the final outcomes, not intermediary outputs. Webpage hits and signifiers of program participation (e.g., hats or certificates) are good and are necessary for outreach, but simply measuring such outputs without examining the actual changes in opinions or behaviors (outcomes) means that the program is not being fully and properly evaluated.

Another factor affecting the success of programs is inertia. Rather than determine the best approach based on data and research, program providers fall back on the ways things have always been done.

The absence of an evaluation component built into the program is another barrier to success. In some instances, programs are designed with a built-in component, but it is not adequate to properly evaluate the program.

Fear of findings may be another reason for inadequate program implementation. Program providers may be afraid to find that their initiative is not effective.

Lack of resources to properly evaluate a program can also be a problem. It may be that providers would like to evaluate their efforts but simply have no resources to do so. This is an important reason to build evaluation components into programs from the start.

## Spokespersons and Credibility

Not all programs require a spokesperson, but for those that do, the credibility of the person or entity delivering the message is as important as the actual message. Without the necessary credibility, the message will not be properly heard or seen—it will be discounted before it even has time to sink in.

This ties into one of the key principles of persuasion outlined by Aristotle: *ethos*. The term, *ethos*, refers to credibility, which is held by trained professionals like agency biologists and game wardens. (The other two key principles are *pathos*, referring to emotion, and *logos*, which refers to logic. While building support for hunting depends on all three elements, ethos is the first because the other two depend on the first.)

Fish and wildlife agencies themselves are highly credible when providing the public with information about fish and wildlife, including their management, which entails hunting. This has been true for many years—surveys as far back as the 1980s have found that more Americans say that agency personnel are credible than say that other entities, including nonprofits, sportsmen's groups, and environmental groups, are credible. The graph shows the results of a statewide study that is typical of other findings on this topic.

In this statewide survey, the most credible sources, as shown in the graph, are a Game Warden with the Maine Department of Inland Fisheries and Wildlife, a biologist with the same agency, and a biologist with the U.S. Fish and Wildlife Service—all with 70 percent or more of residents saying that the source is *very* credible. Much lower down in credibility are spokespersons from nonprofit organizations, including conservation and sportsmen's organizations.[280]

**Percent of Maine residents who think each of the following are a very credible source of information on fish and wildlife and outdoor recreation:**

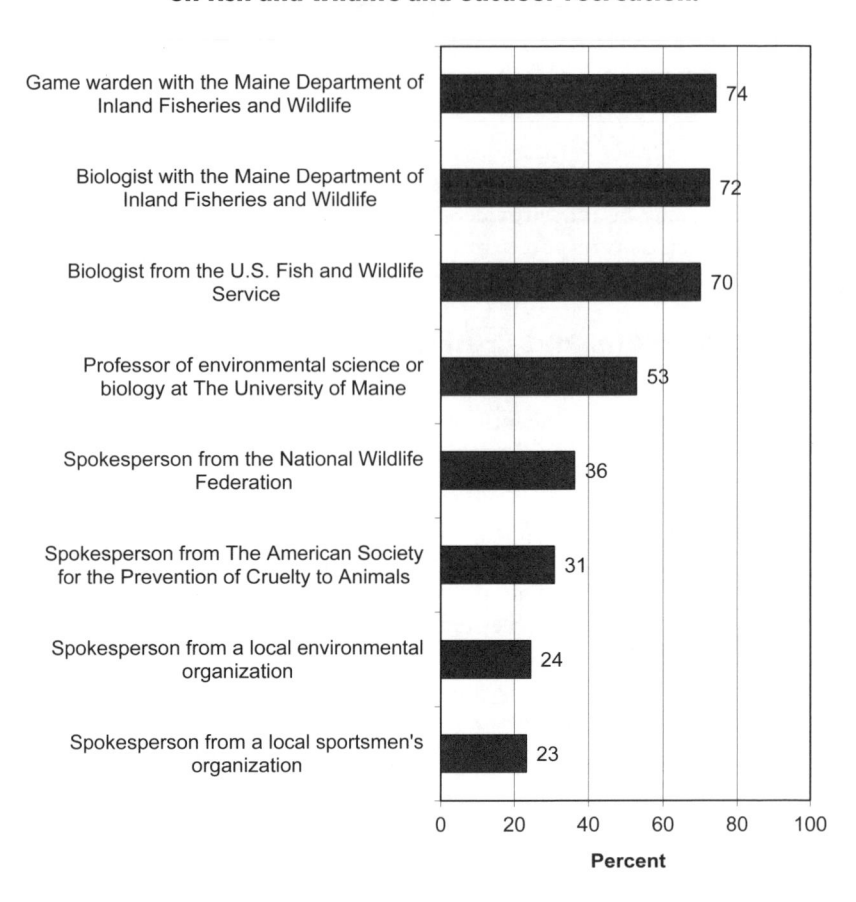

| Source | Percent |
|---|---|
| Game warden with the Maine Department of Inland Fisheries and Wildlife | 74 |
| Biologist with the Maine Department of Inland Fisheries and Wildlife | 72 |
| Biologist from the U.S. Fish and Wildlife Service | 70 |
| Professor of environmental science or biology at The University of Maine | 53 |
| Spokesperson from the National Wildlife Federation | 36 |
| Spokesperson from The American Society for the Prevention of Cruelty to Animals | 31 |
| Spokesperson from a local environmental organization | 24 |
| Spokesperson from a local sportsmen's organization | 23 |

*Source: Responsive Management.*[281]

## Communications Case Studies

This section includes a review of four case studies of effective communications campaigns in support of hunting, as well as a fifth case study regarding fishing participation. The first hunting case study is a look at the Nimrod Society, followed by an examination of the Colorado Wildlife Council and the Michigan Wildlife Council regarding cultural acceptance of hunting—both of these Councils stemmed from the Nimrod Society. A fourth case study pertains to the cultural acceptance of alligator hunting and farming in the U.S. The fifth case study is on a program to increase fishing participation—it does not concern the cultural acceptance of an activity and does not concern hunting—but is included here because it is an excellent example of a successful program in action based on research.

## CASE STUDY #1: NIMROD SOCIETY

The Nimrod Society's goal is to educate the general public about the positive role sportsmen play in wildlife conservation. The Nimrod Society, based in Colorado, seeks to expand public education programs to all states, based on the education program in Colorado.

In the 1990s, after several anti-hunting ballot initiatives were passed in Colorado, concerned sportsmen in the state joined forces to develop a media-based program to "educate the urban, non-hunting public about the scientific, economic, and conservation benefits of hunting and fishing." Through their efforts, legislation was passed establishing a Wildlife Council, funded through a surcharge on licenses, that was dedicated to a pro-hunting public awareness campaign.

The Nimrod Society also helped Michigan pass similar legislation that established a surcharge on hunting and fishing licenses to fund an outreach campaign to educate Michigan's urban, non-sporting public about the benefits of hunting, fishing, and wildlife management. The Nimrod Society's ultimate goal is to reach all 50 states with similar programs.

In short, the Nimrod Society facilitates the establishment of educational campaigns and programs in all the states. Its resources are made available to organizations to start outreach programs at the state level across the United States.

The Nimrod Society itself followed the steps outlined previously, as discussed below. Note that the Nimrod Society also uses those steps in the state-level programs it helps develop; in a sense, the Nimrod Society is a *meta-program* because it spawns state-level programs itself.

*Identify Issues Related to Cultural Acceptance of Hunting:* The primary issue was that Americans were uninformed about the role that hunting and fishing played in conservation, which was allowing other organizations to fill the information gap with misinformation. The end result was that voters were making decisions that were contrary to sound wildlife management and conservation and that were harmful to hunting and fishing—decisions made based on emotion instead of factual knowledge.

*Identify Outreach Issues:* One issue that became immediately apparent was that there was a dearth of organizations to conduct this outreach, and agencies often did not have resources to do these programs on their own (i.e., without a funding mechanism).

*Define Goals and Objectives:* The overarching goal is to establish a self-sufficient (i.e., funded) program in each state to inform the public of the important role that hunting and fishing play in conservation in that state.

*Identify Publics:* Several publics were identified. One consisted of those who did not come from a hunting culture and who were often ill-informed about hunting. However, another "public" had to be reached first: legislators and conservation/hunting/fishing activists who wished to get involved and start a program in their state. While the Nimrod Society implements outreach to get state programs started, it is these state programs that ultimately conduct outreach to the wider public(s).

*Understand the Publics:* Those who started the Nimrod Society understood that some non-hunters were ill-informed. But stepping back into their role in administering a *meta-program* designed to spawn state programs, they also understood that legislators might not have known the best program to support and that the state agency might not have had the resources to conduct a program on its own. They also understood that conservation and hunting/fishing activists might not have known how to go about starting a state program. These were its audiences to reach—those who could start a state program.

*Identify, Develop, and Pre-Test Messages:* The Nimrod Society's primary messages went out to legislators and conservation and hunting/fishing activists to start a Wildlife Council in Colorado, which in turn would create an outreach campaign for the state. So messages at this stage were not widely disseminated to the public but were ultimately directed at the Colorado state legislature to enact the necessary legislation. The medium used and the messages in this context are much different than a program aimed at a wider public audience. See the next two sections for actual messages that were developed for a wider audience.

*Consider Trends:* Those who started the Nimrod Society recognized that a smaller percentage of Americans were hunting and fishing, which was leading to ignorance about the role that those activities played in

# DEVELOPING FORMAL COMMUNICATIONS PROGRAMS IN SUPPORT OF HUNTING

conservation, which in turn was leading to anti-hunting and anti-fishing measures being considered.

*Get the Message Across:* The Nimrod Society consisted of concerned conservationists, sportsmen and women, and livestock and agricultural producers. Their message was directed at the Colorado legislature, and they obviously had influence with those in a position to start a program, as their message was heard. The legislature enacted a state law in 1998 that created the Colorado Wildlife Council and provided it with a source of funding from hunting and fishing license sales.

*Evaluate the Effort:* One part of the evaluation of the Nimrod Society in its role as a meta-program is to look at the number of states in which it has been able to establish a program. The second part of the evaluation would be an examination of residents of the states in which programs have been started to see if their opinions on and knowledge about hunting have changed. This second part of the evaluation would need to be done on a state-by-state basis, and these evaluations are discussed where each state-level program is discussed in the next two sections.

## CASE STUDY #2: THE COLORADO WILDLIFE COUNCIL

Colorado's legislature enacted House Bill 98-1409 (§ 33-4-120) to create the Wildlife Management Public Education Advisory Council, whose mission was to "design a media-based public information program to educate the public about wildlife management and wildlife-related recreation opportunities, particularly hunting and fishing."[282] The name of the Council was later changed to the Colorado Wildlife Council.

The Council's campaigns were initially funded by a 75-cent surcharge added to hunting and fishing licenses (through the efforts of the Council, this surcharge was later raised to $1.50, folded into an overall license fee increase). The Council membership included hunters, anglers, an agricultural producer, representatives of rural counties and municipalities whose economies are boosted by hunting and fishing, a media/marketing expert, and a staff member of Colorado Parks and Wildlife (then the Colorado Division of Wildlife; further references to the agency will use its current name, and this is meant to include its previous incarnation as the Division of Wildlife).[283]

The Colorado Wildlife Council's stated goal is to educate the general public about the benefits of wildlife, wildlife management, and wildlife-related recreational opportunities in Colorado, specifically hunting and fishing. The Council follows the steps that are necessary in creating formal communications efforts, as discussed in detail below.

*Identify Issues Related to Cultural Acceptance of Hunting:* The necessity of a public information campaign was examined by Colorado Parks and Wildlife prior to the enactment of Colorado House Bill 98-1409, as documented in the agency's *Communications Audit, August 1998*. The pressing issue that was identified was that the public knew little about wildlife management and how hunting and fishing played an important role in it.

This lack of knowledge on the public's part was identified as being critical because the public as a whole was voting on wildlife-related ballot initiatives, and separate bans on trapping and a spring bear hunt had already passed in the state. Again, one of the primary hunting issues that was identified at the outset became the impetus for the creation of the Council.

*Identify Outreach Issues:* The Nimrod Society's efforts to get the Colorado Wildlife Council started was, in part, because of the identified outreach issue: the state agency could not, without a steady, reliable funding source, conduct this level of outreach on its own.

The Council also identified proper timing as an important outreach issue. Outreach has to be relevant to the issues that are contemporary, and it must be given time to work. Another outreach issue that the Council recognized was the need to avoid message drift—to avoid having the message sidetracked through pressure to change or modify it by those who were not keeping an eye on the primary goals.

*Define Goals and Objectives:* The Council's overall goal was to educate the public about the benefits of wildlife management and, importantly, the tools used to manage wildlife. An important aspect of the overall goals—as specifically directed in the legislation—was that outreach be designed to *increase the cultural acceptance* of hunting and fishing, not to *recruit new hunters and anglers*. This aspect of the goals is ingrained in the Council and its outreach—the Council by law cannot conduct efforts primarily for recruitment.

*Identify Publics:* The Council's initial communications efforts were directed at the general public, followed by outreach that focused specifically on "the non-hunting, non-fishing Colorado public."[284] Outreach was deemed to be of most importance to those not engaged in these wildlife-related activities.

## DEVELOPING FORMAL COMMUNICATIONS PROGRAMS IN SUPPORT OF HUNTING

Research under the aegis of the Council showed the difficulty in changing the opinions of somebody with a negative perception of hunting, so that audience was not to be a focus. Another segment of society consisted of hunters and those already supportive of hunting, so there was no need to spend resources reaching them. That left people who only moderately supported hunting—i.e., they were not particularly strong in that opinion—and those who were neutral about hunting. These people were referred to as the "in the wind" audience because their opinions were not firmly fixed (besides not having strong opinions on hunting and fishing, the "in the wind" crowd largely consisted of younger likely voters who were new to Colorado and who engaged in other forms of outdoor recreation). These together formed the audience deemed to be of the most importance for focused outreach efforts. As outlined in the Colorado Wildlife Council's *Strategic Communications Toolkit*, getting a hunting opponent to support hunting is a much longer "pull" than getting somebody neutral about hunting to support it.

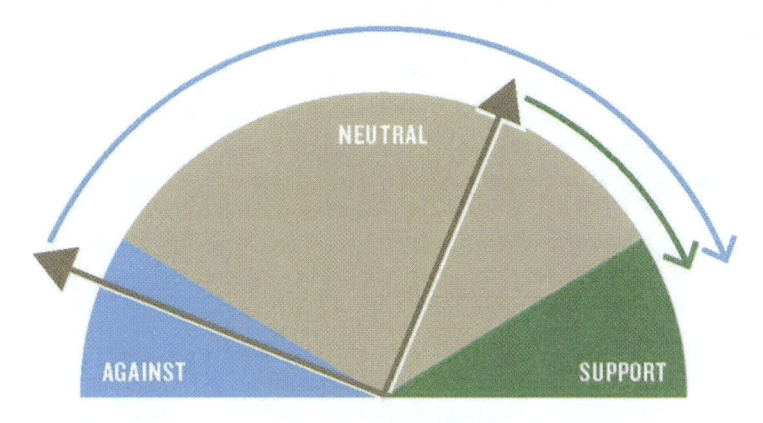

Energy spent trying to convince those completely against hunting to then support hunting is wasted, when those in the middle are an easier pull through education.

*Source: Colorado Wildlife Council* [285]

*Understand the Publics:* As authorized and directed by the legislation that created the Council, the Council's advertising firm continually conducts research to help understand the target audiences that are identified. This research shows which messages resonate with the target audiences as well as which types of media best reach them. As evidenced by the Council's approach, ongoing research to understand audiences is critical, as opinions, knowledge levels, and media preferences shift over time.

Understanding audiences requires understanding how they consume media, including their preferred formats (for instance, cable television versus other streaming services). Another component of understanding audiences is to know the activities that they like, including outdoor activities such as hiking and camping, to aid in establishing a connection with them. This allows targeting that is quite specific in both the messaging and the format of the messaging.

For instance, the Council, through the research it sponsored, found that a large portion of Colorado residents come from out of state (68 percent were born out of state including some born outside of the U.S.), that the overwhelming majority of them live within one urban corridor (the Pueblo to Fort Collins urban corridor accounts for 85 percent of state residents), and that the majority of those moving into the state from elsewhere are between 20 and 29 years old.[285] This information is important when considering whom to target and how to target them.

*Identify, Develop, and Pre-Test Messages:* The Council releases individual campaigns that rely on message testing and the use of professional research and marketing services. One of its research efforts found that audiences reacted positively to a message that sought to link hunting to the conservation and protection of species: Hug-a-Hunter. The campaign used various mediums, including television and radio spots, print and digital advertisements, and billboards.

When evaluation (discussed later) showed that the campaign, despite being well known and getting positive reactions, no longer resonated with one of the primary target audiences (the "in the wind" people), a new campaign was initiated. This change of direction was informed by research and identification of a more focused target audience—research that included surveys and focus groups. This research looked into how the public reacts to words and phrases as well as to images. For instance, much of the non-hunting public did not react well to seeing firearms prominent in the imagery. The campaign was adjusted to address this.

The ongoing research found that two themes resonated well with the target audiences. These are the economic benefits of hunting and fishing to the state of Colorado and the conservation benefits of hunting and fishing. These are the themes that are emphasized in outreach directed at non-hunters and non-anglers.

*Consider Trends:* Continuing research looks at trends in opinions of the various audiences, as well as the characteristics of those audiences. This research allows the outreach effort to be altered according to changing conditions. For instance, it allowed for a change of media in outreach when the research suggested that the target audience could be better reached outside of traditional cable television—this audience consumed most of its television shows outside of traditional cable television. The ongoing research allowed for the format to be changed to meet the audience needs.

*Get the Message Across:* The various campaigns have used a variety of media, including television, billboards, internet ads, and social media, depending on the preferences and consumption patterns of the audience. Specific audiences are targeted as well, including the "in the wind" market previously identified. The campaigns have included conservation success stories.

In addition to using mass media, the Council's campaigns have included a person-to-person effort (manned by temporary Council staff) that was designed to simply inform people attending public events that hunting and fishing played an important role in wildlife management and, therefore, conservation itself.

*Evaluate the Effort:* The initial 1998 communications plan of the Colorado Wildlife Council explicitly stated that the "plan is a living document that should be reviewed annually and updated as necessary." It accounted for evaluations of the efforts from the very start.

The ongoing research ensures that the goals are being met or that the outreach is adjusted to better reach those goals. This ongoing evaluation includes a look at whether the target audience is changing in knowledge levels and opinions. The research also evaluates whether the outreach is most effectively reaching the target audiences.

Specifically, these evaluations look at how perceptions are changed—not simply how many people might have seen a particular message. The Council set up goals for these perceptions and provided that measurements be taken through surveys and focus groups. Such an evaluation is necessary because even negative results need to be known to allow the outreach to evolve as necessary.

A good example of evaluation of efforts included surveys conducted of those who were reached in the aforementioned person-to-person outreach. The surveys evaluated if the person-to-person efforts were effective and helped inform adjustments to those efforts.

## CASE STUDY #3: MICHIGAN WILDLIFE COUNCIL

The goal of the Michigan Wildlife Council is to educate the public about the benefits of hunting and fishing and to promote the essential role that sportsmen and sportswomen play in furthering conservation. The Council is dedicated to increasing public knowledge and appreciation of the impact hunting and fishing have on wildlife and the natural resources all Michiganders enjoy.

The Council is a Governor-appointed public body, with nine members, established by a legislative act in 2013. The Michigan Public Act No. 246 set up the funding structure for the Council—a surcharge of $1 from the sale of every hunting and fishing license.

Its primary message is that hunting and fishing dollars fund Michigan's waters, forests, and wildlife conservation.

> When people purchase a hunting or fishing license, they are actually funding wildlife conservation and management activities across the state. Hunting and fishing licenses—not state taxes—fund efforts to protect endangered species, maintain wildlife habitats and help keep Michigan's natural resources abundant so they can be used and enjoyed for generations to come.

One of its outreach videos states the following:

> No matter where you're from, chances are you love Michigan's forests, waters, and wildlife. But how do we pay to care for it all? You might be surprised to find that it comes from hunting and fishing licenses and not your taxes. Every year, over $61 million from the sale of hunting and fishing licenses conserves and protects our natural resources, ensuring it will be here for all of us for generations. Learn more at HereForMiOutdoors.org.

The Michigan Wildlife Council has permanent, steady, reliable funding based on license sales. Its campaigns use imagery of hunters and anglers as well as non-hunters and non-anglers, showing the connection. Its communications link conservation that benefits all Michigan residents to hunting and fishing. The discussion on the next page shows how the Council followed the previously outlined steps in the creation of one of its campaigns.

## DEVELOPING FORMAL COMMUNICATIONS PROGRAMS IN SUPPORT OF HUNTING

*Identify Issues Related to Cultural Acceptance of Hunting:* The primary issues on which the Council focused were understanding public opinion on hunting and fishing, the motivators linked to approval of the activities, and the fundamental knowledge gaps of the non-hunting and non-fishing public regarding the benefits of hunting and fishing.

The population of Michigan was examined using a survey that was conducted in 2015 to obtain baseline information about residents of the state and to assist in all phases of the outreach effort.[286] Some misconceptions that were identified in this research were that many people think that *everyone funds wildlife protection work through taxes* (very little general taxes are actually used for this), that *wildlife does not require management by humans to thrive* (they do in the modern world[287]), and that *regulated hunting and fishing lead to the extinction of species* (regulated hunting does not endanger species—that is part of what the regulations are for).

*Identify Outreach Issues:* As indicated previously, part of the Nimrod Society's efforts to get the Michigan Wildlife Council started was the identified outreach issue that the state agency could not, without a steady, reliable funding source, conduct the outreach on its own. Beyond this outreach issue, the Council examined and addressed all other outreach issues, using in-house expertise as well as with the assistance of a marketing firm, Güd Marketing, that was retained for the effort.

*Define Goals and Objectives:* The Michigan legislature identified goals at the outset of the overall outreach effort, and the scheduled meetings of the Council allow existing goals to be adjusted as necessary and further goals to be set. From these goals, objectives were set—based on improvements in key measures from the baseline survey research that was conducted.

*Identify Publics:* The aforementioned baseline survey that was conducted in 2015 assisted in audience segmentation. There is no single "Michigan resident"; rather, there are many audiences in the state. This segmentation is both geographic—for instance, Detroit and Grand Rapids were targeted separately—and by opinion. In particular, the outreach effort identified audiences who were already moderately approving of hunting (but not strongly approving) or neutral about hunting. These audience segments were approached differently, using different media and different messages. Interestingly, one audience that was not ignored consisted of hunters themselves, not to get them to support hunting, as they obviously already do, but to inform them about how they could better portray hunting to non-hunters. Outreach to hunters also focused on informing them of all the benefits hunting provides to the state, including funding support for conservation and jobs and tax revenue from hunter expenditures.

*Understand the Publics:* A baseline survey was conducted, along with focus group research, to help understand each of the audiences that were identified above. Part of understanding the audience is to know what resonates in a *negative* way or to identify things with which the audience is unfamiliar. For instance, it was discovered that those in the Metro Detroit area who were neutral about hunting or who only moderately approved of it did not recognize a hunting blind in the campaign imagery; they also appeared unfamiliar with hunting using archery equipment as well as hunting for species other than deer.

The use of a professional marketing firm allowed the in-house knowledge and data about Michigan's publics to be used in the outreach effort. It is critical to understand the public so that the message and media match the audience—as was meticulously done in this effort. Every state is different, and outreach has to be tailored to both the state as well as the sub-populations within the state.

*Identify, Develop, and Pre-Test Messages:* The messages were crafted by a collaborative effort of the Council and its marketing firm. Through survey and focus group research, these messages and the media to deliver them were thoroughly tested to identify which messages to deliver to which audiences using which media. Part of developing the messages was considering where there was the greatest lack of knowledge—to help prioritize whom to target, which affects which messages to use.

The research showed that terms that resonated include *future generations* and *healthy and thriving wildlife*. Additionally, hunting was overwhelmingly accepted for population control, for food, for habitat protection, and protection of people. The research also showed that the target audience perceived hunting (the activity) differently from hunters (the participants), with many people more supportive of the former than the latter, thinking of hunters as often irresponsible and reckless and even cruel and inhumane.

*Consider Trends:* Ongoing surveys are conducted annually, which started in 2017 (after the initial baseline survey in 2015). Each of these surveys looks at trends in the characteristics of various audiences, as well as trends in their opinions and knowledge levels. Other forms of research are also conducted, such as online bulletin boards and focus groups. These trend surveys and the other research allow the outreach effort to be adjusted in any way necessary.

*Get the Message Across:* The formal campaign started in 2016 and continues today. The outreach effort uses multiple types of media—such as radio, billboards, videos, the Pandora music service, side street billboards, and social media—and targets specific audiences—such as the Detroit metro area, the Grand Rapids area, and people who are only moderately supportive or who are neutral regarding hunting. Importantly, this is not a blanket statewide campaign but is an effort that focuses on specific audiences.

The initial messaging was simple, establishing a connection with the audience, with later phases of the outreach to include more detail about the specific role that hunters and anglers play in conservation. The first phase, in 2016, introduced the Michigan Wildlife Council to the public as a credible source of information and established a connection to the public through wildlife and outdoor enjoyment. The 2017 phase of the outreach introduced the idea that wildlife management is necessary. In 2018, the next phase introduced the message that hunting and fishing licenses are what fund wildlife management. In 2019, the campaign began to introduce other benefits of hunting and fishing, including jobs supported and revenue generated.

*Evaluate the Effort:* Finally, an evaluation component was built into the overall outreach effort, with surveys and other research conducted to see how the audiences are reacting to the outreach and to help assess the effects of the outreach. Key measures are looked at each year to help in the assessment. This allows the outreach to be focused as necessary to reach those who might not have been fully reached previously. This evaluation is necessary, whether it ultimately shows positive results or not.

In this case, several key measures show positive results: for instance, between the baseline survey in 2015 and the first of the continuing annual surveys in 2017, among non-hunters there was a 25 percent increase in the belief that wildlife management by humans is necessary. Additionally, there was an increase in approval of hunting of 14 percent in West Michigan. The annual survey done in 2019 found that half of the state recognizes that wildlife management by humans is necessary, which is a large increase from the 39 percent who agreed with this in 2015. Additionally, between 2015 and 2019, the percentage of state residents agreeing that the hunting and fishing industry contributes significantly to Michigan's economy, and that the hunting and fishing industry creates a significant number of jobs in Michigan, increased by 10 percent. There was also a 10 percent increase in the percentage of residents saying that hunting is an important part of Michigan's culture and heritage.[288]

The ongoing evaluation is important so that necessary adjustments can be made along the way. As indicated by Güd Marketing, "This is a marathon, not a sprint. It takes time to build relevant connections to a relatively disconnected audience. Our belief is that the more informed an audience is on how hunting and fishing impact the things they care about, the greater appreciation they will have for our outdoor activities."[289]

## CASE STUDY #4: LOUISIANA ALLIGATOR MANAGEMENT PROGRAM

Another state-specific case study demonstrates how a deliberate planning and research process can be used to develop specific messages that fill a public knowledge gap. This case study[290] concerns the legal, regulated hunting and farming of alligators in Louisiana and a ban on alligator products that California was considering. In this case, misperceptions and a general lack of knowledge about the health of the American alligator population contributed to public opposition to the use of alligators, despite the current stability and overall health of the alligator population.

Although the ban on alligators and crocodiles in California was to apply to several species, this section primarily concerns the American alligator (*Alligator mississippiensis*) because that is the species in the wild in Louisiana as well as in the state's farms. Any references to alligator are to the American alligator unless otherwise indicated. In the United States, the alligator's range includes all or parts of Alabama, Arkansas, Florida, Georgia, Louisiana, Mississippi, North Carolina, Oklahoma, South Carolina, and Texas.

While the current population of alligators in the United States is stable or increasing, this was not always so. Unregulated harvest of alligators in the early to middle part of the 1900s—note that this is before hunting regulations were instituted, so it is decidedly *not* regulated hunting—had led to its being considered endangered. Louisiana banned the hunting of alligators in 1962 and began a program for alligator recovery.

From that date, there was no alligator season until 1972, when the Louisiana Department of Wildlife and Fisheries (LDWF) instituted an alligator season in some parishes. Hunting was then allowed statewide in 1981 because, by that time, recovery of the American alligator was well underway due to the efforts of the State of Louisiana. Also at this time, alligator farms were raising alligators for harvest in Louisiana.

Alligator populations in Louisiana steadily increased from the 1970s to 1999. Since that time, they have remained stable or have slightly increased from year to year. Today, there are approximately 5 million alligators in the wild in the U.S. Estimates are that over 2 million live in the wild in Louisiana (from a low of about 150,000 in the early 1970s) and 1.5 million live in the wild in Florida (from a low of 100,000 in the early 1970s). Additionally, 500,000 live in the wild in Texas (from a low of 100,000). Now, the LDWF manages the alligator as a commercial, renewable natural resource to be harvested both by hunting them in the wild and through raising them on farms. The harvest of American alligators in Louisiana (and in the other range states) is highly regulated and closely monitored by both state and federal officials.

The Alligator Management Program's overarching goal is to manage and conserve Louisiana's wild alligator populations. Secondary goals that stem from the overarching goal are to benefit wetland ecosystems, benefit associated wildlife species, and benefit coastal landowners and state residents. The philosophy of the Program is species protection, habitat stewardship, sustained use, regulation of harvest, and the provision of economic benefits.

The evidence above shows that the Louisiana Alligator Management Program was a sustainable use program that did not harm alligator populations, but instead helped them. Additionally, other species benefit from the conservation of alligator habitat, including the eastern black rail, alligator snapping turtle, Calcasieu painted crawfish, Pascagoula map turtle, frecklebelly madtom, western chicken turtle, whooping crane, ringed map turtle, and the West Indian manatee. Additionally, alligators help control the populations of marshland herbivores, such as nutria and muskrat, that, if unchecked, would denude the marshes of important plants. Nonetheless, a ban of alligator products was set to become law in California.

In an effort to lift the ban, the state of Louisiana and private industry representatives filed suit in Federal Court (Eastern District of California) seeking an injunction to stop the ban from going into effect, contending that the ban violates the Supremacy Clause, the Commerce Clause, and the Due Process Clause of the U.S. Constitution. On December 27, 2019, a Federal judge temporarily blocked the California ban from taking effect through a temporary restraining order.

At the same time, the Louisiana Wildlife and Fisheries Foundation funded a project to implement an outreach campaign to garner more support of alligator hunting and farming—including among Californians and those who were to vote on the ban.

> People who know that alligator populations are healthy are three times more likely to approve of alligator hunting and three times more likely to approve of alligator farming, compared to those who do not think that alligator populations are healthy. In fact, that correlation—approval of alligator hunting and farming and knowing that the populations are healthy—exceeds in importance almost every demographic characteristic and is almost as important as if the person wears fur.

The formulation of the campaign entailed hiring Responsive Management to conduct research on messaging and audience characteristics. Responsive Management conducted focus groups and a survey to explore the issues. Data from the survey was used to help craft the primary messages, with extensive analyses to find what would resonate.

As part of the overall study, logistic regression analyses were performed on survey data to find the variables most closely linked to approval of alligator hunting and alligator farming. The research found that people who know that alligator populations are healthy are three times more likely to approve of alligator hunting and three times more likely to approve of alligator farming, compared to those who do not think that alligator populations are healthy.[291] In fact, that correlation—approval of alligator hunting and farming and knowing that the populations are healthy—exceeds in importance almost every demographic characteristic and is almost as important as if the person wears fur. Therefore, materials were developed for outreach that included the important message that the alligator population is healthy and stable. This message is one of the most important of all to win support for the utilization of alligators.

This was an incredibly powerful finding—the link between disapproving of alligator hunting and farming and thinking that the alligator was endangered. This misinformation was driving many people's opposition to the alligator industry. Correcting this misinformation was key to

# DEVELOPING FORMAL COMMUNICATIONS PROGRAMS IN SUPPORT OF HUNTING

garnering support of alligator hunting and farming. All the subsequent materials for outreach on this issue emphasized that alligator populations are healthy and stable, putting the science and the methodical steps used to create that campaign into practical use.

**Do you approve or disapprove of legal, regulated hunting of wild alligators?**

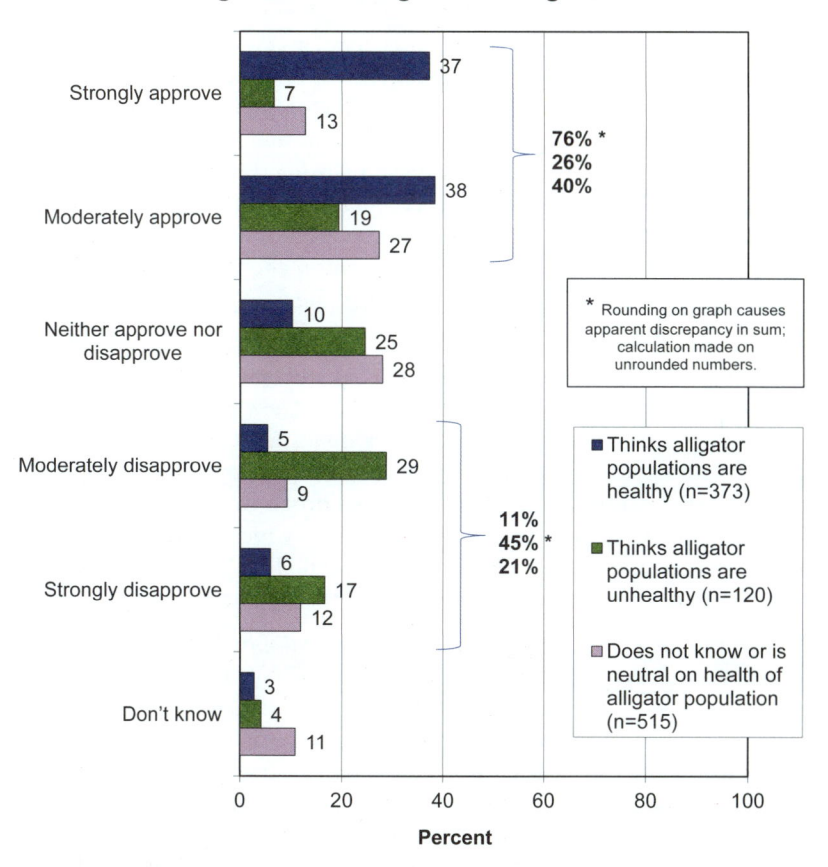

| Response | Thinks alligator populations are healthy (n=373) | Thinks alligator populations are unhealthy (n=120) | Does not know or is neutral on health of alligator population (n=515) |
|---|---|---|---|
| Strongly approve | 37 | 7 | 13 |
| Moderately approve | 38 | 19 | 27 |
| Neither approve nor disapprove | 10 | 25 | 28 |
| Moderately disapprove | 5 | 29 | 9 |
| Strongly disapprove | 6 | 17 | 12 |
| Don't know | 3 | 4 | 11 |

Approve totals: 76%* / 26% / 40%
Disapprove totals: 11% / 45%* / 21%

\* Rounding on graph causes apparent discrepancy in sum; calculation made on unrounded numbers.

*Source: Responsive Management.*[292]

## CASE STUDY #5: RECREATIONAL BOATING AND FISHING FOUNDATION

Participation in fishing and boating declined in the 1980s and 1990s.[293] In response to these declines, states, fisheries administrators, and industry leaders provided input to the Sport Fishing and Boating Partnership Council (SFBPC) in 1997-1998.[294] Congress then passed the Sportfishing and Boating Safety Act, which required the Secretary of the Department of the Interior to implement a National Outreach and Communication Program to address recreational boating and fishing participation and promote conservation and responsible use of the nation's aquatic resources. In response, the Sport Fishing and Boating Partnership Council (SFBPC) developed a strategic plan for the Program, and the Recreational Boating and Fishing Foundation (RBFF) was established in October 1998 to carry out that plan. Dedicated funding for the RBFF is provided through the Sport Fish Restoration and Boating Trust Fund and administered by U.S. Fish and Wildlife Service.

The RBFF's mission is to implement a national outreach strategy to increase participation in recreational fishing and boating. To accomplish this, the RBFF focuses on strategies that recruit new participants, retain current ones, and reactivate lapsed individuals. Increased participation benefits state and federal agencies by increasing license sales and funds to improve conservation and management efforts. Greater participation also benefits the fishing and boating industry by increasing the number of customers and thus increasing revenue. Finally, the RBFF's mission engages consumers to become involved in fishing and boating.

The RBFF utilizes a variety of strategies to support state agencies. To reactivate boaters, agencies employ direct-mail campaigns that encourage individuals to renew their boating license. Similarly, emails are used to remind anglers to renew their fishing license prior to expiration. The RBFF also has a robust grant program that provides agencies with funds to develop or evaluate new R3 programs. *Vamos a Pescar* is another grant that funds agency R3 efforts to increase participation of Hispanics. Additionally, the RBFF directs consumers to agency websites and encourages the purchase of fishing and boating licenses. Finally, the RBFF supports state agencies by providing workshops and webinars to assist agencies with marketing, customer service and consumer engagement.

Recognizing the importance of industry in fishing and boating participation, the RBFF supports manufacturers and retailers with the development and implementation of marketing projects to increase growth. The RBFF's industry support is accomplished through research and partnerships. Consumer research aids industry stakeholders to help them understand the changing demographics of the sport, new markets, and customer trends to inform their decision-making processes. Similarly, the RBFF can also reach new markets by developing partnerships with industry manufacturers and retailers.

The RBFF's takemefishing.org and VamosAPescar.org initiatives may be the most critical ways to engage consumers. These year-long efforts help anglers and boaters learn, plan, and equip for successful experiences. Both websites feature a variety of information including "how-to" videos, state fishing license and boat registration links, and interactive maps that allow visitors to find local fishing and boating locations. The RBFF has also partnered with the Walt Disney World Resort as well as the Boy Scouts of America to diversify the target audiences for fishing and boating information.

Since 1998, the RBFF has taken a strategic approach to increasing participation in fishing and boating. Research, assessments and specific evaluations have allowed the RBFF to employ an adaptive process to identify strengths and weaknesses of efforts, refine programs, and recommend the most effective strategies to increase the recruitment, retention, and reactivation of anglers and boaters.

One example of a strategic effort by the RBFF is the "60 in 60" campaign. The objective of "60 in 60" is to have 60 million anglers in 60 months (2017-2021). At the end of 2019, there were an estimated 49.4 million anglers in the United States.[295] To achieve the objective, the RBFF is working with agencies and industry professionals to increase the number of anglers by 10 million in the final two years of the campaign. This requires strategic efforts based on knowledge and experience from years of R3 activities across the country. For example, the most effective recruitment efforts should target youth, families, and women.[296] The RBFF will also continue to partner with agencies to utilize the best approaches to retain and reactivate anglers. The "60 in 60" campaign exemplifies a results-oriented effort designed to increase fishing.

Fishing participation has increased during the time when R3 angling efforts intensified. In the last three years as of this writing, fishing participation has increased 7.4 percent among youth and 6.6 percent among women, and it has doubled among Hispanics.[297] The sale of fishing licenses nationwide increased 4 percent between the periods 1994-1998 (an average of 37.5 million license sales in those years) to 2015-2019 (an average of 39.1 million license sales in those years).[298]

A variety of factors contribute to the RBFF's successes. Since its beginning, the RBFF has sought to understand what types of anglers and boaters are participating, why they participate, and what drives satisfaction in those participants. Perhaps more importantly, the RBFF strives to understand the issues with non-participation as well as declining participation. Changing demographics in the U.S. have required the RBFF to continually study the effects of societal factors. This greater understanding has allowed the RBFF to prioritize these issues to effectively develop outreach strategies. Implementation of these strategies is the results of goals and clearly defined objectives. Developing specific objectives requires specifying target audiences (i.e., which demographic is the target of a particular R3 activity?). The RBFF encourages program evaluation to assess effectiveness and further refine programs. The RBFF has expertly utilized marketing strategies that have effectively increased awareness and participation. Finally, the RBFF activities focus on program outcomes (did we increase participation, avidity, and investment of anglers) as opposed to program outputs (how many individuals participated in an event).

The number of fishing and boating participants has increased during the past 20 years. Through partnerships with agencies and industry professionals, the RBFF's strategic efforts have played a critical role in recruiting, retaining, and reactivating anglers and boaters.

## Key Takeaways

- Formal communications programs in support of hunting must be developed through a deliberate, orderly, scientific process.

- Organizations should use social science research to develop and test messages, campaign themes, and other outreach material.

- Programs must be evaluated based on outcomes (e.g., actual changes in attitudes or increases in knowledge) and not outputs (e.g., website hits or program registrations).

- States should look to the models of the Michigan Wildlife Council and the Colorado Wildlife Council as effective communications programs that build cultural support for hunting using a systematic planning process.

- Don't rely on the same messages for every audience. While an earlier chapter ranked the most effective arguments for and against hunting, it is inevitable that certain concepts will resonate differently depending on the intended audience of the message or program.

- Use the credibility of fish and wildlife agencies—especially agency personnel in uniform.

- Incorporate an emotional component. Hunting is not just about killing, but includes naturalistic, relaxation, familial, and other social values.

- Enlist a friendly face for hunting advocacy.

- Use messages that rely on strong nature- and wildlife-related imagery.

- Maintain positivity in messaging. Messages that use strong imagery and an emotional component are generally more effective than confrontational messages, which are often distrusted and viewed with skepticism.

- Show the entire face of hunting. The image of a hunter should not be limited to the stereotypical older white male.

## Key Takeaways (continued)

- Do not assume you know the messages and delivery methods that will work without testing them. Revisit, retest, and adapt as you move forward with formal communication strategies.

- Allow outreach time to do its work. Do not expect results overnight.

- Repeat the messages—redundancy works in getting messages across to an audience. Do not forget that, by the time you are tired of giving the same message, your audience may just be catching on.

- Do not plan only for big media. Think of all the media available for messaging. In particular, do not ignore social media.

- Enlist the help of marketing and communications professionals, if your organization needs assistance.

# CHAPTER 11

# *Talking About Hunting: Don'ts and Dos*

**THIS CHAPTER USES ALL OF** *the lessons of the research and information presented up to this point to explain the most effective ways to talk about hunting. The chapter details what to say and how to say it, including the most important points and concepts to communicate in order to build cultural support for hunting. The chapter is straightforward, giving concrete advice on communicating about hunting, based on all of the research detailed in the previous chapters. As a compendium of all the research, few citations are included in this chapter—most of the information given is fully cited in previous chapters.*

## General Comments

Promoting hunting is not a matter of dramatically changing most Americans' hearts and minds; rather, it is about affirming core values that they already have (about meat consumption, about the use of animals, about conservation, about family and friends, about ethics) and bringing to the forefront widely held opinions and attitudes about hunting.

Therefore, remember what the current research says. Hunters already have the facts on their side. Most of the American public consents to the use of animals, provided that the animals do not experience undue pain and suffering. Most of the American public approves of hunting in general; approval of hunting specifically for the meat is even higher. The overwhelming majority of Americans consume meat and use products derived from animals. Just under half of all Americans live in a household with a firearm. And more than 11 million Americans go hunting each year—hunting is not a fringe activity.

**How to Talk About Hunting** ⊕ *Research-Based Communications Strategies*

The following specific advice for how to talk about hunting covers the tone and types of messages that resonate—the things to talk about—as well as the words and phrases to use.

## Tone of Discussion

- Be patient when speaking about hunting. While Americans care about conservation, they do not know much about wildlife or hunting, including even basic information about wildlife management. Consider that almost half of Americans feel that hunting as practiced today can cause some species to become endangered or extinct. Many people do not understand how highly regulated hunting is.

- Remember the importance of *ethos*, *pathos*, and *logos*. Ethos refers to credibility; pathos refers to emotion; and logos refers to logic. Building support for hunting depends on communications that incorporate all three elements. This extends even to the tone of discussions about hunting: strengthening cultural acceptance of hunting requires advocates who are trustworthy and knowledgeable but, as importantly, empathetic.

- When talking to non-hunters about hunting, focus on common values and motivations rather than just providing information about hunting. Values shared by hunters and non-hunters might include self-sufficiency and social responsibility; common motivations might include the desire to maintain stable wildlife populations and healthy habitat, or interest in finding healthy organic foods. Encouraging non-hunters to think about hunting in terms of values and motivations they share with hunters will help position hunting as the best method of achieving a common goal.

- View all communications through the animal rights-animal welfare-dominionism continuum explained in detail in Chapter 5. Communications that are perceived as dominionistic (exerting mastery and control over animals) will be rejected. Communications that are based on an animal welfare philosophy (that animals can be used as long as they do not suffer undue pain and suffering) are more likely to be accepted. This includes how you talk about wildlife (avoid inflammatory expressions like, "if it flies, it dies" or "if it's brown, it's down"). Hunters must show respect for wildlife and the animals they harvest. Viewing communications through this continuum also should affect your behavior in the field (always practice ethical hunting within the boundaries of laws and regulations). Most importantly, hunters must not cede the middle ground of animal welfare to animal rights extremists: hunting is consistent with animal welfare and the views of the vast majority of Americans; the animal rights philosophy, on the other hand, is not.

- Keep in mind that, as the United States continues to modernize in terms of urbanization and increases in education, income, and overall population, wildlife values are likely to continue shifting: Americans have moved from having primarily traditionalist views about wildlife (that wildlife should be managed by humans) to more mutualistic views (that wildlife and humans ought to coexist). This shift impacts how people view the need for wildlife management—as professor of wildlife management Dr. David E. Samuel notes, the North American Model of Wildlife Conservation revolves around the utilitarian use of animals, which is incompatible with the increasingly common sentiment of wanting to protect individual animals.[299] Advocates of hunting must be prepared to thoughtfully respond to this mindset.

- Peer influence matters. Don't be afraid to talk about hunting. For many people, hunting must be demystified. Hunters should be open about the reasons why they hunt and the benefits hunting provides.

- Tell stories. A story is generally the best way to transmit information. Non-hunters will gain a better understanding of hunting through firsthand stories from hunters that emphasize knowledge and love of wildlife and nature.

- Maintain positivity in communications. A positive tone communicates openness, inclusivity, and optimism. Messages delivered in a positive tone will make people more likely to *hear* what is being said. Positive messages are more effective than confrontational messages, the latter which are often distrusted and viewed with skepticism.

- Don't use inflammatory language or a defensive or combative tone. Don't denigrate or disparage someone for having a different viewpoint on hunting than you do. In posts and in conversation, communicate respect for others and for wildlife.

- Assist people in making a direct connection to hunting—by sharing game meat, serving game at dinners and parties, and helping them recall relatives or friends they know who hunt.

*Black bear populations are increasing due to successful management efforts by state fish and wildlife agencies. These efforts include forest management programs to provide more food for bears, regulated hunting seasons, ongoing population surveys, and conservation easements from private landowners to increase bear habitat.*[300]

## Messages and Outreach

The above looked at the way the communications should be framed. Now we look at the messages and themes that are effective at building more support for hunting. This starts with the benefits that hunting provides, which are important to emphasize, particularly to non-hunters. As botanist and zoologist Ann Causey notes, it is reasonable for non-hunters to insist that "non-trivial reasons be given for intentional human-inflicted injuries or deaths [to animals]."[301] Explaining the benefits of hunting is the way to supply these non-trivial reasons. This discussion starts with the benefits in general before moving to more specific benefits.

### BENEFITS OF HUNTING IN GENERAL

- Focus on the benefits of hunting, not the fallacies of anti-hunters. Promotion of hunting should communicate the activity as a source of food, as a wildlife management tool, and as a stimulus for conservation.

## CONSERVATION

- Inform non-hunters that regulated hunting does not cause species to become endangered or extinct. Thinking that this is so is a very important factor in some people's opposition to hunting. Emphasize that no wildlife species in the United States has become endangered or extinct from hunting during modern wildlife management times. As author James Swan notes, "Since the early 1900s, many of the most popular game species in the United States have become more abundant, thanks to the curtailing of market hunting, the development of scientific wildlife management to determine seasons and limits, and the help from revenues generated by the sales of hunting licenses and equipment that have been used for habitat protection and restoration."[302]

- Emphasize the integral role that hunting plays in conservation, both historically as well as today. Bridge the gap between hunters and conservationists who do not hunt. People who identify as environmentalists or conservationists but who do not hunt still share many values with hunters. For example, both groups care about the protection of lands from development for future generations, and both groups care about the health of habitat and species populations. This again highlights the importance of common interests and motivations that demonstrate that hunters are not out of step with mainstream Americans.

- Communicate that hunters were at the forefront of the conservation movement that brought many species back from being endangered to being healthy and stable. Hunters contribute to the long-term sustainability of both game and non-game species. This latter point is important, as a common anti-hunting fallacy is the idea that hunters only care about (and provide funding for) species that they can hunt—this is not the case.

- Hunting pays for much of the funding for conservation throughout the United States, as well as North America as a whole and many places in the world.

- Every fish and wildlife agency in the U.S. is legally mandated to sustainably manage wildlife and provide hunting opportunities. These agencies have been charged to protect the wildlife resource from the wanton exploitation of wildlife before regulations were put in place. These agencies and the laws, regulations, and wildlife management efforts put in place are responsible for bringing back numerous wildlife species from the brink of extinction. Hunting is an important wildlife management tool that federal and state fish and wildlife agencies use to the benefit of both species that are hunted and non-game species. Hunting is also used to help manage habitats that benefit all species.

- Remember that an expansion of the conservation base benefits everyone, wildlife most of all. As state and federal agencies increasingly consider diversified sources of funding to pay for wildlife management, hunters should be prepared to welcome and encourage support from non-hunters who are similarly committed to conservation. In turn, non-hunters must recognize the commitments and contributions of hunters. With this in mind, it is less important for hunters to prove that they contribute the *most* to conservation than to simply show that they contribute *substantially* to conservation (the figures regarding hunters' financial contributions to wildlife management cited in Chapter 1 speak for themselves). The most important point is that hunting has been a vital part of the overall web of wildlife conservation measures in the United States for a century—hunters and non-hunting conservationists are not working at cross purposes; rather, they are enjoined by the common goal of maintaining healthy wildlife populations and habitat.

## WILDLIFE MANAGEMENT

- This topic is related to conservation in that wildlife management is a tool used in conservation as a whole. Hunting is one of the most important tools used by agencies to manage wildlife and habitat.

- Emphasize the ecological and habitat benefits of hunting over the human-centered ones (with the exception of food as an acceptable human-centered reason to hunt). While hunting for recreation, for instance, is supported by most Americans, more Americans support wildlife-centered reasons for hunting over human-centered reasons.

- One of the most supported reasons for hunting, among those who do not initially approve of hunting, is if hunting "means that the overall health of the ecosystem will be better"—a concept entirely dependent on properly balanced wildlife populations.

- Some people will not support hunting, even when used as a wildlife management tool and even if the absence of hunting means that some species will become overpopulated. To these people, emphasize the harm that overbrowsing by deer, for instance, can do to ecosystems—to the detriment of many other species including the extirpation of some of these other species because they have no food.

## FOOD FOR THE TABLE

- Among Americans as a whole, approval of hunting is highest when it is done for the meat. Of all the reasons people hunt, this one has the highest approval—nine out of ten Americans approve of hunting for food. Messaging to promote hunting should capitalize on the existing strong rate of approval among Americans for this motivation for hunting.

- One way to emphasize that hunting provides food and to connect non-hunters with hunters is to share game meat with others.

- Many people prefer that their meat be from hunting rather than from modern farming. Hunting is a source of quality, organic, naturally replenished food from free-range animals. Talk about the quality of the game meat.

  + Factory farming and the practices of the industrialized meat industry are a major concern among many Americans. Some say that animals that are hunted live better lives than domesticated livestock. Use this existing concern in communications; make comparisons of the life of a game species versus life of livestock on a factory farm.

- Hunting is integral to the locavore diet. The locavore movement—a blanket phrase describing support for any locally sourced foods, including hunting one's own food—is considered by many to be a solution to the problem of "food miles" (the distance food travels from producer to consumer) and the problem of meat being produced through inhumane methods or unsanitary conditions. Hunting satisfies the desire to become more self-sufficient in procuring one's own food. There are also important food security issues involved in obtaining one's own meat.

- As an element of a communications campaign, the locavore theme can unite disparate groups (e.g., mainstream Americans, animal rights supporters, millennials, hunter/angler conservationists) by capitalizing on a common interest and belief. Even some ardent animal rights proponents support the idea of people hunting for their own food.

## ETHICS

- Emphasize that hunting is highly regulated. Furthermore, the funds to pay for the enforcement of those regulations are paid for by the hunters themselves.

- Show how hunters are ethical, responsible, and compassionate (and hunt that way, as well). Show that hunters care about species as a whole and that they respect the wildlife they hunt. This goes hand in hand with conservation.

  + Note that many Americans dislike social media posts of hunters posing with their animals. This is not to say that hunters should not post such photos, but the poses with the animals should show respect. And hunters should at least be aware that not all people will look favorably on the posts. Hunters should also consider photo subjects other than the harvested animal, such as nature scenery, fellow hunters and family members, or prepared game meat.

- Link hunting in America to fair chase. Any hunting in America that does not involve fair chase is a fringe hunting activity—not widely done and opposed by many hunters themselves. Emphasizing fair chase is very important in all communications about hunting.

- Emphasize that hunters seek to limit the pain and suffering of animals. Ethical hunters track any game that they have wounded to complete the hunt. Hunters are keenly aware of the importance of a quick, clean kill.

- Nearly all hunters consume the meat obtained from hunting. The meat represents a local, natural source of food. Meat sourced through hunting is often seen as more ethical than meat obtained through factory farming. Hunting that does not include the consumption of the animal is less supported than hunting where food is one of the primary reasons for hunting.

  + The locavore movement—an environmental movement at heart as well as a dietary lifestyle—embraces hunting to supply organic, local meat.

- Separate hunting in general from trophy hunting. Support for trophy hunting among Americans is low relative to support for hunting for any other reason. Only 1 percent of U.S. hunters hunt primarily for a trophy. However, defining all hunting as trophy hunting is a powerful communications tool for anti-hunters because of the pervasive assumption that trophy hunting includes the wanton waste of wildlife, is done largely for human-centered benefits, and is responsible for the decimation of wildlife populations. In reality, this is not what trophy hunting is; however, this is a widely held belief among most Americans and a belief that communications must confront when the term is used as a weapon against ethical, legal, regulated hunting.

+ When necessary in a debate about hunting, have your opponent define "trophy hunting." This can show that most hunting in America is not trophy hunting.

+ In clarifying trophy hunting, inform people that all states have strict laws against the wanton waste of game harvested through hunting—in other words, it is not legal to harvest an animal for its trophy horns or antlers while leaving the rest of the animal.

+ When trophy hunting is discussed, link it to the benefits it provides—including the monetary and conservation benefits it provides to local communities.

⊕ Assure non-hunters that ethical hunting is a safe activity. Although surveys show that a slight majority of Americans think that hunting is more dangerous than other popular sports, the statistics actually show that hunting has a low rate of injury compared to many of these other sports. Just as many non-hunters do not realize the extent to which hunting is regulated, many also do not realize that new hunters are required to complete an extensive safety education course. Hearing about hunter education requirements can be eye-opening for non-hunters.

⊕ Separate *poaching* from *hunting*. Legal, regulated hunting is the antithesis of poaching. In fact, funding from hunters is what pays the salaries of game wardens and wildlife officers who fight against poaching. As part of this strategy, the phrase, "illegal hunting," should never be used, as the illegal hunting of animals should always be referred to as what it is—poaching. Poachers are criminals, the opposite of law-abiding people engaging in state-sanctioned regulated hunting.

⊕ Finally regarding ethics, walk the walk. Every current hunter should be aware of the ambassadorship role he or she plays on behalf of hunting. Lead by a good example, and don't be the bad example used by opponents of hunting. Botanist and zoologist Ann Causey notes the importance that hunters both act and think ethically: moral hunting requires not just "a change of appearance or vocabulary but a change in mindset, a deepening of values."[303] Another view comes from writer Jim Posewitz: the ethical hunter is one who "knows and respects the animal hunted, follows the law, and behaves in a way that will satisfy what society expects of him or her as a hunter."[304]

## Customizing the Messages for Certain Audiences

- Attitudes about hunting vary by demographic segment of the American population. For this reason, messages should be customized and targeted whenever possible.

- The general messaging themes that work the best in support of hunting are hunting as a food source, hunting as conservation (i.e., hunting as a form of wildlife management that produces ecological benefits to both game and non-game species), and hunting as a right.

- The general messaging themes that garner the most *opposition* to hunting are hunting as a violation of fair chase, hunting being linked to trophy hunting, and hunting resulting in diminished wildlife populations. Advocates of hunting should be knowledgeable about ways to rebut these concepts.

- Don't rely on the same messages for every audience. While an earlier chapter ranked the most effective arguments for and against hunting, it is inevitable that certain concepts will resonate differently depending on the group or person. What is compelling in a conversation with a neighbor may not win over the crowd at a formal debate. The key is to know the audience and adjust the message accordingly.

- Research regarding the stages of children's perceptions of animals should guide communications about hunting with youth: the period from second to fifth grade is marked primarily by emotional concern for animals; factual and cognitive understanding of animals increases between fifth and eighth grades; finally, ethical and ecological concerns about animals develop between eighth and eleventh grades.

- Acknowledge that hunting participation may not be for everyone; focus on getting support for hunting. It is not necessary to make hunters out of all non-hunters; the primary focus of hunting communications should be to garner more support for hunting. Participation may follow but is secondary to increasing cultural support for hunting.

- Bridge the gap between hunters and non-hunting recreationists. While a relatively small percentage of Americans hunt, tens of millions of Americans enjoy hiking, camping, and viewing wildlife. These activities benefit from the healthy habitat and wild, undeveloped areas made possible through the funding provided by hunters. These audiences need to hear that part of the hunting story. The expansion of the wildlife conservation community to include non-hunting groups is not a bad thing since the result will be what hunters themselves have always strived for: the effective conservation of the nation's wildlife resources.

## Persuasive Strategies and Tactics

- Frame discussions about hunting around the need to manage and maintain wildlife in the first place (i.e., it is not a question of *whether* people should intervene in nature, but *how*). If people are receptive to the need to manage wildlife, hunting can be shown as a logical way to go about doing this.

- Keep in mind the difference between *offensive* arguments (which explain why something is good) and *defensive* arguments (which explain why something is *not that bad*). Defensive arguments can help rebut damaging claims against hunting, but offensive arguments are ultimately what change minds. This underscores the importance of using offensive arguments to clearly articulate the benefits of hunting.

- Don't let anti-hunters use offensive arguments to claim the moral high ground. Hunting advocates should lead with their own strong offensive arguments explaining why hunting is the ethical thing to do (not merely a defensible thing to do).

- Practice rebutting points made by anti-hunters using *link turns* (which communicate the idea, "the thing you think we cause, we actually prevent") or *impact turns* (which communicate the idea, "the thing you think we decrease, we actually increase"). For example, a skillful rebuttal in defense of hunting might point out that hunting, instead of leading to diminished wildlife populations, actually funds wildlife conservation and ensures the sustainability of both game and nongame species.

- When discussing hunting, stay on point and remain focused on the relevant topics. Hunting opponents will sometimes intentionally make

- comments to derail the discussion; it is not necessary to humor every nonsensical or outlandish claim with a thoughtful response.
- Be prepared to reframe discussions or debates about hunting if anti-hunters lead the conversation astray. Practice pivoting to the true issue at stake through which hunting is a means to an end (e.g., hunting as an effective wildlife management tool or hunting as a way to obtain food).
- To strengthen arguments about hunting, consider appealing to credible historical figures such as Aldo Leopold or Theodore Roosevelt, or employing useful examples that demonstrate hunting to be a necessity (e.g., instances in which hunting has reduced deer-vehicle collisions).
- Listen carefully to arguments from the opposing side and identify any common ground with anti-hunters (e.g., concern for healthy wildlife populations). However, be consistent when arguing for hunting—do not undermine the legitimacy of legal, regulated hunting by flip-flopping on points.
- Communicate that conservation requires a pragmatic focus on wildlife populations as a whole, not selective outrage over certain animals or events. Do not let anti-hunters frame discussions about hunting in terms of a narrow definition of morality.

## Words and Phrases That Resonate

- When talking about hunting, use the phrase, *legal, regulated hunting*. It is well received because it separates ethical hunting from poaching. It conveys that hunting is carefully managed.
- Employ other words and phrases known to resonate—for example, use the phrase, *healthy wildlife populations*. Other terms known to resonate with Americans include *lifestyle, efficient, investment, balance,* and *independent*. (See Chapter 2 for more detail on this.)
- Ecological reasons for hunting are well supported. Use terms that show the ecological benefits of hunting.
- Many Americans have a high concern for habitat in the United States. Talk about *healthy habitat* and that hunting plays a role in protecting habitat.
- When talking about huntable wildlife, the term, *game*, may turn some people off by appearing to trivialize the animal (again, note

the importance of avoiding terms and actions that are seen as dominionistic). The term, *wildlife*, often can substitute.

- One concept that many Americans respond well to is "does not use taxpayer dollars." There is much concern about taxes and government spending in today's world. The fact that many fish and wildlife agencies do not use general taxes will be well received; communications should emphasize that "general taxes are not used" by many fish and wildlife agencies.

## Formal Communications Programs and Spokespersons

- Programs to improve cultural acceptance of hunting should not be confused with programs to increase participation in hunting. These are different types of programs with different goals.
- Formal communications programs in support of hunting must be developed through a deliberate, orderly, scientific process.
- Organizations should use social science research to develop and test messages, campaign themes, and other outreach material.
- States should look to the models of the Michigan Wildlife Council and the Colorado Wildlife Council as effective creators of communications programs that build cultural support for hunting using a systematic planning process. These organizations are also excellent models because they are funded through automatic surcharges on hunting licenses, meaning that they have dedicated and reliable funding for their communications efforts.
- The most effective communications will be concise, positive messages that make strong use of imagery and include language that extols the key benefits of hunting: above all, hunting as a good food source and hunting as a tool for conservation and wildlife management.
- Fortunately, hunting, as an activity to be promoted through imagery, has a clear advantage over many other activities: intrinsic to the activity is the imagery of the natural world—landscapes, forests, vistas, water bodies, and wildlife all make potentially strong and eye-catching subjects. Indeed, the captivating and appealing nature of wildlife/nature imagery will likely be appreciated even more as America becomes increasingly urbanized.

- Incorporate an emotional component in messaging. *Pathos,* or emotion, is one of the critical components of any argument or message that resonates. In the case of hunting, the emotional component might relate to compassion for wildlife or strong family ties, to name two examples. Hunting is not just about killing—it encompasses naturalistic, familial, and other social values that hold emotional resonance with Americans.

- Positive communications are more effective than negative communications. However, the time to "go negative" on behalf of hunting is in courtrooms and capitol buildings, when legal decisions and legislative victories depend on the strength of the argument. But the potentially vociferous nature of arguments about hunting in these venues should be separated from the tone of promotional campaign messages (and general communications), which should remain positive.

- When possible, use the trustworthiness that fish and wildlife agency personnel have among Americans in general—including non-hunting Americans. Personnel from both federal and state agencies are seen as credible, especially game wardens and biologists in uniform. Unfortunately, local sportsmen's organizations and some nonprofits are not as widely respected, as they are generally seen as having biases. Use of an organization that is not trusted runs the risk of turning off people before they even hear the message.

- Diversity in spokespersons will help reach audiences that need outreach. People are more receptive to messages when they feel that they have a connection with the speaker. If hunting is to survive into the future, it cannot be viewed as being strictly the province of older white men—hunting is for everyone. As noted in Chapter 10, people buy things and engage in activities in which they see themselves.

- Be mindful that social media is a double-edged sword. It provides a cost-effective way to disseminate messages and imagery, but it can also provide an avenue for backlash. At the same time, responses on social media can give the impression that certain views (such as vocal opposition to hunting) are more widely held than they actually are. Perhaps most important is the need for advocates of hunting to maintain control over the messages and images they post to social media: promoting hunting through social media means being ready to correct misperceptions, explain the benefits of hunting, and demonstrate that hunters share many of the same values and motivations as most Americans.

# Endnotes

[1] Desmond Tutu, at an address at the Nelson Mandela Foundation in Houghton, Johannesburg, South Africa, on November 23, 2004. The quotation has also been attributed to the prophet Micah.

[2] Almost all active hunters (97 percent) in one study indicated that they and/or their family eat the animals they kill, as documented in: Responsive Management / National Shooting Sports Foundation. 2008. *The Future of Hunting and the Shooting Sports: Research-Based Recruitment and Retention Strategies*. Produced for the U.S. Fish and Wildlife Service under Grant Agreement CT-M-6-0. Harrisonburg, VA.

[3] Basic nationwide hunter characteristics, including expenditures, were taken from the most recent *National Survey of Fishing, Hunting, and Wildlife-Associated Recreation*. Additionally, the total multiplier effect of employee wages and other economic activity is closer to $36 billion—as documented in the 2018 Southwick/NSSF report *Hunting in America: An Economic Force for Conservation*, available at https://www.southwickassociates.com/wp-content/uploads/2018/09/Hunting-in-America-2018.pdf.

[4] Kellert, S.R. 1996. *The Value of Life: Biological Diversity and Human Society*. Island Press/Shearwater Books, Washington D.C.

[5] See "Florida's Bear Control Plan Leaves Hunting on the Table" https://www.orlandoweekly.com/Blogs/archives/2019/12/12/floridas-bear-control-plan-leaves-hunting-on-the-table and "Bear Hunting Petition Reignites 20-Year-Old Debate Over Baiting" https://www.pressherald.com/2020/07/08/bear-hunting-petition-reignites-20-year-old-debate-over-baiting/#.

[6] Intelligence Squared debate: "Do hunters conserve wildlife?" https://www.intelligencesquaredus.org/debates/hunters-conserve-wildlife#:~:text=Hunters%20conserve%20wildlife%2C%20they%20say%2C%20they%20argue.&text=%22No%2C%22%20to%20this%20statement,U.S.%20I'm%20John%20Donvan.

[7] Two studies were used for this finding:
Responsive Management. 2017. *The American Public's Attitudes Toward Animal Rights, Animal Welfare, and Hunting*. Harrisonburg, VA.
Responsive Management. 2019. *Sport Shooting Participation in the United States in 2018*. Produced for the NSSF. Harrisonburg, VA.

[8] Two sources are used here:
McKie, R. 2012, September 22. "Humans Hunted for Meat 2 Million Years Ago." *The Guardian*. Accessed online August 24, 2020. Available at https://www.theguardian.com/science/2012/sep/23/human-hunting-evolution-2million-years.

Ghose, T. 2013, May 14. "Earliest Evidence of Human Hunting Found." *LiveScience*. Accessed online August 17, 2020. Available at https://www.livescience.com/31974-earliest-human-hunters-found.html#:~:text=Archaeologists%20have%20unearthed%20what%20could,least%202%20million%20years%20ago.

[9] Two sources are used here:
Specific data on the amount of game meat produced by hunters annually are available in *The Wild Harvest Initiative's Annual Report No. 3*—2018, produced by Conservation Visions. Accessed online August 18, 2020. Available at https://www.apos.ab.ca/media/community/2018%20WHI%20Annual%20Report.pdf.
The extrapolation of individual meals is from a March 2020 press release from the National Wildlife Federation detailing its partnership with The Wild Harvest Initiative; see https://www.nwf.org/Outdoors/Blog/3_23_20_NWF_Partner_with_the_Wild_Harvest_Initiative_to_Promotes_Wild_Food_and_Conservation.

[10] Responsive Management, 2011. *Americans' Attitudes Toward Hunting, Fishing, and Target Shooting*. Conducted for the National Shooting Sports Foundation. Harrisonburg, VA.

[11] Duda, M.D.; M.F. Jones; and A. Criscione. 2010. *The Sportsman's Voice: Hunting and Fishing in America*. Venture Publishing, PA.

[12] Responsive Management / National Shooting Sports Foundation. 2008. *The Future of Hunting and the Shooting Sports: Research-Based Recruitment and Retention Strategies*. Produced for the U.S. Fish and Wildlife Service under Grant Agreement CT-M-6-0. Harrisonburg, VA.

[13] 2020 survey of fish and wildlife agency personnel conducted by Responsive Management in partnership with the American Sportfishing Association under a Multistate Conservation Grant. Overall, the survey found 95% of agency employees approving of legal hunting. Other survey questions found 97% approving of hunting for the meat, 95% approving of hunting for wildlife management, 91% approving of hunting to get locally sourced food, 86% approving of hunting to get organic meat, 78% approving of hunting for the challenge, 74% approving of hunting for the sport, 73% approving of hunting to protect property, 65% approving of hunting to protect humans from harm, and 53% approving of hunting for a trophy.

[14] Congressional Sportsmen's Foundation overview of "Right to Hunt, Fish, and Harvest Wildlife." Retrieved at http://congressionalsportsmen.org/policies/state/right-to-hunt-fish.

[15] Organ, J.F.; V. Geist; S.P. Mahoney; S. Williams; P.R. Krausman; G.R. Batcheller; T.A. Decker; R. Carmichael; P. Nanjappa; R. Regan; R.A. Medellin; R. Cantu; R.E. McCabe; S. Craven; G.M. Vecellio; and D.J. Decker. 2012. "The North American Model of Wildlife Conservation." *The Wildlife Society Technical Review* 12-04. The Wildlife Society, Bethesda, Maryland.

[16] Shane Mahoney is a wildlife conservation writer, lecturer, scientist, and hunter. This is taken from an article, "The Myth of Eden" in his series, "Conservation Matters" written for the Fall 2011 *Mountain Hunter Magazine*, pages 32-37.

## ENDNOTES

[17] For an overview of the Wildlife Restoration Act, including the amendments listing the various excise taxes, see the summary from the U.S. Fish and Wildlife Service at https://www.fws.gov/laws/lawsdigest/FAWILD.HTML.

[18] This quotation from Senator Malcolm Wallop is from the May 26, 1983, *Congressional Record* as recounted in Lonnie L. Williamson's "Evolution of a Landmark Law" from *Restoring America's Wildlife*, published in 1987 to commemorate the 50th anniversary of the Pittman-Robertson Act. Sen. Wallop co-sponsored an amendment to the Act (the Wallop-Brieux Amendment) that also taxed motorboat fuel and boating/boating-related sales analogous to the Pittman-Robertson tax on ammunition and firearms.

[19] Pittman-Robertson Wildlife Restoration budget justification document (2013). See https://www.fws.gov/budget/2013/PDF%20Files%20FY%202013%20Greenbook/24.%20Wildlife%20Restoration.pdf.

[20] The summary of the requirement that hunting license revenue be used only for the work of state fish and wildlife agencies, and the observation that Pittman-Robertson has done more for wildlife than any other legislation, are from the essay "Evolution of a Landmark Law," by Lonnie L. Williamson—the essay appeared in the book *Restoring America's Wildlife* (1987), prepared in cooperation with the wildlife agencies of the states and territories and published by the U.S. Department of the Interior and the U.S. Fish and Wildlife Service. U.S. Government Printing Office, Washington, D.C.

[21] Summary of the two Multistate Conservation Grant Programs from the Association of Fish and Wildlife Agencies; see https://www.fishwildlife.org/afwa-informs/multi-state-conservation-grants-program.

[22] The figures cited in this paragraph are from the Congressional Research Service report *Pittman-Robertson Wildlife Restoration Act: Understanding Apportionments for States and Territories*. 2019, April. Accessed online August 14, 2020. Available at https://fas.org/sgp/crs/misc/R45667.pdf.

[23] Data on acreage set aside is from a Pittman-Robertson Wildlife Restoration budget justification document, 2013. See page WR-3 in the document available at https://www.fws.gov/budget/2013/PDF%20Files%20FY%202013%20Greenbook/24.%20Wildlife%20Restoration.pdf. State acreage was obtained from the U.S. Census Bureau.

[24] Sources: National Wild Turkey Federation (wild turkey pop.); Quality Deer Management Association (white-tailed deer pop.); Ducks Unlimited, https://www.ducks.org/Conservation/Waterfowl-Research-Science/Wood-Duck-Boxes, and the U.S. Fish and Wildlife Service, https://www.fws.gov/southeast/wildlife/birds/wood-duck/ (duck pop.); Rocky Mountain Elk Foundation (Rocky Mountain elk pop.); World Wildlife Fund (pronghorn antelope pop.); Wild Sheep Foundation (bighorn sheep pop.); U.S. Fish and Wildlife Service (bald eagle pop.).

[25] The State Conservation Machine 2017. Product of the Association of Fish & Wildlife Agencies and the Arizona Game and Fish Department. Data collected September 2014–August 2015, published 2017.

[26] US Fish and Wildlife Service National Hunting License Data—Calculation Year 2020. See https://www.fws.gov/wsfrprograms/subpages/licenseinfo/Natl%20Hunting%20License%20Report%202020.pdf.

27 The State Conservation Machine. 2017. Product of the Association of Fish & Wildlife Agencies and the Arizona Game and Fish Department. Data collected September 2014–August 2015.

28 U.S. Fish and Wildlife Service Kulm WMD overview of the Federal Duck Stamp program. Accessed online August 21, 2020. Available at https://www.fws.gov/nwrs/threecolumn.aspx?id=2147537855#:~:text=Since%201934%2C%20the%20sales%20of,Service's%20National%20Wildlife%20Refuge%20System.

29 U.S. Department of the Interior press release: "Visitor Spending at National Wildlife Refuges Boosts Local Economies by $3.2 Billion." 2019, July 9. Accessed online August 21, 2020. Available at https://www.doi.gov/pressreleases/visitor-spending-national-wildlife-refuges-boosts-local-economies-32-billion.

30 Rocky Mountain Elk Foundation press release: "RMEF Celebrates 35 Years of Conservation." 2019, May 14. Accessed online August 21, 2020. Available at https://www.rmef.org/elk-network/rmefcelebrates35yearsofconservation/.

31 Delta and American Ban Big Game Trophies as Airline Freight. August 3, 2015; see https://www.npr.org/sections/thetwo-way/2015/08/03/429088940/delta-will-ban-big-game-trophies-as-airline-freight.

32 Chaney, R. 2019, May 9. Google clarifies: Hunting ads OK. Accessed online August 18, 2020. Available at https://www.spokesman.com/stories/2019/may/09/google-clarifies-hunting-ads-ok/.

33 The Maine Department of Inland Fisheries and Wildlife opposed Question 1, a 2014 bear hunting referendum. The referendum received funding and support from the Humane Society of the United States. See https://www.nhpr.org/post/maine-opposing-sides-gear-battle-over-bear-hunting-referendum#stream/0. For more on the agency's opposition to the bear hunting referendum, see https://bangordailynews.com/2014/10/22/politics/elections/judge-maine-wildlife-department-can-campaign-on-bear-hunting-question/.

34 Several sources are used here:
Holyoke, J. 2013, September 23. "Maine Bear Hunting Referendum Opponents Unveil Coalition." *Bangor Daily News*. Accessed online August 15, 2020. https://bangordailynews.com/2013/09/23/news/maine-bear-hunting-referendum-opponents-unveil-coalition/.
Holyoke, J. 2013, August 7. "Groups Join in Effort for New Maine Bear Hunting Referendum." *Bangor Daily News*. Accessed online August 15, 2020. https://bangordailynews.com/2013/08/07/news/groups-join-in-effort-for-new-maine-bear-hunting-referendum/.
Sarnacki, A. 2014, August 11. "Visit by U.S. Humane Society President Brings National View to Maine's Bear Baiting Vote." *Bangor Daily News*. Accessed online August 15, 2020. https://bangordailynews.com/2014/08/11/news/visit-by-u-s-humane-society-president-brings-national-view-to-maines-bear-baiting-vote/.

35 Lautenschlager, R.A., and R.T. Bowyer. 1985. "Wildlife Management by Referendum: When Professionals Fail to Communicate." *Wildlife Society Bulletin*, Vol. 13, No. 4. (Winter, 1985), pp. 564-570. Available at http://links.jstor.org/sici?sici=0091-7648%28198524%2913%3A4%3C564%3AWMBRWP%3E2.0.CO%3B2-F.

# ENDNOTES

36   Intelligence Squared debate held in May 2016, available at http://intelligencesquaredus.org/debates/past-debates/item/1496-hunters-conserve-wildlife.

37   The reference is to the live audience poll only, as the online audience poll continued to receive votes well after the debate (and is therefore less reliable as an indicator). The live audience poll results are available via the Intelligence Squared website: https://www.intelligencesquaredus.org/debates/hunters-conserve-wildlife.

38   Heberlein, T.A. 2012. *Navigating Environmental Attitudes*. Oxford University Press: New York, NY.

39   Responsive Management. 2017. *The American Public's Attitudes Toward Animal Rights, Animal Welfare, and Hunting*. Harrisonburg, VA.

40   Manfredo, M.J.; L. Sullivan; A.W. Don Carlos; A.M. Dietsch; T.L. Teel; A.D. Bright; and J. Bruskotter. 2018. "America's Wildlife Values: The Social Context of Wildlife Management in the U.S." National report from the research project titled *America's Wildlife Values*. Fort Collins, CO: Colorado State University, Department of Human Dimension of Natural Resources.

41   Schultz, P.W. 2011. "Conservation Means Behavior." *Conservation Biology*, 25(6):1080-1083.

42   Stern, P.C. 2000. "Toward a Coherent Theory of Environmentally Significant Behavior." *Journal of Social Issues*, 56:407–424.

43   Hinke-Sacilotto, I. 2005. *Chincoteague National Wildlife Refuge: An Ecological Treasure*. Big Earth Publishing, Boulder, CO.

44   The list was provided by the U.S. Fish and Wildlife Service.

45   Digest of Federal Resource Laws of Interest to the U.S. Fish and Wildlife Service. 2020. *Federal Aid in Wildlife Restoration Act*. Accessed online August 7, 2020. https://www.fws.gov/laws/lawsdigest/FAWILD.HTML.

46   Rocky Mountain Elk Foundation. 2017. *Hunting Is Conservation – Paid for by Hunters*. Elk Network. Accessed online August 6, 2020. https://www.rmef.org/elk-network/hunting-conservation-paid-hunters/.

47   Two sources discuss the recovery of the bald eagle:
South Carolina Department of Natural Resources. 2020. *South Carolina's Bald Eagles – Past Surveys*. Accessed online August 10, 2020. http://www.dnr.sc.gov/wildlife/baldeagle/pastsurveys.html.
Smithsonian's National Zoo & Conservation Biology Institute. 2020. *Adopt a Bald Eagle*. Accessed online August 10, 2020. https://nationalzoo.si.edu/support/adopt/adopt-bald-eagle.

48   Two sources discuss steps to save the bald eagle:
U.S. Fish and Wildlife Service. 2020. *History of Bald Eagle Decline, Protection and Recovery*. Accessed online August 10, 2020. https://www.fws.gov/midwest/eagle/History/index.html.
American Eagle Foundation. 2020. *Bald Eagle Facts and Information*. Archived from the original on December 6, 2007. Accessed online August 10, 2020. https://web.archive.org/web/20071206030939/http://www.eagles.org/moreabout.html.

49   Two sources are used here:
U.S. Fish and Wildlife Service. 2020. *Fact Sheet: Natural History, Ecology and Recovery*. Accessed online August 10, 2020. https://www.fws.gov/midwest/eagle/Nhistory/biologue.html.
Richie, M. and Edelson, N. 2017, July 3. *Bald Eagles Soaring After Recovery*. Accessed from The National Wildlife Federation online August 10, 2020. https://blog.nwf.org/2017/07/bald-eagles-soaring-after-recovery/.

50   Richie, M. and Edelson, N. 2017, July 3. *Bald Eagles Soaring After Recovery*. Accessed from The National Wildlife Federation online August 10, 2020. https://blog.nwf.org/2017/07/bald-eagles-soaring-after-recovery/.

51   Three sources are cited here:
National Research Council (US) Committee on Agricultural Land Use and Wildlife Resources. 1970. *Land Use and Wildlife Resources, Chapter 8: Legislation and Administration*. Washington (DC): National Academies Press (US). Accessed online August 10, 2020. https://www.ncbi.nlm.nih.gov/books/NBK208748/.
U.S. Fish and Wildlife Service. 2020. *Introduction to Wildlife and Sport Fish Restoration Online Course*. Accessed online August 10, 2020. https://training.fws.gov/courses/WSFR/INT/resources/WSFRnarration.pdf.
Duda, M. D.; M. Jones; and T. Beppler. 2016 September 13. *Hunters' Contributions to U.S. Wildlife Conservation*. https://www.nrahlf.org/articles/2016/9/13/hunters-contributions-to-us-wildlife-conservation/.

52   National Wild Turkey Federation. 2020. *Wild Turkey Population History and Overview*. Accessed online August 10, 2020. https://www.nwtf.org/_resources/dyn/files/75706989za3010574/_fn/Wild+Turkey+Population+History+and+Overview.pdf?Compare.

53   Miller, M. L. 2013, November 26. *Wild Turkey Restoration: The Greatest Conservation Success Story?* Accessed online August 10, 2020. https://blog.nature.org/science/2013/11/26/wild-turkey-restoration-the-greatest-conservation-success-story/.

54   National Wild Turkey Federation. 2020. *Wild Turkey Population History and Overview*. Accessed online August 10, 2020. https://www.nwtf.org/_resources/dyn/files/75706989za3010574/_fn/Wild+Turkey+Population+History+and+Overview.pdf?Compare.
Miller, M. L. 2013, November 26. *Wild Turkey Restoration: The Greatest Conservation Success Story?* Accessed online August 10, 2020. https://blog.nature.org/science/2013/11/26/wild-turkey-restoration-the-greatest-conservation-success-story/.

55   Responsive Management, 2006. *Wyoming Residents' Use of Information Sources Regarding Wildlife Issues*. Conducted for the Wyoming Game and Fish Department. Harrisonburg, VA.

56   Luntz, F. 2006. *Words That Work: It's Not What You Say, It's What People Hear*. Hachette Book Group, New York, NY.

57   Responsive Management / National Shooting Sports Foundation. 2019. *Americans' Attitudes Toward Hunting, Fishing, Sport Shooting, and Trapping*. Conducted for AFWA under Grant Number F19AP00100. Harrisonburg, VA.

# ENDNOTES

[58] Responsive Management. 2017. *The American Public's Attitudes Toward Animal Rights, Animal Welfare, and Hunting.* Harrisonburg, VA.

[59] Responsive Management. 2017. *The American Public's Attitudes Toward Animal Rights, Animal Welfare, and Hunting.* Harrisonburg, VA.

[60] The two studies referenced here include the following:
Cornell University Survey Research Institute. 2013. *Cornell National Social Survey 2013.* CISER version 1. Ithaca, NY: Cornell Institute for Social and Economic Research. (This study measured approval of "regulated hunting.")
Responsive Management. 2013. Unpublished data from study conducted for the Professional Outdoor Media Association. Harrisonburg, VA. (This study measured approval of "legal hunting.")

[61] Responsive Management. 2014. *Washington Residents' Opinions on Bear and Wolf Management and Their Experiences with Wildlife That Cause Problems.* Conducted for the Washington Department of Fish and Wildlife. Harrisonburg, VA.

[62] All material referenced in this section is from the following source: Luntz, Frank. 2007. *Words That Work.* New York, NY: Hyperion.

[63] Responsive Management and Mile Creek Communications. 2016. *Marketing, Communications, and Public Relations Plan for the Maine Department of Inland Fisheries and Wildlife, Division of Information & Education.* Produced for the Maine Department of Inland Fisheries and Wildlife. Harrisonburg, VA.

[64] Responsive Management. 2001. *The Future of Fishing in the United States: Assessment of Needs to Increase Sport Fishing Participation.* Conducted for the International Association of Fish and Wildlife Agencies under Grant Agreement 1448-98210-98-G048. Harrisonburg, VA.

[65] Nunes, Keith. 2020, June 10. "Organic food sales reach $50 billion in 2019." *Food Business News.* Accessed online August 24, 2020. Available at https://www.foodbusinessnews.net/articles/16202-organic-food-sales-reach-50-billion-in-2019

[66] Responsive Management. 2012. *Pennsylvania Residents' Opinions on and Attitudes Toward Deer and Deer Management.* Conducted for the Pennsylvania Game Commission. Harrisonburg, VA.

[67] U.S. Fish and Wildlife Service/U.S. Census Bureau. 2016. *National Survey of Fishing, Hunting, and Wildlife-Associated Recreation.* Washington, D.C.

[68] In addition to the National Survey (cited above), another source was used: U.S. Census Bureau. Age and Sex Composition in the United States: 2016, Table 1. Population by Age and Sex: 2016. Accessed August 13, 2020.

[69] The sources are:
the U.S. Fish and Wildlife Service and the U.S. Census Bureau from the 2016 *National Survey*;
the U.S. Fish and Wildlife Service, which maintains the records of hunting licenses sold in each state;
the National Sporting Goods Association, which is a retailer association that includes tracking participation rates among its efforts on behalf of retailers; and (for the Cornell study) Decker, D.J.; R.C. Stedman; L.R. Larson; and W.F.

Siemer. 2013. "Hunting for Wildlife Management in America." In *The Wildlife Professional*. Published by The Wildlife Society. Spring 2015, pp. 24-29.

70   Responsive Management / National Shooting Sports Foundation. 2008. *The Future of Hunting and the Shooting Sports: Research-Based Recruitment and Retention Strategies*. Produced for the U.S. Fish and Wildlife Service under Grant Agreement CT-M-6-0. Harrisonburg, VA.

71   Decker, D.J.; R.C. Stedman; L.R. Larson; and W.F. Siemer. 2013. "Hunting for Wildlife Management in America." In *The Wildlife Professional*. Published by The Wildlife Society. Spring 2015, pp. 24-29. (https://lrl.people.clemson.edu/WebFiles/Decker.etal.2015_TWP-HuntinginAmerica.pdf)

72   U.S. Census Bureau. Age and Sex Composition in the United States: 2013, Table 1. Population by Age and Sex: 2013. Accessed August 13, 2020: https://www.census.gov/data/tables/2013/demo/age-and-sex/2013-age-sex-composition.html.

73   U.S. Fish and Wildlife Service/U.S. Census Bureau. 1991 through 2011. *National Surveys of Fishing, Hunting, and Wildlife-Associated Recreation*. Washington, D.C.

74   U.S. Fish and Wildlife Service/U.S. Census Bureau. 1991 through 2011. *National Surveys of Fishing, Hunting, and Wildlife-Associated Recreation*. Washington, D.C.

75   The U.S. Fish and Wildlife Service tracks hunting license sales in each state.

76   Three sources are used:
Applegate, J.E. 1977. "Dynamics of the New Jersey Sport Hunting Population." *Transactions of the North American Wildlife and Natural Resources Conference* 42:103-16.
Decker, D.J.; T.L. Brown; and J.W. Enck. 1992. "Factors Affecting the Recruitment and Retention of Hunters: Insights from New York." *Proceedings of the Twentieth Congress of the International Union of Game Biologists*, ed. S. Csanyi and J. Erhnhaft, 670-677. Godollo, Hungary: University of Agricultural Sciences.
Decker, D.J.; R.W. Provencher; and T.L. Brown. 1984. *Outdoor Recreation Research Unit Publication 84-6: Antecedents to Hunting Participation: An Exploratory Study of the Social- Psychological Determinants of Initiation, Continuation, and Desertion in Hunting*. Ithaca, NY: Cornell University.

77   Responsive Management / National Shooting Sports Foundation. 2008. *The Future of Hunting and the Shooting Sports: Research-Based Recruitment and Retention Strategies*. Produced for the U.S. Fish and Wildlife Service under Grant Agreement CT-M-6-0. Harrisonburg, VA.

78   According to data from the *National Survey of Fishing, Hunting, and Wildlife-Associated Recreation*, the proportion of hunters who are female increased from 9 percent in 2001 to 10 percent in 2016. Additionally, the National Sporting Goods Association, in its report *Sports Participation in 2016—Shooting Sports*, found that hunting participation by women grew from 2.7 million in 2007 to 3.7 million in 2016, a rate of growth higher than that of men. Furthermore, the same study found that women made up 13 percent of all hunters in 2007 but 20 percent of all hunters in 2016. Also, the *National*

# ENDNOTES

*Survey of Fishing, Hunting, and Wildlife-Associated Recreation* found that 32 percent of all hunters in 2016 hunted with a bow and arrow.

[79] Decker, D.J.; T.L. Brown; and W.F. Siemer. (eds.) 2001. *Human Dimensions of Wildlife Management in North America*. Published by The Wildlife Society: Bethesda, MD.

[80] U.S. Fish and Wildlife Service/U.S. Census Bureau. 2016. *National Survey of Fishing, Hunting, and Wildlife-Associated Recreation*. Washington, D.C.

[81] Responsive Management / National Shooting Sports Foundation. 2008. *The Future of Hunting and the Shooting Sports: Research-Based Recruitment and Retention Strategies*. Produced for the U.S. Fish and Wildlife Service under Grant Agreement CT-M-6-0. Harrisonburg, VA.

[82] Responsive Management / National Shooting Sports Foundation. 2018. *Sport Shooting Participation in the United States in 2018*. Harrisonburg, VA.

[83] These NSGA data were compiled and used in the following report that was used as a reference:
Responsive Management / National Shooting Sports Foundation. 2017. *Hunting, Fishing, Sport Shooting, and Archery Recruitment, Retention, and Reactivation: A Practitioner's Guide*. Harrisonburg, VA.
The NSGA data can be found in:
National Sporting Goods Association / National Shooting Sports Foundation. 2020. *Sports Participation in 2019: Shooting Sports*. Des Plaines, IL.

[84] Responsive Management / Archery Trade Association. 2017. *Bowhunting in the United States: A Market Study*. Harrisonburg, VA

[85] National Shooting Sports Foundation / Southwick Associates / Responsive Management. 2011. *Understanding Activities That Compete With Hunting and Target Shooting*. Harrisonburg, VA.

[86] Sources: Kellert, S. 1980. *Public Attitudes Toward Critical Wildlife and Natural Habitat Issues: Phase I of the U.S. Fish and Wildlife Service Study*. Washington, D.C.: Government Printing Office.
Responsive Management. 1995. *Factors Related To Hunting and Fishing Participation in the United States: Final Report*. Harrisonburg, VA.
Responsive Management / National Shooting Sports Foundation. 2008. *The Future of Hunting and the Shooting Sports: Research-Based Recruitment and Retention Strategies*. Produced for the U.S. Fish and Wildlife Service under Grant Agreement CT-M-6-0. Harrisonburg, VA.
Responsive Management. 2013. *Nationwide Survey of Hunters Regarding Participation in and Motivations for Hunting*. Harrisonburg, VA.
Responsive Management. 2017. Unpublished data from a nationwide survey.

[87] International Hunter Education Association. Accessed August 18, 2020. http://www.ihea-usa.org/news-and-events/ihea-news-releases/256-hunting-qsafe-and-getting-safer.

[88] Williams, M. 2018, June 30. "State-Required Hunter Education Continues to Reduce Mishaps, Improve Safety." *The Dallas Morning News*. Accessed August 18, 2020. https://www.dallasnews.com/sports/other-sports/2018/06/30/state-required-hunter-education-continues-to-reduce-mishaps-improve-safety/.

[89] U.S. Fish and Wildlife Service/U.S. Census Bureau. 2016. *National Survey of Fishing, Hunting, and Wildlife-Associated Recreation*. Washington, D.C.

[90] National Shooting Sports Foundation / Southwick Associates. 2018. *Hunting in America: An Economic Force*.

[91] Rocky Mountain Elk Foundation. 2017. *Hunting Is Conservation – Paid for by Hunters*. Elk Network. Accessed online August 6, 2020. https://www.rmef.org/elk-network/hunting-conservation-paid-hunters/.

[92] National Shooting Sports Foundation / Southwick Associates. 2018. *Hunting in America: An Economic Force*.

[93] Two sources are used:
U.S. Census Bureau. Population and Housing Unit Estimates Datasets, 1970-2019.
Population Reference Bureau. 2020. U.S. Population and Percentage Increase in Population Between Census Years, 1790 to 2060. Accessed August 20, 2020: https://www.prb.org/the-u-s-population-is-growing-at-the-slowest-rate-since-the-1930s/.

[94] Two sources are used:
Decker, D.J.; T.L. Brown; and W.F. Siemer. (eds.) 2001. *Human Dimensions of Wildlife Management in North America*. Published by The Wildlife Society: Bethesda, MD.
Duda, M.D.; M.F. Jones; and A. Criscione. 2010. *The Sportsman's Voice: Hunting and Fishing in America*. Venture Publishing, PA.

[95] In addition to the two sources in the endnote above, this was also used: Heberlein, T.A.; and E. Thomson. 1992. "Socioeconomic Influences on Declining Hunter Numbers in the United States, 1977-1990." Pages 699-705 in S. Csanyi and J. Emhaft, eds. *Transactions of the 20th Congress of the International Union of Game Biologists, Part 2*. University of Agricultural Science, Godollo, Hungary.

[96] Responsive Management / National Shooting Sports Foundation. 2009. *Issues Related to Hunting Access in the United States: National Results*. Harrisonburg, VA.

[97] Responsive Management. 2006. *National Wildlife Federation: National Opinion Survey of Hunters and Anglers*. Harrisonburg, VA.

[98] Mark Damian Duda and Tom Beppler wrote an article for the NRA Hunters' Leadership Forum that included multiple research projects conducted by Responsive Management; the article is titled "The Dirty Dozen Threats to Hunting: 21st Century Implications for Recruitment, Retention, and Reactivation."

[99] This is from the above-mentioned article, "The Dirty Dozen Threats to Hunting: 21st Century Implications for Recruitment, Retention, and Reactivation."

[100] The live audience poll results are available via the Intelligence Squared website: https://www.intelligencesquaredus.org/debates/hunters-conserve-wildlife.

[101] The information was obtained from the Wildlife Management Institute.

# ENDNOTES

[102] This information was obtained from the Trust for Public Land and the National Conference of State Legislatures.

[103] Responsive Management. 2005. *Public Opinion on Fish and Wildlife Management Issues and the Reputation and Credibility of Fish and Wildlife Agencies in the Southeastern United States*. Conducted for the Southeastern Association of Fish and Wildlife Agencies under Multistate Conservation Grant VA M-10-R.

[104] Responsive Management / National Shooting Sports Foundation. 2019. *Americans' Attitudes Toward Hunting, Fishing, Sport Shooting, and Trapping*. Conducted for AFWA under Grant Number F19AP00100. Harrisonburg, VA.

[105] Duda, M.D.; M.F. Jones; and A. Criscione. 2010. *The Sportsman's Voice: Hunting and Fishing in America*. Venture Publishing, PA.
Kellert, S.R. 1978. "Attitudes and Characteristics of Hunters and Antihunters." *Transactions of the North American Wildlife Natural Resources Conference*. 43:412-23.

[106] Responsive Management / National Shooting Sports Foundation. 2019. *Americans' Attitudes Toward Hunting, Fishing, Sport Shooting, and Trapping*. Conducted for AFWA under Grant Number F19AP00100. Harrisonburg, VA.

[107] Responsive Management / National Shooting Sports Foundation. 2019. *Americans' Attitudes Toward Hunting, Fishing, Sport Shooting, and Trapping*. Conducted for AFWA under Grant Number F19AP00100. Harrisonburg, VA.

[108] Responsive Management / National Shooting Sports Foundation. 2019. *Americans' Attitudes Toward Hunting, Fishing, Sport Shooting, and Trapping*. Conducted for AFWA under Grant Number F19AP00100. Harrisonburg, VA.

[109] Responsive Management / National Shooting Sports Foundation. 2019. *Americans' Attitudes Toward Hunting, Fishing, Sport Shooting, and Trapping*. Conducted for AFWA under Grant Number F19AP00100. Harrisonburg, VA.

[110] Responsive Management / National Shooting Sports Foundation. 2019. *Americans' Attitudes Toward Hunting, Fishing, Sport Shooting, and Trapping*. Conducted for AFWA under Grant Number F19AP00100. Harrisonburg, VA.

[111] Responsive Management / National Shooting Sports Foundation. 2019. *Americans' Attitudes Toward Hunting, Fishing, Sport Shooting, and Trapping*. Conducted for AFWA under Grant Number F19AP00100. Harrisonburg, VA.

[112] Responsive Management has conducted surveys on this in 1995, 2003, 2006, 2011, 2013, 2015, 2016, and 2019. They are compiled in:
Responsive Management/NSSF. 2019. *Americans' Attitudes Toward Hunting, Fishing, Sport Shooting, and Trapping*. Conducted for AFWA under Grant Number F19AP00100. Harrisonburg, VA.

[113] Responsive Management / National Shooting Sports Foundation. 2019. *Americans' Attitudes Toward Hunting, Fishing, Sport Shooting, and Trapping*. Conducted for AFWA under Grant Number F19AP00100. Harrisonburg, VA.

[114] Responsive Management / National Shooting Sports Foundation. 2019. *Americans' Attitudes Toward Hunting, Fishing, Sport Shooting, and Trapping*. Conducted for AFWA under Grant Number F19AP00100. Harrisonburg, VA.

[115] The graph itself is from:
Responsive Management / National Shooting Sports Foundation. 2019. *Americans' Attitudes Toward Hunting, Fishing, Sport Shooting, and Trapping.* Conducted for AFWA under Grant Number F19AP00100. Harrisonburg, VA.
The other study cited, where those who did not know a hunter were less likely than Americans overall to approve of hunting, was taken from:
Responsive Management. 2017. *The American Public's Attitudes Toward Animal Rights, Animal Welfare, and Hunting.* Harrisonburg, VA.

[116] Responsive Management / National Shooting Sports Foundation. 2019. *Americans' Attitudes Toward Hunting, Fishing, Sport Shooting, and Trapping.* Conducted for AFWA under Grant Number F19AP00100. Harrisonburg, VA.

[117] Responsive Management / National Shooting Sports Foundation. 2019. *Americans' Attitudes Toward Hunting, Fishing, Sport Shooting, and Trapping.* Conducted for AFWA under Grant Number F19AP00100. Harrisonburg, VA.

[118] Responsive Management / National Shooting Sports Foundation. 2019. *Americans' Attitudes Toward Hunting, Fishing, Sport Shooting, and Trapping.* Conducted for AFWA under Grant Number F19AP00100. Harrisonburg, VA.

[119] Responsive Management. 2016. *The American Public's Attitudes Toward Animal Rights, Animal Welfare, and Hunting: Focus Group Report.* Harrisonburg, VA.

[120] Ducarme, F.; G.M. Luque; F. Courchamp. 2013. "What Are 'Charismatic Species' for Conservation Biologists?" *BioSciences Master Reviews.* 10: 1–8. http://biologie.ens-lyon.fr/biologie/ressources/bibliographies/pdf/m1-11-12-biosci-reviews-ducarme-f-2c-m.pdf?lang=en.

[121] Responsive Management / National Shooting Sports Foundation. 2019. *Americans' Attitudes Toward Hunting, Fishing, Sport Shooting, and Trapping.* Conducted for AFWA under Grant Number F19AP00100. Harrisonburg, VA.

[122] Responsive Management / National Shooting Sports Foundation. 2019. *Americans' Attitudes Toward Hunting, Fishing, Sport Shooting, and Trapping.* Conducted for AFWA under Grant Number F19AP00100. Harrisonburg, VA.

[123] Responsive Management. 2016. *The American Public's Attitudes Toward Animal Rights, Animal Welfare, and Hunting: Focus Group Report.* Harrisonburg, VA.

[124] Responsive Management / National Shooting Sports Foundation. 2019. *Americans' Attitudes Toward Hunting, Fishing, Sport Shooting, and Trapping.* Conducted for AFWA under Grant Number F19AP00100. Harrisonburg, VA.

[125] Responsive Management / National Shooting Sports Foundation. 2019. *Americans' Attitudes Toward Hunting, Fishing, Sport Shooting, and Trapping.* Conducted for AFWA under Grant Number F19AP00100. Harrisonburg, VA.

[126] Responsive Management / National Shooting Sports Foundation. 2019. *Americans' Attitudes Toward Hunting, Fishing, Sport Shooting, and Trapping.* Conducted for AFWA under Grant Number F19AP00100. Harrisonburg, VA.

[127] Duda, M.D.; M.F. Jones; and A. Criscione. 2010. *The Sportsman's Voice: Hunting and Fishing in America.* Venture Publishing, PA.

# ENDNOTES

[128] Cornell University Survey Research Institute. 2013. *Cornell National Social Survey 2013.* CISER version 1. Ithaca, NY: Cornell Institute for Social and Economic Research.

[129] Responsive Management / National Shooting Sports Foundation. 2019. *Americans' Attitudes Toward Hunting, Fishing, Sport Shooting, and Trapping.* Conducted for AFWA under Grant Number F19AP00100. Harrisonburg, VA.

[130] Responsive Management. 2017. *The American Public's Attitudes Toward Animal Rights, Animal Welfare, and Hunting.* Harrisonburg, VA.

[131] Responsive Management. 2016. *The American Public's Attitudes Toward Animal Rights, Animal Welfare, and Hunting: Focus Group Report.* Harrisonburg, VA.

[132] Two sources were used for this finding:
Curran, O. *How Does Trophy Hunting Work?* HowStuffWorks, a division of InfoSpace Holdings, LLC. Accessed online August 5, 2020. https://adventure.howstuffworks.com/outdoor-activities/hunting/game-handling/trophy-hunting.htm.
*Rowland Ward.* Wikipedia. Accessed online August 5, 2020. https://en.wikipedia.org/wiki/Rowland_Ward.

[133] Responsive Management. 2016. *The American Public's Attitudes Toward Animal Rights, Animal Welfare, and Hunting: Focus Group Report.* Harrisonburg, VA.

[134] Mahoney, S. 2017. *The Power of a Word.* The P&Y Ethic: The Journal of the Pope and Young Club. Accessed online September 2, 2020. https://www.conservationvisions.com/work/power-word-0.

[135] Luntz, F. 2006. *Words That Work: It's Not What You Say, It's What People Hear.* Hachette Book Group, New York, NY.

[136] Responsive Management/NSSF. 2017. *Hunting, Fishing, Sport Shooting, and Archery Recruitment, Retention, and Reactivation: A Practitioner's Guide.* Harrisonburg, VA.

[137] Responsive Management. 2017. Unpublished data from a nationwide survey.

[138] Three sources are cited here:
Curran, O. *How Does Trophy Hunting Work?* HowStuffWorks, a division of InfoSpace Holdings, LLC. Accessed online August 5, 2020. https://adventure.howstuffworks.com/outdoor-activities/hunting/game-handling/trophy-hunting.htm.
*Theodore Roosevelt.* Wikipedia. Accessed online August 5, 2020. https://en.wikipedia.org/wiki/Theodore_Roosevelt.
Spomer, R. 2019. *Sport Hunting Defined.* NRA Hunters Leadership Forum. Accessed online August 5, 2020. https://www.nrahlf.org/articles/2019/1/6/sport-hunting-defined/.

[139] The quotation is from James Swan's book, *In Defense of Hunting.*

[140] Three sources are cited:
Responsive Management / National Shooting Sports Foundation. 2017. *Hunting, Fishing, Sport Shooting, and Archery Recruitment, Retention, and Reactivation: A Practitioner's Guide.* Harrisonburg, VA
Responsive Management. 2017. Unpublished data from a nationwide survey.

Responsive Management / National Shooting Sports Foundation. 2008. *The Future of Hunting and the Shooting Sports: Research-Based Recruitment and Retention Strategies*. Produced for the U.S. Fish and Wildlife Service under Grant Agreement CT-M-6-0. Harrisonburg, VA.

[141] Hunters for the Hungry. Accessed online August 6, 2020. https://www.h4hungry.org/about-us-2/.

[142] Responsive Management. 2017. *The American Public's Attitudes Toward Animal Rights, Animal Welfare, and Hunting*. Harrisonburg, VA.

[143] This was obtained from https://www.nssf.org/hunting-is-safer-than-golf-and-most-other-recreational-activities/.

[144] Responsive Management. 2017. *The American Public's Attitudes Toward Animal Rights, Animal Welfare, and Hunting*. Harrisonburg, VA.

[145] Causey, A. 1995. "Is Hunting Morally Acceptable?" *High Country News*. Accessed from www.hcn.org/issues/49/1495 on August 31, 2020.

[146] National Association of Conservation Law Enforcement Chiefs / Responsive Management / University of Wisconsin-Stevens Point. 2020. *Planning for the Future of Conservation Law Enforcement in the United States: National Report*. Harrisonburg, VA.

[147] Responsive Management. 2017. *The American Public's Attitudes Toward Animal Rights, Animal Welfare, and Hunting*. Harrisonburg, VA.

[148] Overview of NRA hunter education course at https://nra.yourlearningportal.com/Course/HuntersEdActivityInfoPage

[149] Duda, M.D.; M.F. Jones; and A. Criscione. 2010. *The Sportsman's Voice: Hunting and Fishing in America*. Venture Publishing, PA. The quotation in this sidebar is from the following: Samuel, D.E. 1999. *Know Hunting:* Truths, Lies & Myths. Know Hunting Publications, Cheat Lake, WV.

[150] Responsive Management / National Shooting Sports Foundation / Hunting Heritage Trust. 2012. *Understanding the Impact of Peer Influence on Youth Participation in Hunting and Target Shooting*. Harrisonburg, VA.

[151] Responsive Management / National Shooting Sports Foundation / Hunting Heritage Trust. 2012. *Understanding the Impact of Peer Influence on Youth Participation in Hunting and Target Shooting*. Harrisonburg, VA.

[152] Responsive Management / National Shooting Sports Foundation / Hunting Heritage Trust. 2012. *Understanding the Impact of Peer Influence on Youth Participation in Hunting and Target Shooting*. Harrisonburg, VA.

[153] Responsive Management / National Shooting Sports Foundation / Hunting Heritage Trust. 2012. *Understanding the Impact of Peer Influence on Youth Participation in Hunting and Target Shooting*. Harrisonburg, VA.

[154] Responsive Management. 2017. *The American Public's Attitudes Toward Animal Rights, Animal Welfare, and Hunting*. Harrisonburg, VA.

[155] In a 1996 nationwide survey of Americans for the Fur Information Council of America, Responsive Management found that 79 percent of respondents agreed that animals can be used by humans, as long as the animal does not experience undue pain and suffering; meanwhile, 21 percent of Americans

said that animals are here for human use and can be utilized regardless of the animal's welfare. Other Responsive Management research from 2006 found 85 percent of Americans agreeing that animals can be used by humans, as long as the animal does not experience undue pain and suffering (by comparison, 18 percent agreed that animals have rights like humans and should not be used in any way, and 30 percent agreed that animals are here for human use and can be utilized regardless of the animal's welfare or rights—as detailed in: Duda, M.D.; M.F. Jones; and A. Criscione. 2010. *The Sportsman's Voice: Hunting and Fishing in America*. Venture Publishing, PA.). Additionally, a 2015 Gallup survey found the following: "Almost a third of Americans, 32 percent, believe animals should be given the same rights as people, while 62 percent say they deserve some protection but can still be used for the benefit of humans. ... Very few Americans, 3 percent, believe animals require little protection from harm and exploitation 'since they are just animals.'" https://news.gallup.com/poll/183275/say-animals-rights-people.aspx

[156] Responsive Management. 2017. *The American Public's Attitudes Toward Animal Rights, Animal Welfare, and Hunting*. Harrisonburg, VA.

[157] Responsive Management. 2017. *The American Public's Attitudes Toward Animal Rights, Animal Welfare, and Hunting*. Harrisonburg, VA.

[158] Responsive Management. 2017. *The American Public's Attitudes Toward Animal Rights, Animal Welfare, and Hunting*. Harrisonburg, VA.

[159] Responsive Management. 2017. *The American Public's Attitudes Toward Animal Rights, Animal Welfare, and Hunting*. Harrisonburg, VA.

[160] Responsive Management. 2017. *The American Public's Attitudes Toward Animal Rights, Animal Welfare, and Hunting*. Harrisonburg, VA.

[161] Responsive Management. 2017. *The American Public's Attitudes Toward Animal Rights, Animal Welfare, and Hunting*. Harrisonburg, VA.

[162] The mission statement of People for the Ethical Treatment of Animals explicitly states that the organization operates under the principle that "animals are not ours to eat, wear, experiment on, or use for entertainment." Another prominent animal rights organization, the Humane Society of the United States (HSUS), states its intent to "end suffering for all animals." HSUS also prominently advertises its goal to stop trophy hunting, broadly defining the practice as hunting "not to get food, but simply to obtain animal parts for display and for bragging rights."

[163] Responsive Management. 2017. *The American Public's Attitudes Toward Animal Rights, Animal Welfare, and Hunting*. Harrisonburg, VA.

[164] Responsive Management. 2017. *The American Public's Attitudes Toward Animal Rights, Animal Welfare, and Hunting*. Harrisonburg, VA.

[165] Responsive Management. 2017. *The American Public's Attitudes Toward Animal Rights, Animal Welfare, and Hunting*. Harrisonburg, VA.
There is also research from Pew showing that Americans are essentially divided about the use of animals in scientific research, although it is important to note that this survey wording did not specify whether the animals would be harmed or killed: see https://www.pewresearch.org/fact-tank/2018/08/16/americans-are-divided-over-the-use-of-animals-in-scientific-research/.

[166] Responsive Management. 2017. *The American Public's Attitudes Toward Animal Rights, Animal Welfare, and Hunting.* Harrisonburg, VA.

[167] Responsive Management. 2017. *The American Public's Attitudes Toward Animal Rights, Animal Welfare, and Hunting.* Harrisonburg, VA.

[168] Responsive Management. 2017. *The American Public's Attitudes Toward Animal Rights, Animal Welfare, and Hunting.* Harrisonburg, VA.

[169] Responsive Management. 2017. *The American Public's Attitudes Toward Animal Rights, Animal Welfare, and Hunting.* Harrisonburg, VA.

[170] Responsive Management. 2016. *The American Public's Attitudes Toward Animal Rights, Animal Welfare, and Hunting: Focus Group Report.* Harrisonburg, VA.

[171] Responsive Management / National Shooting Sports Foundation. 2019. *Americans' Attitudes Toward Hunting, Fishing, Sport Shooting, and Trapping.* Conducted for AFWA under Grant Number F19AP00100. Harrisonburg, VA.

[172] Responsive Management. 2016. *The American Public's Attitudes Toward Animal Rights, Animal Welfare, and Hunting: Focus Group Report.* Harrisonburg, VA.

[173] Responsive Management. 2016. *The American Public's Attitudes Toward Animal Rights, Animal Welfare, and Hunting: Focus Group Report.* Harrisonburg, VA.

[174] Responsive Management. 2016. *The American Public's Attitudes Toward Animal Rights, Animal Welfare, and Hunting: Focus Group Report.* Harrisonburg, VA.

[175] The major finding and supporting observations come from the CSU / WAFWA / Responsive Management study "America's Wildlife Values." https://sites.warnercnr.colostate.edu/wildlifevalues/wp-content/uploads/sites/124/2019/01/AWV-National-Final-Report.pdf
Also supporting these points is research from Jeremy T. Bruskotter, John A. Vucetich and Michael Paul Nelson in *The Wildlife Professional*: "Animal Rights and Conservation: Conflicting or Compatible?" https://www.researchgate.net/publication/318275505_Animal_Rights_and_Conservation_Conflicting_or_Compatible

[176] See "Demographic Turning Points for the United States: Population Projections for 2020 to 2060" from the U.S. Census Bureau. Available at https://www.census.gov/content/dam/Census/library/publications/2020/demo/p25-1144.pdf

[177] Responsive Management. 2017. *The American Public's Attitudes Toward Animal Rights, Animal Welfare, and Hunting.* Harrisonburg, VA.

[178] Responsive Management. 2017. *The American Public's Attitudes Toward Animal Rights, Animal Welfare, and Hunting.* Harrisonburg, VA.

[179] Responsive Management. 2017. *The American Public's Attitudes Toward Animal Rights, Animal Welfare, and Hunting.* Harrisonburg, VA.

[180] Responsive Management / National Shooting Sports Foundation. 2019. *Americans' Attitudes Toward Hunting, Fishing, Sport Shooting, and Trapping.* Conducted for AFWA under Grant Number F19AP00100. Harrisonburg, VA.

# ENDNOTES

[181] Responsive Management / National Shooting Sports Foundation. 2019. *Americans' Attitudes Toward Hunting, Fishing, Sport Shooting, and Trapping.* Conducted for AFWA under Grant Number F19AP00100. Harrisonburg, VA.

[182] Responsive Management. 2016. *The American Public's Attitudes Toward Animal Rights, Animal Welfare, and Hunting: Focus Group Report.* Harrisonburg, VA.

[183] Piaget, J. 1926. *Judgment and Reasoning in the Child.* New York, NY: Harcourt & Brace.

[184] See Kellert, S. and M. Westervelt. 1983. *Children's Attitudes, Knowledge and Behaviors Toward Animals.* Phase V of U.S. Fish and Wildlife Service Study, U.S. Government Printing Office. 024-010-006-412, Washington, D.C. 202pp. See also Roediger, H. L., Rushton, J. P., Capaldi, E. D., & Paris, S. G. 1986. *Psychology.* (2nd ed.) Canada: Little, Brown & Company (Canada) Limited.

[185] All focus group findings discussed here are from Responsive Management. 2016. *The American Public's Attitudes Toward Animal Rights, Animal Welfare, and Hunting: Focus Group Report.* Harrisonburg, VA.

[186] Two sources are used:
Responsive Management. 2017. *The American Public's Attitudes Toward Animal Rights, Animal Welfare, and Hunting.* Harrisonburg, VA.
Responsive Management / National Shooting Sports Foundation. 2019. *Americans' Attitudes Toward Hunting, Fishing, Sport Shooting, and Trapping.* Conducted for AFWA under Grant Number F19AP00100. Harrisonburg, VA.

[187] Unless otherwise noted, all of the results in this chapter regarding arguments that were tested for and against hunting were taken from the Responsive Management study, *The Effectiveness of Pro- and Anti-Hunting Arguments Among the American Public*, produced for the NRA Hunters' Leadership Forum in 2019.

[188] Hunting in a high fence preserve as a method of hunting was supported by only 23 percent of hunters, as documented in:
Responsive Management / National Shooting Sports Foundation. 2008. *The Future of Hunting and the Shooting Sports: Research-Based Recruitment and Retention Strategies.* Produced for the U.S. Fish and Wildlife Service under Grant Agreement CT-M-6-0. Harrisonburg, VA.

[189] Responsive Management. 2017. *The American Public's Attitudes Toward Animal Rights, Animal Welfare, and Hunting.* Harrisonburg, VA. The species population data are from the following sources: Quality Deer Management Association, Ducks Unlimited, the U.S. Fish and Wildlife Service, and the Rocky Mountain Elk Foundation.

[190] Hunting in a high fence preserve as a method of hunting was supported by only 23 percent of hunters, as documented in:
Responsive Management / National Shooting Sports Foundation. 2008. *The Future of Hunting and the Shooting Sports: Research-Based Recruitment and Retention Strategies.* Produced for the U.S. Fish and Wildlife Service under Grant Agreement CT-M-6-0. Harrisonburg, VA.

[191] Smith, M.E.; and D.A. Molde. 2014. "Wildlife Conservation & Management Funding in the U.S." *Nevadans for Responsible Wildlife Management.*

[192] As an example, the Maine Department of Inland Fisheries and Wildlife notes that the agency "preserves, protects, and enhances the inland fisheries and wildlife resources of the state. Established in 1880 to protect big game populations, MDIFW has since evolved in scope to include protection and management of fish, non-game wildlife, and habitats, as well as restoration of endangered species like the bald eagle." (from its website at https://www.maine.gov/ifw/news-events/media.html#:~:text=MDIFW%20Mission%20Statement,recreation%2C%20sport%2C%20and%20science). Many other states have similar missions vis-à-vis nongame wildlife.

[193] The Bureau of Land Management's own website reports that its 2020 budget includes spending $139.2 million on its oil and gas programs, as well as $18.9 million on its Coal Management Program, and $11.8 million on programs associated with mining other minerals. Downloaded from https://www.blm.gov/about/budget on September 15, 2020.

[194] The management used sterilization in addition to a limited hunting program, so the management was not without a hunting component anyway, and this still did not reduce the deer population. This is discussed in:
Boulanger, J.R.; P.D. Curtis; and B. Blossey. 2014. *An Integrated Approach for Managing White-Tailed Deer in Suburban Environments: The Cornell University Study*. A publication of the Cornell University Cooperative Extension and the Northeast Wildlife Damage Research and Outreach Cooperative.

[195] In 2014 dollars; this information comes from the Boulanger et al. study cited above.

[196] Boulanger et al. cited above.

[197] Goldfarb, B. 2016. "Birth Control for Bambi." *Undark*. Downloaded September 16, 2020, from https://undark.org/2016/04/15/birth-control-for-bambi/.

[198] USA Today. 2014. "City Uses Birth Control to Limit Nuisance Deer Herd." Published on USA Today's website, originally taken from the *Westchester County Journal News*. Downloaded on September 16, 2020, from https://www.usatoday.com/story/news/nation/2014/03/18/deer-birth-control-reduce-herd/6555093/.

[199] Thomson, C. 2006. "Taking a Shot at Deer Contraception." *The Baltimore Sun*, from October 8, 2006. Downloaded September 16, 2020, from https://www.baltimoresun.com/news/bs-xpm-2006-10-08-0610080163-story.html.

[200] Samuel, D.E. 1999. *Know Hunting: Truths, Lies & Myths*. Know Hunting Publications, Cheat Lake, WV.

[201] Brennan, O. 2018. "Wildlife Contraception." *Wild Animal Suffering Research*. Downloaded on September 16, 2020, from https://was-research.org/paper/wildlife-contraception/.

[202] LaSharr, T.N.; R.A. Long; J.R. Heffelfinger; V.C. Bleich; P.R. Krausman; R.T. Bowyer; J.M. Shannon; R.W. Klaver; C.E. Brewer; M. Cox; A.A. Holland; A. Hubbs; C.P. Lehman; J.D. Muir; B. Sterling; and K.L. Monteith. 2019. "Hunting and Mountain Sheep: Do Current Harvest Practices Affect Horn Growth?" *Evolutionary Applications*. John Wiley & Sons Ltd.

## ENDNOTES

[203] Heffelfinger, J. 2014. "Selective Harvest in Ungulates" (Letters to the Editor section.) *Wildlife Professional* 8(4). p. 8.

[204] Boyce, M.S.; and P.R. Krausman. 2018. "Special Section: Controversies in Mountain Sheep Management." *Journal of Wildlife Management* 82(1), pp5-7.

[205] Coulson, T.; S. Schindler; L.Traill; and B.E. Kendall. 2018. "Predicting the Evolutionary Consequences of Trophy Hunting on a Quantitative Trait." *Journal of Wildlife Management* 82(1) pp. 46-56.

[206] Monteith, K.L.; R.A. Long; V.C. Bleich; J.R. Heffelfinger; P.R. Krausman; and R.T. Bowyer. 2013. "Effects of Harvest, Culture, and Climate on Trends in Size of Horn-Like Structures in Trophy Ungulates." *Wildlife Monographs* 183, pp 1-26.

[207] Mahoney, S. 2017. *The Power of a Word*. The P&Y Ethic: The Journal of the Pope and Young Club. Accessed online September 2, 2020. https://www.conservationvisions.com/work/power-word-0.

[208] Newkirk, I. 2016. "The Pastime of Psychopaths." *Huffpost*. Accessed September 17, 2020 from https://www.huffpost.com/entry/the-pastime-of-psychopath_b_8084410.

[209] Kellert, S.R. 1996. *The Value of Life: Biological Diversity and Human Society*. Island Press/Shearwater Books, Washington D.C.

[210] Causey, A. 1989. "On the Morality of Hunting." *Environmental Ethics*. Volume 11, Issue 4.

[211] The Gallup poll was one of its series called, *Gallup Poll Social Series* (one of twelve polls that encompass this series). Downloaded from https://news.gallup.com/poll/264932/percentage-americans-own-guns.aspx on July 29, 2020.

[212] This finding is from the Pew Research Center's *Factank* page on its website, "7 facts about guns in the U.S." by J. Gramlich and K. Schaeffer, downloaded from https://www.pewresearch.org/fact-tank/2019/10/22/facts-about-guns-in-united-states/ on July 29, 2020.

[213] Responsive Management. 2017. *The American Public's Attitudes Toward Animal Rights, Animal Welfare, and Hunting*. Harrisonburg, VA.

[214] Responsive Management. 2019. *Sport Shooting Participation in the United States in 2018*. Harrisonburg, VA.

[215] These studies were conducted by Responsive Management for the NSSF:
*Sport Shooting Participation in the United States in 2009*
*Sport Shooting Participation in the United States in 2012*
*Sport Shooting Participation in the United States in 2014*
*Sport Shooting Participation in the United States in 2016*
*Sport Shooting Participation in the United States in 2018*

[216] The NSSF reports cited above were the source for this.

[217] Zogby Analytics online survey of likely voters conducted in 2015. Downloaded from: http://origin-qps.onstreammedia.com/origin/multivu_archive/ENR/177704-Jan-2015-Survey_ID-a444af529b00_.pdf on August 3, 2020.

218 This incident is detailed in a book by John R. Lott, Jr., *The Bias Against Guns: Why Almost Everything You've Heard About Gun Control Is Wrong*, published in 2003 by Regnery Publishing, Inc., an Eagle Publishing Company.

219 The NSSF reports cited above were the source for this.

220 The NSSF reports cited above, excluding the 2009 report, were the source for this.

221 The Sports & Fitness Industry Association publishes participation data in conjunction with the Outdoor Foundation. The SFIA was formerly the Sporting Goods Manufacturers Association (SGMA).

222 The National Sporting Goods Association publishes participation data, available for purchase from that organization.

223 Responsive Management. 2019. *Sport Shooting Participation in the United States in 2018*. Harrisonburg, VA.

224 Responsive Management. 2019. *Sport Shooting Participation in the United States in 2018*. Harrisonburg, VA.

225 Responsive Management. 2019. *Sport Shooting Participation in the United States in 2018*. Harrisonburg, VA.

226 Responsive Management. 2019. *Sport Shooting Participation in the United States in 2018*. Harrisonburg, VA.

227 Four of the five NSSF reports cited previously (excluding the 2009 report) were the source for this.

228 Responsive Management. 2019. *Sport Shooting Participation in the United States in 2018*. Harrisonburg, VA.

229 The Federal Aid in Wildlife Restoration Act, commonly called the Pittman-Robertson Act (named after the Congressmen who sponsored the original legislation), provides funds for the acquisition and improvement of wildlife habitat, introduction of wildlife into suitable habitat, research into wildlife problems, surveys and inventories of wildlife problems, acquisition and development of access facilities for public use, and hunter education programs, as well as the aforementioned construction and operation of shooting ranges. The funds come from an excise tax on sporting goods such as firearms, ammunition, and archery equipment.

230 National Shooting Sports Foundation/Southwick Associates/Responsive Management. 2011. *Understanding Activities That Compete With Hunting and Target Shooting*. Harrisonburg, VA.

231 Responsive Management. 2017. *The American Public's Attitudes Toward Animal Rights, Animal Welfare, and Hunting*. Harrisonburg, VA.

232 If the authors wanted to belabor the point, they could list nearly every survey that Responsive Management has conducted where this constraints question was asked of hunters and sport shooters, a list that would fill this entire page of endnotes. A good representative example of these studies is the following: Responsive Management / National Shooting Sports Foundation. 2008. *The Future of Hunting and the Shooting Sports: Research-Based Recruitment and Retention Strategies*. Produced for the U.S. Fish and Wildlife Service under Grant Agreement CT-M-6-0. Harrisonburg, VA.

# ENDNOTES

Responsive Management. 2018. *Iowa Residents Participation in and Opinion on Outdoor Recreation*. Study conducted for the Iowa Department of Natural Resources. Harrisonburg, VA.

Responsive Management. 2018. *Maryland Residents', Landowners', and Deer Hunters' Attitudes Toward Deer Hunting and Deer Management*. Study conducted for the Maryland Department of Natural Resources. Harrisonburg, VA.

[233] Responsive Management. 2017. *Reactivating Non-Shooting Firearm Owners*. Harrisonburg, VA.

[234] Responsive Management. 2017. *Reactivating Non-Shooting Firearm Owners*. Harrisonburg, VA.

[235] Responsive Management / National Shooting Sports Foundation. 2017. *Hunting, Fishing, Sport Shooting, and Archery Recruitment, Retention, and Reactivation: A Practitioner's Guide*. Harrisonburg, VA.

[236] Responsive Management / National Shooting Sports Foundation. 2019. *Americans' Attitudes Toward Hunting, Fishing, Sport Shooting, and Trapping*. Conducted for AFWA under Grant Number F19AP00100. Harrisonburg, VA.

[237] Responsive Management / National Shooting Sports Foundation. 2019. *Americans' Attitudes Toward Hunting, Fishing, Sport Shooting, and Trapping*. Conducted for AFWA under Grant Number F19AP00100. Harrisonburg, VA.

[238] Responsive Management / National Shooting Sports Foundation. 2019. *Americans' Attitudes Toward Hunting, Fishing, Sport Shooting, and Trapping*. Conducted for AFWA under Grant Number F19AP00100. Harrisonburg, VA.

[239] Responsive Management / National Shooting Sports Foundation. 2019. *Americans' Attitudes Toward Hunting, Fishing, Sport Shooting, and Trapping*. Conducted for AFWA under Grant Number F19AP00100. Harrisonburg, VA.

[240] Responsive Management / National Shooting Sports Foundation. 2018. *Sport Shooting Participation in the United States in 2018*. Harrisonburg, VA.

[241] Responsive Management / National Shooting Sports Foundation. 2019. *Americans' Attitudes Toward Hunting, Fishing, Sport Shooting, and Trapping*. Conducted for AFWA under Grant Number F19AP00100. Harrisonburg, VA.

[242] Responsive Management / National Shooting Sports Foundation. 2019. *Americans' Attitudes Toward Hunting, Fishing, Sport Shooting, and Trapping*. Conducted for AFWA under Grant Number F19AP00100. Harrisonburg, VA.

[243] Pew Research Center. 2017, June 22. *America's Complex Relationship With Guns*. Accessed at https://www.pewsocialtrends.org/2017/06/22/americas-complex-relationship-with-guns/.

[244] Responsive Management / National Shooting Sports Foundation. 2019. *Americans' Attitudes Toward Hunting, Fishing, Sport Shooting, and Trapping*. Conducted for AFWA under Grant Number F19AP00100. Harrisonburg, VA.

[245] Pew Research Center. 2017, June 22. *America's Complex Relationship With Guns*. Accessed at https://www.pewsocialtrends.org/2017/06/22/americas-complex-relationship-with-guns/.

[246] Gallup. 2019, August 14. *What Percentage of Americans Own Guns?* Accessed at https://news.gallup.com/poll/264932/percentage-americans-own-guns.aspx.

[247] Based on consultation from A-Game Speech and Debate Consulting.

[248] Based on consultation from A-Game Speech and Debate Consulting.

[249] Responsive Management / Recreational Boating and Fishing Foundation. 2018. *Actionable Strategies for Angler Recruitment, Retention, and Reactivation.* Produced for the U.S. Fish and Wildlife Service under Grant Agreement F18AP00165. Harrisonburg, VA

[250] Based on consultation from A-Game Speech and Debate Consulting.

[251] Based on consultation from A-Game Speech and Debate Consulting. Instruction on debating about hunting also comes from the following source: Responsive Management / Rocky Mountain Elk Foundation / Appleseed Marketing Consulting, LLC. 2019. *How to Debate and Communicate About Hunting: Communications Action Plan.* Produced for the U.S. Fish and Wildlife Service under Grant Agreement F18AP00170. Harrisonburg, VA.

[252] Responsive Management. 2017. *The American Public's Attitudes Toward Animal Rights, Animal Welfare, and Hunting.* Harrisonburg, VA.

[253] Toulmin, S.E. 1958. *The Uses of Argument.* Cambridge, MA: University Press.

[254] Shell, G.R.; and M. Moussa. 2007. *The Art of Woo: Using Strategic Persuasion to Sell Your Ideas.* New York, New York: Portfolio/Penguin Group.

[255] Based on consultation from A-Game Speech and Debate Consulting. Instruction on debating about hunting also comes from the following source: Responsive Management / Rocky Mountain Elk Foundation / Appleseed Marketing Consulting, LLC. 2019. *How to Debate and Communicate About Hunting: Communications Action Plan.* Produced for the U.S. Fish and Wildlife Service under Grant Agreement F18AP00170. Harrisonburg, VA.

[256] Based on consultation from A-Game Speech and Debate Consulting. Instruction on debating about hunting also comes from the following source: Responsive Management / Rocky Mountain Elk Foundation / Appleseed Marketing Consulting, LLC. 2019. *How to Debate and Communicate About Hunting: Communications Action Plan.* Produced for the U.S. Fish and Wildlife Service under Grant Agreement F18AP00170. Harrisonburg, VA.

[257] Responsive Management. 2019. *The Effectiveness of Pro- and Anti-Hunting Arguments Among the American Public.* Produced for the NRA Hunters' Leadership Forum. Harrisonburg, VA.

[258] Based on consultation from A-Game Speech and Debate Consulting. Instruction on debating about hunting also comes from the following source: Responsive Management / Rocky Mountain Elk Foundation / Appleseed Marketing Consulting, LLC. 2019. *How to Debate and Communicate About Hunting: Communications Action Plan.* Produced for the U.S. Fish and Wildlife Service under Grant Agreement F18AP00170. Harrisonburg, VA.

[259] Responsive Management / Rocky Mountain Elk Foundation / Appleseed Marketing Consulting, LLC. 2019. *How to Debate and Communicate About Hunting: Communications Action Plan.* Produced for the U.S. Fish and Wildlife Service under Grant Agreement F18AP00170. Harrisonburg, VA.

[260] Based on consultation from A-Game Speech and Debate Consulting. Instruction on debating about hunting also comes from the following source:

# ENDNOTES

Responsive Management / Rocky Mountain Elk Foundation / Appleseed Marketing Consulting, LLC. 2019. *How to Debate and Communicate About Hunting: Communications Action Plan*. Produced for the U.S. Fish and Wildlife Service under Grant Agreement F18AP00170. Harrisonburg, VA.

[261] Based on consultation from A-Game Speech and Debate Consulting. Instruction on debating about hunting also comes from the following source: Responsive Management / Rocky Mountain Elk Foundation / Appleseed Marketing Consulting, LLC. 2019. *How to Debate and Communicate About Hunting: Communications Action Plan*. Produced for the U.S. Fish and Wildlife Service under Grant Agreement F18AP00170. Harrisonburg, VA.

[262] Based on consultation from A-Game Speech and Debate Consulting. Instruction on debating about hunting also comes from the following source: Responsive Management / Rocky Mountain Elk Foundation / Appleseed Marketing Consulting, LLC. 2019. *How to Debate and Communicate About Hunting: Communications Action Plan*. Produced for the U.S. Fish and Wildlife Service under Grant Agreement F18AP00170. Harrisonburg, VA.

[263] Based on consultation from A-Game Speech and Debate Consulting. Instruction on debating about hunting also comes from the following source: Responsive Management / Rocky Mountain Elk Foundation / Appleseed Marketing Consulting, LLC. 2019. *How to Debate and Communicate About Hunting: Communications Action Plan*. Produced for the U.S. Fish and Wildlife Service under Grant Agreement F18AP00170. Harrisonburg, VA.

[264] Based on consultation from A-Game Speech and Debate Consulting. Instruction on debating about hunting also comes from the following source: Responsive Management / Rocky Mountain Elk Foundation / Appleseed Marketing Consulting, LLC. 2019. *How to Debate and Communicate About Hunting: Communications Action Plan*. Produced for the U.S. Fish and Wildlife Service under Grant Agreement F18AP00170. Harrisonburg, VA.

[265] Based on consultation from A-Game Speech and Debate Consulting. Instruction on debating about hunting also comes from the following source: Responsive Management / Rocky Mountain Elk Foundation / Appleseed Marketing Consulting, LLC. 2019. *How to Debate and Communicate About Hunting: Communications Action Plan*. Produced for the U.S. Fish and Wildlife Service under Grant Agreement F18AP00170. Harrisonburg, VA.

[266] Based on consultation from A-Game Speech and Debate Consulting. Instruction on debating about hunting also comes from the following source: Responsive Management / Rocky Mountain Elk Foundation / Appleseed Marketing Consulting, LLC. 2019. *How to Debate and Communicate About Hunting: Communications Action Plan*. Produced for the U.S. Fish and Wildlife Service under Grant Agreement F18AP00170. Harrisonburg, VA.

[267] Based on consultation from A-Game Speech and Debate Consulting. Instruction on debating about hunting also comes from the following source: Responsive Management / Rocky Mountain Elk Foundation / Appleseed Marketing Consulting, LLC. 2019. *How to Debate and Communicate About Hunting: Communications Action Plan*. Produced for the U.S. Fish and Wildlife Service under Grant Agreement F18AP00170. Harrisonburg, VA.

[268] Based on consultation from A-Game Speech and Debate Consulting.

[269] Two sources are used here:
Responsive Management / National Shooting Sports Foundation. 2019. *Americans' Attitudes Toward Hunting, Fishing, Sport Shooting, and Trapping.* Harrisonburg, VA.
Responsive Management. 2017. *The American Public's Attitudes Toward Animal Rights, Animal Welfare, and Hunting.* Harrisonburg, VA.

[270] A-Game Speech and Debate Consulting analysis of the Intelligence Squared debate held May 4, 2016. Debate recording accessed online August 28, 2020. Available at https://www.intelligencesquaredus.org/debates/hunters-conserve-wildlife#:~:text=Hunters%20conserve%20wildlife%2C%20they%20say%2C%20they%20argue.&text=%22No%2C%22%20to%20this%20statement,U.S.%20I'm%20John%20Donvan.

[271] Manfredo, M.J.; T.L. Teel; and A.M. Dietsch. 2015. "Implications of Human Value Shift and Persistence for Biodiversity Conservation." *Conservation Biology* (30)2.

[272] Responsive Management. 1998. *Women's, Hispanics', and African-Americans' Participation in, and Attitudes Toward, Boating and Fishing: Focus Group Report.* Study conducted for the Sport Fishing and Boating Partnership Council. Harrisonburg, VA.

[273] Kellert, S.R. 1996. *The Value of Life: Biological Diversity and Human Society.* Island Press/Shearwater Books, Washington D.C.

[274] Two sources are used here:
Teel, T.; A. Dayer; M. Manfredo; and A. Bright. 2005. *Regional Results From the Research Project Entitled, "Wildlife Values in the West."* Project Report No. 58 submitted to the Western Association of Fish and Wildlife Agencies. Human Dimensions in Natural Resources Unit, Colorado State University, Fort Collins, CO.
Manfredo, M. 2008. *Who Cares About Wildlife? Social Science Concepts for Exploring Human-Wildlife Relationships and Conservation Issues.* New York.

[275] Two sources are used here:
Teel, T.; A. Dayer; M. Manfredo; and A. Bright. 2005. *Regional Results From the Research Project Entitled, "Wildlife Values in the West."* Project Report No. 58 submitted to the Western Association of Fish and Wildlife Agencies. Human Dimensions in Natural Resources Unit, Colorado State University, Fort Collins, CO.
Manfredo, M. 2008. *Who Cares About Wildlife? Social Science Concepts for Exploring Human-Wildlife Relationships and Conservation Issues.* New York.

[276] Henderson, C. 1984. "Publicity Strategies and Techniques for Minnesota's Nongame Wildlife Checkoff." *Transactions of the North American Wildlife and Natural Resources Conference* 49: 181-189.

[277] The ideas were brainstormed in a *Crucial to Conservation* workshop held in Atlanta, Georgia, in August 2016, as detailed in *Crucial to Conservation Workshop: Final Report* produced in 2016.

[278] The National Hunting and Shooting Sports Action Plan was developed by the Wildlife Management Institute and the Council to Advance Hunting and Shooting Sports in 2016. It is available at https://cahss.org/national-hunting-shooting-sports-action-plan/.

# ENDNOTES

[279] Duda, M.; S.J. Bissell; and K.C. Young. 1998. *Wildlife and the American Mind: Public Opinion on and Attitudes Toward Fish and Wildlife Management.* Responsive Management, Harrisonburg, VA.

[280] In addition to being supported by various Responsive Management studies, this point is supported by other research that found that those who are neutral about hunting desire "sound, balanced, science-based information" from professional wildlife managers, and that persuasive communications that appear self-serving are best left to special interest groups such as sportsmen's organizations. This research includes:
Campbell, M.; and K.J. Mackay. 2009. "Communicating the Role of Hunting for Wildlife Management." *Human Dimensions of Wildlife* (14)1, pp. 21-36.

[281] Responsive Management. 2015. *Maine Residents' and Outdoor Recreationists' Attitudes Toward Wildlife Management and Participation in Wildlife-Related Recreation.* Harrisonburg, VA.

[282] The information in this section was obtained in part through a personal interview with Jennifer Anderson of the Colorado Wildlife Council. Additional information if from the following:
(Colorado) Wildlife Management Public Education Advisory Council. 1998. *Wildlife Management Public Education Plan.* This document was presented to the Director of the Colorado Division of Wildlife.

[283] Specifically, the Council was composed of two hunters who purchase big game licenses on a regular basis (one being from the Western Slope), two anglers who purchase fishing licenses on a regular basis (one being from the Western Slope), one representative of rural counties whose economies have substantial income from hunting and fishing, one representative of rural municipalities whose economies receive substantial input from hunting and fishing, an agricultural producer, a person with background in media and marketing, and one staff member of the Division of Wildlife.

[284] This comes directly from the identified scope of the initial *Wildlife Management Public Education Plan* created by the Wildlife Management Public Advisory Council in 1998.

[285] Colorado Wildlife Council. 2019. *Strategic Communications Toolkit.*

[286] This research and other background information about the Michigan Wildlife Council were provided by Güd Marketing, including internal documents prepared for the Council and stakeholders. These materials are used extensively in this section about the Council and are the source for any statistics or facts that are presented, unless otherwise indicated.

[287] The researchers acknowledge that wildlife would not need any management in a world untouched by humans; however, humans need land and therefore alter the land and habitats in necessary ways, so we do not live in a world untouched by humans. To coexist with nature in a world that does include humans, wildlife and habitats will need management—even if some of that management includes keeping some areas completely wild, as that in itself can be part of an overall management strategy.

[288] These specific statistics were provided by Güd Marketing based on its surveys conducted in 2015 and then annually from 2017 through 2019.

## How to Talk About Hunting ⊕ *Research-Based Communications Strategies*

[289] The first part of this quotation was obtained from a telephone conference call with Güd Marketing representatives (Ally Caldwell and Jill Holden) about this outreach campaign; the call was conducted on August 25, 2020. Additional comments from Ally Caldwell, Jill Holden, and Chelsea Maupin were subsequently provided.

[290] Information throughout this section on the Louisiana Alligator Program was taken from the Louisiana Department of Wildlife and Fisheries website and from lawsuits filed on behalf of the alligator industry, as well as from outreach materials prepared by and on behalf of the Foundation and the Department.

[291] Responsive Management. 2020. *How to Talk About Alligators: Words Matter.* Harrisonburg, VA.

[292] Responsive Management. 2020. *How to Talk About Alligators: Words Matter.* Harrisonburg, VA.

[293] U.S. Department of the Interior, U.S. Fish and Wildlife Service, and U.S. Census Bureau. 2016. *National Survey of Fishing, Hunting, and Wildlife-Associated Recreation.* Washington, D.C.: U.S. Government Printing Office.

[294] Fedler, A.J., and R.B. Ditton. 2000. "Developing a National Outreach Strategy for Recreational Fishing and Boating." *Fisheries* 25:22-28.

[295] Recreational Boating and Fishing Foundation. 2020. "What Is 60 in 60?" Accessed from www.takemefishing.org/60in60/ August 18, 2020.

[296] Take Me Fishing. 2018. "What Three Things Will Help Us Reach 60 in 60?" Accessed from www.youtube.com/watch?v=eLDzeJyLXLY August 18, 2020.

[297] Recreational Boating and Fishing Foundation. 2020. "60 in 60 Overview." Accessed from www.slideshare.net/takemefishing/60-in-60-overview?ref=https://www.slideshare.net/takemefishing/slideshelf August 18, 2020.

[298] U.S. Fish and Wildlife Service. 2020. Historical Fishing License Data. Retrieved from its license database on August 18, 2020 at the following: www.fws.gov/wsfrprograms/Subpages/LicenseInfo/Fishing.htm.

[299] This point is made in Dr. David E. Samuel's book, *Know Hunting: Truths, Lies & Myths.*

[300] Holland, J.S. 2015. "Black Bears Are Rebounding—What Does That Mean for People?" *National Geographic* from its website, accessed September 23, 2020, from: https://www.nationalgeographic.com/news/2015/06/150626-black-bears-animals-science-nation-conservation/#close.

[301] Causey, A. 1995. "Is Hunting Morally Acceptable?" *High Country News.* Accessed from www.hcn.org/issues/49/1495 on August 31, 2020.

[302] The quotation is from James Swan's book, *In Defense of Hunting.*

[303] Causey, A. 1995. "Is Hunting Morally Acceptable?" *High Country News.* Accessed from www.hcn.org/issues/49/1495 on August 31, 2020.

[304] The quotation is from Jim Posewitz's book, *Beyond Fair Chase: The Ethic and Tradition of Hunting.*

# About the Authors & Consultants

**Mark Damian Duda** is the founder and executive director of Responsive Management. He has led Responsive Management since the firm's inception in 1990. Mark holds a master's degree with an emphasis on natural resource policy and planning from Yale University, where he attended on two academic scholarships. Mark has conducted more than 1,000 studies on how people relate to the outdoors. He is the author of more than 150 publications and four books on wildlife and outdoor recreation, including *The Sportsman's Voice: Hunting and Fishing in America* and *Watching Wildlife*.

Mark is a Certified Wildlife Biologist® whose research has been upheld in U.S. Courts, used in peer-reviewed journals, and presented at major natural resource and outdoor recreation conferences around the world. His work has been featured in many of the nation's top media, including NPR's Morning Edition, Fox News, CNN, *The New York Times*, *Newsweek*, and the front pages of *The Wall Street Journal*, *The Washington Post*, and *USA Today*. For seven years, Mark served as a columnist for *North American Hunter* and *North American Fisherman* magazines.

Mark has been named Conservation Educator of the Year by the Florida Wildlife Federation and National Wildlife Federation, was a recipient of the Conservation Achievement Award from the Western Association of Fish and Wildlife Agencies, and was named Wildlife Professional of the Year by the Virginia Wildlife Society. He also received the Conservation Achievement Award in Communications from Ducks Unlimited and the Conservation Service Award from the Potomac Ducks Unlimited Chapter for his contributions as a researcher and writer. Mark was also honored as Researcher of the Year by the National Shooting Sports Foundation and received the Distinguished Leadership Award from the National Rifle Association. Mark is an avid hunter, sport shooter, angler, boater, and birdwatcher.

How to Talk About Hunting ⊕ *Research-Based Communications Strategies*

**Peter Churchbourne** is an avid outdoorsman, conservationist, and steadfast advocate for all hunters. His passion is anything to do with the outdoors, but most important to him is hunting waterfowl with his labs, chasing turkeys, bowhunting, and introducing new people to the life outside. Peter has hunted in 42 states, Canada, and South America. Before becoming the director of Hunter Services at the NRA, where he was responsible for developing the award-winning online hunter education program, Peter worked at Ducks Unlimited for 17 years in various positions around the United States. Peter is currently a director with the NRA Hunters' Leadership Forum where he is engaged in building new NRA hunting programs and fighting for hunters' rights.

**Martin Jones** is Senior Quantitative Research Associate with Responsive Management. Martin has researched and written exclusively about natural resource, wildlife, hunting, and outdoor recreation issues for the past 20 years. He has written more than 500 reports covering survey results and other quantitative research findings from hunting and wildlife management studies. Martin was a co-author of *The Sportsman's Voice: Hunting and Fishing in America*. Martin holds a master's degree from the University of Vermont.

**Samuel Nelson** is a founding partner of A-Game Speech and Debate Consulting. Sam is also a senior lecturer at Cornell University's School of Industrial and Labor Relations. Since taking charge in 2009, he has grown Cornell's Speech and Debate team to one of the largest and most competitive teams in the world. In addition, he has a long career helping politicians, policy makers, and business leaders become better advocates for their respective causes. He teaches Argumentation and Debate at Cornell, taken by over 100 students every semester to improve their critical thinking and persuasive speaking skills. Sam has a bachelor's degree from the University of Southern California as well has an M.A. in Speech Communication and a JD from Syracuse University. He resides in Trumansburg, NY, with his family, where he also owns a bookstore.

**John Stowell** is a founding partner of A-Game Speech and Debate Consulting. John is a marketing communications and research professional with thirty years of experience in large and mid-sized businesses. He has built three beverage brands from scratch, one now exceeding $1 billion in revenue for Coca-Cola, and brings a brand marketer's eye to the positioning of interpersonal and group communication. John earned a Doctor of Business Administration at Georgia State University, an M.B.A. at UNC Chapel Hill, and a B.A. at Oklahoma University. John also served in the U.S. Army for four years, resigning as a Captain with the Army Commendation Medal for service overseas. He loves long hikes in the woods with his wife, Laura, travel, the history of anything, and spending time with their three daughters.

**Armands Revelins** is a researcher and consultant with A-Game Speech and Debate Consulting. Armands is Assistant Director of Speech & Debate Programs and Director of Policy Debate at Cornell University. Armands holds a master's degree in philosophy from the University of Illinois and has previously coached nationally ranked teams at both the high school and collegiate levels. As a college debater for the University of Southern California, he qualified for the highly competitive National Debate Tournament four times and was a high school Tournament of Champions winner.

**Karen Mehall Phillips** is the director of communications for the NRA Hunters' Leadership Forum and senior editor of NRA's American Hunter. An avid rifle and bow hunter, she has hunted for 30 years and in 29 states, Canada, Italy, Finland, Germany, Spain, New Zealand, Greenland and Africa, including for two of the Big Five.

An NRA Endowment member, Karen worked in the NRA public relations arena prior to joining NRA Publications in 1998. She is the founding editor of two NRA official journals: America's 1st Freedom and Woman's Outlook. National writing awards include being named the 2015 Carl Zeiss Sports Optics Writer of the Year. She actively promotes women and families in the outdoors. She is also a member of the Washington metropolitan area's Fairfax Rod & Gun Club, a founding member of the Professional Outdoor Media Association, a member of Safari Club International and a Life member of the Dallas Safari Club and the Mule Deer Foundation.